Cambridge Monographs in African Archaeology
85
Series Editors: Laurence Smith, Brian Stewart and Stephanie Wynne-Jone

The Ancient Red Sea Port of Adulis and the Eritrean Coastal Region

Previous investigations and museum collections

Chiara Zazzaro

BAR International Series 2569
2013

Published in 2016 by
BAR Publishing, Oxford

BAR International Series 2569

Cambridge Monographs in African Archaeology 85
Series Editors: Laurence Smith, Brian Stewart and Stephanie Wynne-Jone

The Ancient Red Sea Port of Adulis and the Eritrean Coastal Region

ISBN 978 1 4073 1190 6

© C Zazzaro and the Publisher 2013

The author's moral rights under the 1988 UK Copyright,
Designs and Patents Act are hereby expressly asserted.

All rights reserved. No part of this work may be copied, reproduced, stored,
sold, distributed, scanned, saved in any form of digital format or transmitted
in any form digitally, without the written permission of the Publisher.

BAR Publishing is the trading name of British Archaeological Reports (Oxford) Ltd.
British Archaeological Reports was first incorporated in 1974 to publish the BAR
Series, International and British. In 1992 Hadrian Books Ltd became part of the BAR
group. This volume was originally published by Archaeopress in conjunction with
British Archaeological Reports (Oxford) Ltd / Hadrian Books Ltd, the Series principal
publisher, in 2013. This present volume is published by BAR Publishing, 2016.

Printed in England

PUBLISHING

BAR titles are available from:

        BAR Publishing
        122 Banbury Rd, Oxford, OX2 7BP, UK
EMAIL   info@barpublishing.com
PHONE +44 (0)1865 310431
FAX   +44 (0)1865 316916
        www.barpublishing.com

Contents

List of Figures ii
Preface and acknowledgements v
Introduction vi
Environmental and Historical Background 1
    The Red Sea environment and sailing conditions 1
    The recent settlers of the Eritrean North and South Red Sea Regions 2
    The maritime component of Eritrean coastal people 2
    Adulis and the Aksumite maritime hegemony in the Red Sea 3
    The port facilities and the caravan route 6
    Navigational skills, ships and boat technology 6
    Subsistence, economy and religious beliefs of ancient Eritrean coastal people 7
The Eritrean coast in Italian and other European travellers' accounts and previous investigations 10
    The coast and the islands 11
    The eastern lowlands and the Danakil depression 21
    Water storage installations in the wider context of the south-central and southern Red Sea 26
The museum collections of Adulitan materials 31
    History of the museum collections 31
    Ceramic artefacts 32
    The local ceramic artefacts in the National Museum of Eritrea 34
    The imported ceramic artefacts in the National Museum of Eritrea 45
    The local ceramic artefacts in the National Museum of Addis Ababa 48
    The imported ceramic artefacts in the National Museum of Addis Ababa 59
    Vessel Stoppers 65
    Metal artefacts 71
    Metal artefacts kept in the National Museum of Eritrea 74
    Metal artefacts kept in the National Museum of Addis Ababa 75
    Metal artefacts kept in the African Museum in Rome 75
    Glass artefacts 82
    Glass artefacts kept in the National Museum of Eritrea 83
    Glass artefacts kept in the Addis Ababa Museum 86
    Stone artefacts kept in the Addis Ababa Museum 90
    Stone artefacts kept in the British Museum 90
    Shell artefacts and red coral kept in the National Museum of Eritrea 96
    Bone and ivory artefacts kept in the National Museum of Eritrea 96
Conclusion 99
Bibliography 101
    Primary Sources 101
    Secondary Sources 101
    Cartographic Sources 107

List of Figures

Fig. 1 Map of the Red Sea showing the location of Adulis and of the mainstay ports of the Roman (Myos Hormos and Berenike) and of the Byzantine (Clysma and Ayla) trade in the Red Sea. To the left: the hypothetical caravan route heading to the main urban settlements of the Eritrean-Ethiopian highland. 4
Fig. 2 General map of the Eritrean coast showing the location of bays and islands mentioned in the text........................8
Fig. 3 Mosaic of aerial photos, taken in the 1960-70s and covering the territory from Zula to Arafali from 15°N to 15°20'N and from 39°30'E to 39°45'E. 12
Fig. 4 Topographic map of Adulis showing the location of excavated trenches (modified from Bigliardi, Cappelli, Cocca 2013). 14
Fig. 5 Manuscript page from Sauter 1957-1961 (unpublished) showing the area in the Gulf of Zula surveyed underwater by a French team in 1957. 17
Fig. 6 A globular vessel found on the Island of Assarca during a visit by the author in 2004...19
Fig. 7 Map of the Eritrean coast, central sector, showing the location of modern and ancient places and ruins, wells and water sources, volcanic areas and salines mentioned in the sources and on the colonial maps. 20
Fig. 8 Map of the Eritrean coast, southern sector, showing the location of modern and ancient place and ruins, wells and water sources, volcanic areas and salines mentioned in the sources and on the colonial maps. 22
Fig. 9 Materials collected on the surface at Raheita by Francis Anfray in 1965, now kept in the National Museum of Addis Abeba. 23
Fig. 10 Map of the Eritrean coast, northern sector, showing the location of modern and ancient place and ruins, wells and water sources, volcanic areas and salines mentioned in the sources and on the colonial maps. 25
Fig. 11.1-7 Ceramic artefacts in the National Museum of Eritrea...36
Fig. 11.8-14 Ceramic artefacts in the National Museum of Eritrea...37
Fig. 11.15-22 Ceramic artefacts in the National Museum of Eritrea...38
Fig. 11.23-32 Ceramic artefacts in the National Museum of Eritrea...40
Fig. 11.33-40 Ceramic artefacts in the National Museum of Eritrea...41
Fig. 11.41-49 Ceramic artefacts in the National Museum of Eritrea...42
Fig. 11.50-57 Ceramic artefacts in the National Museum of Eritrea...44
Fig. 11.58 Ceramic artefacts in the National Museum of Eritrea. 45
Fig. 11.59-67 Imported Ceramic artefacts in the National Museum of Eritrea. 47
Fig. 11.68-75 Imported Ceramic artefacts in the National Museum of Eritrea. 49
Fig. 11.76-81 Imported Ceramic artefacts in the National Museum of Eritrea. 50
Fig. 12.1-10 Local Ceramic artefacts in the National Museum of Addis Ababa. 51
Fig. 12.11-21 Local Ceramics in the National Museum of Addis Ababa. 53
Fig. 12.22-39 Local Ceramics in the National Museum of Addis Ababa. 54
Fig. 12.40-54 Local Ceramics in the National Museum of Addis Ababa. 55
Fig. 12.55-67 Local Ceramics in the National Museum of Addis Ababa. 56
Fig. 12.68-85 Local Ceramics in the National Museum of Addis Ababa. 58
Fig. 12.86-103 Local Ceramics in the National Museum of Addis Ababa. 60
Fig. 12.104-121 Local and Imported Ceramics in the National Museum of Addis Ababa...62
Fig. 12.122-139 Imported Ceramics in the National Museum of Addis Ababa. 63
Fig. 12.140-154 Imported Ceramics in the National Museum of Addis Ababa. 64
Fig. 13.1-5 Vessel Stoppers in the National Museum of Eritrea...66
Fig. 13.6-10 Vessel Stoppers in the National Museum of Eritrea...67
Fig. 13.11-15 Vessel Stoppers in the National Museum of Eritrea...68
Fig. 13.16-20 Vessel Stoppers in the National Museum of Eritrea...69
Fig. 13.21-25 Vessel Stoppers in the National Museum of Eritrea...70
Fig. 13.26-30 Vessel Stoppers in the National Museum of Eritrea and in the National Museum of Addis Ababa. 72
Fig. 13.31-34 Vessel Stoppers in the National Museum of Eritrea and in the National Museum of Addis Ababa. 73
Fig. 14.1-6 Metal artefacts in the National Museum of Eritrea...75
Fig. 14.7-11 Metal artefacts in the National Museum of Eritrea, in the National Museum of Addis Ababa......................76
Fig. 14.12 Metal artefacts in the African Museum in Rome...78
Fig. 14.13 Metal artefacts in the African Museum in Rome...79
Fig. 14.14 Metal artefacts in the African Museum in Rome...80
Fig. 14.15 Metal artefacts in the African Museum in Rome...81
Fig. 14.16 Metal artefacts in the African Museum in Rome...82
Fig. 15.1-3 Glass artefacts in the National Museum of Eritrea. 83
Fig. 15.4-8 Glass artefacts in the National Museum of Eritrea. 84

Fig. 15.9-14 Glass artefacts in the National Museum of Eritrea. 85
Fig. 15.15 Glass artefacts in the National Museum of Eritrea. 86
Fig. 16.1-5 Stone artefacts in the National Museum of Addis Ababa. 88
Fig. 16.6-11 Stone artefacts in the National Museum of Eritrea. 89
Fig. 16.12-17 Stone artefacts in the National Museum of Eritrea. 91
Fig. 16.18-23 Stone artefacts in the National Museum of Eritrea. 92
Fig. 16.24-34 Stone artefacts in the National Museum of Eritrea. 93
Fig. 16.35-45 Stone artefacts in the National Museum of Eritrea and in the National Museum of Addis Ababa. 94
Fig. 16.1-49 Stone artefacts in the the British Museum. 95
Fig. 17.1-7 Shell, red coral, ivory and bone artefacts in the National Museum of Eritrea. 97

Preface and acknowledgements

In conducting research on trade and long distance connections during antiquity I have always been impressed by the complexity of trade networks and by the effect that they had on the knowledge and culture of people that were not directly involved in the trade and indeed of people who could not possibly afford the exotic products. I have wondered about both the people who stayed at home and those who started traveling and why. I always found myself hesitating between money and power, necessity and hunger, curiosity and knowledge, and I finally realized that it always will be a mixture of all these aspects. Adulis, as port, has been the gateway for people, ideas, goods and powers that had a major impact on the history of the Eritrean and Ethiopian highlands at least from the 1st millennium BC onwards. The formation of the early Ethio-Sabean society reflects mutual cultural exchanges occurred among the opposite coasts of the Red Sea. The subsequent introduction of Christian religion is also a consequence of a long time trade and cultural interaction with the Romans and Byzantines through the Red Sea, so as the introduction of coinage. Further, the spreading of the Islamic religion and the early Arab peopling in the Horn came also through the Eritrean coast and islands and coincided with the end of Adulis.

This book is the outcome of main research undertaken while holding a PhD scholarship at the University of Naples "L'Orientale" (completed in 2006), part of a long-term research project started by Rodolfo Fattovich at the University of Naples "L'Orientale" almost twenty years ago, investigating the circuits of exchange in the Red Sea during antiquity. Excavations directed by Fattovich and Kathryn Bard (Boston University) are still ongoing at the pharaonic site of Mersa Gawasis, on the Egyptian Red Sea coast. Excavations led by Andrea Manzo (University of Naples "L'Orientale"), in Sudan and research activities in the southern Red Sea of the MARES project (University of Exeter), are also part of this program of research in which I have been involved for the last ten years. During this time I benefited from working in surveys and excavations and from sharing ideas and suggestions with senior and younger colleagues, to all of whom go my warmest acknowledgements.

I am currently based at the University of Naples "L'Orientale", a most auspicious institution for conducting research on north-east Africa and the Red Sea in relation to past cultures of the Mediterranean and Indian Ocean. I wish to thank Giorgio Banti and Alessandro Triulzi, and especially Jacob Beyene for helping in translating Ge'ez inscriptions, the colleague in the departments of Classics for suggestions on the identification of some imported materials and Cinzia Perlingieri for having introduced me to the study of the pottery.

Original data for this book came from my examination of written sources and collections of materials from different museums and I am grateful to Antonella Martellucci, director of the former African Museum in Rome, the staff of the National Museum of Addis Ababa, Solène Marion de Procé for providing me with some photos of materials kept in this museum, Yosief Libsekal, director of the National Museum of Eritrea, Friar Ezio Tonini, director of the Center of African Studies in Asmara for facilitating my work and Francis Anfray for enabling me to examine the collection of materials from his previous excavations at Adulis now kept in the National Museum of Addis Abeba.

Since 2011 I have been involved in a project of excavation at Adulis, promoted by the Eritrean government and founded by private sponsors, lead by the National Museum of Eritrea and the Ce.RDO (Center for Research on Eastern Desert), in collaboration with the Northern Red Sea Region Museum of Massawa, the University of Naples "L'Orientale", the University Cattolica of Milan and with the patronage of the archaeology magazine Archeologia Viva. I gratefully acknowledge the promotors of this excavation, Yosief Libsekal and Alfredo and Angelo Castiglioni, and the sponsor Officine Piccini, for enabling me to continue the examination of Adulis pottery and to improve the analysis of the museum collections with comparative data from current stratigraphic excavations.

I am particularly grateful to my colleague and friend Luisa Sernicola, now field director of a number of surveys and excavations in the Aksum area, with whom I initially shared the enthusiasm of traveling in Eritrea and exploring the archaeology of this greatest country.

Introduction

The archaeology of the port site of Adulis and of the Eritrean coast is extremely important for many reasons. First of all, on account of its geographical position of passage between the Red Sea and the Indian Ocean, this region has always been a key area for understanding the long term history of contacts among the major state-based entities of Antiquity: the Hellenistic and South-Arabian states, the Roman empire and the Aksumite kingdom, the Byzantine and Sassanian empires. Further, recent excavations at the Pharaonic site of Mersa Gawasis (Red Sea, Egypt) revealed the presence of pottery probably coming from the Ethiopian-Eritrean regions in contexts dating to the 2nd millennium BC (Manzo 2010). These finds confirms the involvement of the Adulis region in the earliest exchange circuits in the Red Sea.

Adulis, the coastal region, the lowlands and the islands of Eritrea have always been considered under the influence, control or as part of the Aksumite kingdom, one of the oldest and largest African kingdoms, which developed on the Ethiopian-Eritrean highlands from the first centuries BC to Late Antiquity. After a preliminary examination of the literary and archaeological evidence, the author realized that, in fact, very little was known about this important port and that available sources on past explorations and past excavations in the area needed to be re-examined, particularly in the light of recent investigations conducted in other contemporary ports of the Egyptian Red Sea coast. Adulis was closely related to the Aksumite kingdom but it maintained a certain independence – conditioned by particular historical events – due to its strong geographical, environmental and cultural differences, which still today distinguish the region of the coastal lowlands from the highlands.[1]

Adulis and the Eritrean coast is a key area for archaeological investigation in the northern Horn of Africa as it has the potential to explain issues concerning the formation, development and end of the Aksumite kingdom, on its territorial assessment, on the contacts with the South-Arabian states and on the diffusion of Christianity. In fact, it is through the coastal regions that contacts with earlier state-based society happened, if we consider, as an example, the early Ethio-Sabean state developed on the Ethiopian-Eritrean highlands and closely related to the South-Arabian states. It was via the sea and the Eritrean coast that Christianity initially penetrated the kingdom of Aksum, influencing the whole future history of this region, while the earliest Muslim caliphates from Saudi Arabia migrated to the Dahlak Islands in Eritrea, starting the Muslim penetration in Africa which also contributed to the collapse of the Aksumite kingdom.

Archaeological (Fattovich 1995; Fattovich 1996: 158-176; Manzo 2005, Zazzaro 2006 and Zazzaro 2009) and historical (Kobischanov 1966; Munro-Hay 1982; Munro-Hay 1991a) sources well attest the overseas contacts of the Aksumites with Greeks, Romans, Egyptians, Nubians, South Arabians, Persians and Indians, starting from the 1st century AD until the Arab occupation of the western shores of the Red Sea and the islands in the 8th century AD. These contacts certainly took place through the port town of Adulis, at least until the 7th century AD when the town was abandoned for unclear reasons, probably either environmental (a flood or an earthquake) or human (the Muslim migration and successive invasions).

The history of Adulis is strongly related to that of other Red Sea ports. A particular connection with the Arabian Peninsula through Farasan Island and the port of Qāni', in the Ḥaḍramawt, has also to be mentioned, although further archaeological excavation are needed in order to better understand the kind of relationship these two regions had in the past. Certainly archaeological and historical evidence well attest that together with other main Red Sea ports like Berenike, Myos Hormos first and Clysma and Ayla later, Adulis articulated the trade among the Mediterranean and the Indian Ocean in the Roman and Byzantine period. According to recent archaeological evidence in the 1st and 2nd centuries AD Berenike and Myos Hormos were clearly the mainstay of Roman presence in the Red Sea, after the 3rd century Myos Hormos declines while Berenike regain its role until the 5th century. From the 4th century onwards a re-organization of the Roman trade had occurred, the northern Red Sea ports, Ayla and Clysma, were more and more directly linked to Adulis especially from the end of the 5th century AD coinciding with the decline of Berenike (Nappo 2009). Adulis had at that time a strong alliance with the Byzantines in the control of the Red Sea and was one of the most powerful ports in the Red Sea and privileged port for trade with India.[2]

In the last twenty years several archaeological research projects have been carried out along the Red Sea coast, particularly in Egypt, Jordan, Sudan and Yemen. The results of these investigations enriched our knowledge of the population, exchanges and contacts among the different regions of the Red Sea. In this period, apart from a short survey conducted by the University of Asmara (Department of Anthropology and Archaeology), the National Museum of Eritrea and Northern Red Sea Regional Museum and the University of Southampton in 2004 and 2005 at Adulis, very little was done on the Eritrean coast and the southern Red Sea coast in general. This is due to the fact that the country was involved in a 30 years war with Ethiopia from 1961 to 1991, when Eritrea gained its independence after various vicissitudes. The country

---

[1] A recent overview on the history and archaeology of the northern Horn of Africa in the 1st millennium BC and 1st millennium AD has been outlined respectively by Fattovich 2013: 1-60 and by Phillipson 2011.
[2] An overview on the history and archaeology of Red Sea and Gulf of Aden ports has been outlined in two recent books respectively by Sidebotham 2011 and by Salles and Sedov 2010.

remained politically sensitive, making it difficult to initiate archaeological projects in the area, until 2011 when the Adulis Project, promoted by the government and led by the National Museum of Asmara, the Northern Red Sea Regional Museum in collaboration with the Ce.RDO (Centro di Studi per il Deserto Orientale, Varese, Italy) and other Italian institutions among which the University of Naples "L'Orientale", started.

Unlike the Egyptian coast, which was generally ignored by scholars until the second half of the 20th century, Adulis was the object of important excavations and visits by a number of travelers at the end of the 19th century and in the early 20th century. In this time the Eritrean coast was also carefully explored and studied in its environmental, social and historical aspects by the Italian colonialists.

The focus of the present book is a re-examination of the archaeology of Adulis and the Eritrean coast through written classical and colonial sources and archaeological finds in the light of more recent excavations conducted in the Red Sea area and on the Ethiopian-Eritrean highlands os as to re-consider and renovate studies on this subject and to facilitate future investigations in the area.

A particular focus of the archaeology of the northern Horn of Africa in the last years was the reconstruction of the paleo-environment in relation to archaeological evidence (Butzer 1981; Bard 1997) as a way to understand the historical process, in opposition to previous studies that were more focused on the analysis of historical and literary sources (Kobischanov 1965, Kobischanov 1966, Munro-Hay 1982 and Munro-Hay 1991a and b). A similar approach has been in part adopted in this book. So far, very little has been written in archaeology on the maritime environment and sailing conditions in the southern Red Sea, which the author believes are important factors to better understand the dynamics of human modification and adaptation to the sea environment. The investigation of the maritime component of ancient people inhabiting the coastal areas of Eritrea is also a key theme in this book, as well as all the possible implications of the interaction between the human and maritime environment, the technical and practical aspects of the human exploitation of the sea, and the cognitive and mental system related to the perception of the sea. Besides the environmental aspects, historical, literary, archaeological and ethnographic aspects of Red Sea navigation, maritime trade contacts and the technologies adopted to navigate in this sea are also considered.

Eritrea is a very rich country in terms of archaeology, but very little has been published at an international level on the archaeology of Eritrea apart from the work by Schmidt, Curtis and Zelalem Teka (2008), in which the coastal area of Eritrea was almost completely neglected. In this respect, the scattered observations reported in travellers' accounts, colonial documents and archives and more recently by archaeologists who investigated the Eritrean coastal regions, are well worth collecting and re-examining. In fact, these sources have never been properly examined before from the archaeological point of view, and a lot of information is still unpublished. Most of the sources, the documentation and the cartography from the colonial period that the author consulted for this research, were available in a restricted number of specialized Italian libraries, in colonial archives, cartographic companies and in antiquary shops. These sources can by their very nature be vague or contradictory in their description of potential archaeological evidence and they may lack scientific consistency due to the fact that most of the authors were not archaeologists. The coastal areas that have been considered of potential archaeological interest are examined also in relation to their geographical location and environmental aspects. The archaeological evidence mentioned in these sources is of various types: stone structures, tombs, buildings, pottery, lithic etc... The author also considered, in a separate chapter, various sources related to the evidence of water storage installations as they represent an important and widely diffused category of ancient constructions recorded in the southern Red Sea. They are analysed in the wider context of water supply systems adopted in the souther Red Sea in general. Another chapter focuses on the archaeological evidence recorded in the area of the eastern lowland as this area seems to have played a key role in the connection between people of the coast and people of the highlands. The final aim of this section is to illustrate the potential that future archaeological investigations have for investigating and reconstructing dynamics of regional interconnectivity in the northern Horn of Africa during antiquity.

The second part of the book illustrates the collections of materials from previous excavations conducted at Adulis and re-examines the information given for each category of finds in the light of more recent data. Examined material finds were collected by the Swedish archaeologist Richard Sundström in 1906, the Italian archaeologist Roberto Paribeni in 1906 and by the French archaeologist Francis Anfray in the 1960s. These collections are kept in five different museums, in Ethiopia, Eritrea, Italy, United Kingdom and Sweden and they include pottery, jar stoppers, various metal and stone objects, glass vessels and organic materials such as ivory, shell, bone and coral artifacts. Although these materials lack clear stratigraphic information, they still provide important new information on trade contacts and on the subsistence and economy of people who inhabited the site and the region around. The finds and related information have been collected in a database meant to provide a shared record for all the museums in which the Adulis materials are currently kept, in order to prevent the dispersion and disappearance of these data and to facilitate and improve future research. This database is a sort of expanded inventory of almost all the existing material finds from Adulis and is not included in this book as it is rather to be considered an instrument for the museums. In this book, the Adulitan finds are treated as an instrument for better understanding the history of Adulis and of Red Sea trade and contacts and for stimulating future studies.

Environmental and Historical Background

The Red Sea environment and sailing conditions

Environmental aspects, such as the Red Sea coast and seabed topography, tides, currents, winds and their seasonal change, are essential to understand characteristics of the maritime activities conducted in the Red Sea during antiquity. Equally, a brief description of the coastal landscape will help to better understand the development of particular adaptation strategies to the maritime environment and its use as a resource by the inhabitants.

The Red Sea extends for 2300 kilometres from the Suez Canal and the Bab el-Mandeb Strait, varying from 260 to 340 kilometres in width. In such a relatively small area different maritime cultures developed and peoples from the Mediterranean and Indian Ocean regions interacted with one other during antiquity.

The Red Sea was mentioned in Greek, Latin and Arab classical sources as being dangerous for navigation because of coral reefs near the surface in the open sea and close to the shore. In fact the high temperature and salinity of the water cause coral to proliferate. For this reason finds of ancient wooden ships, especially close to the coast, remain very rare.

Nonetheless the Red Sea coast was characterised by a succession of well-protected bays, especially on the western side which is considered more suitable for navigation. In particular, the presence of springs originating from ancient wadyan (rivers) in the north-western coastal sector not only provided fresh water supplies for mariners but also helped to reduce the growth of coral reefs in correspondence to the merse (bays). In the 2nd millennium BC and in the early 1st millennium AD some of these bays formed lagoons developed at the wadi mouths which provided natural access for ships (Blue 2007; Hein et al. 2008). The exploitation of the geomorphology and natural conditions of the coast to establish ports was a common practice in the Indian Ocean-Red Sea area in antiquity and in modern times, as for example the mouth of the Wadi Darabat in Dhofar, according to recent ethnographic sources (Davidde and Petriaggi 1996). However, the same natural conditions may have prevented the long term viability of ancient ports on the Red Sea coast (Heuglin 1877, Krebs 1969).

The merse formed at the mouth of wadyan are usually delimited by ras (headlands), providing good landmarks for ships navigating along the coast. In spite of the danger that the coral reefs represented for navigation, they might also have been useful for mooring during the night. The author's experience of navigating in the north-western sector of the Red Sea with a reconstructed Pharaonic boat and a diver cruiser escorting the boat (Ward 2012), demonstrated that experienced modern mariners do not use any sophisticated equipment to identify coral reefs: they know their exact location by heart and on the basis of the coastal landmarks and observation of the water surface. Today, diver cruisers regularly stop on these coral reefs for underwater explorations and they also anchor there during the night.

The Red Sea basin is characterised by three main deep channels for navigation. The central channel is the deepest, suitable for navigation by large modern ships. The two lateral channels are parallel and separated from the coasts by two sequences of coral reefs; they can take small and medium ships (Red Sea Pilot 1909: 3), as they did during antiquity.

Navigation in the Red Sea was conducted not far from the coast, always keeping sight of the mainland landmarks and such features as islands and coral reefs. Bays, scattered islands and reefs played an important role in the Red Sea navigation, being used as stopping places during the night. The fact that navigation in the Red Sea during Antiquity was mainly conducted at a short distance from the coast, and presumably along the two minor navigable channels, is also demonstrated by the fact that the first century sailors' manual Periplus Maris Erythraei, gives particular emphasis to the description of the coastal landscape and of landmarks which served for orientation to sailing boats.

The Red Sea wind system is regulated by the seasonal cycle of the Indian Ocean monsoons. During the summer season, from June to September, northern winds prevail in the Red Sea, when the southwest monsoon blows in the Indian Ocean. During the winter season, when the northeast monsoon blows in the Indian Ocean, southern winds prevail in the Red Sea. At the same time local breezes (Red Sea Pilot 1909: 12-14) and local variations in wind direction have to be taken into account, particularly in the southern Red Sea where winds are more variable than in the north. Southern winds blowing during the winter season in the Red Sea, from the strait of Bab el-Mandeb to latitude 17°N, and in the central part, from October to May and from November to April, are indeed variable and consistent from the north, especially in January, in the area of the Suez Canal and from latitude 23°N to latitude 19°N. In June, when north-northwest winds prevail in the Red Sea, variable strong winds, usually coming from west or southwest, characterise the southern regions and the Gulf of Aden. In August and September, these same winds are initially not very strong and are characterised by long periods of calm. At that time, at latitude 23°N and at latitude 15°N, north and southeast winds can merge (Red Sea Pilot 1909: 9-14). In the Gulf of Aden, during the winter monsoon, winds blow from the east and become calm at latitude 20°N and in Aden.

Currents in the Red Sea also usually depend on the Indian Ocean monsoons. In January northeast monsoons generate westerly currents in the Gulf of Aden and north-north-westerly throughout the Red Sea. In summer, with the southwest monsoon, currents in the Red Sea are less strong, flowing in a south-south-east direction. Currents can also be locally variable, especially in the south of the Red Sea. Along the Egyptian coast, from November to March, north and northeasterly winds produce a strong western current, but in the absence of wind the current flows in the opposite direction (Red Sea Pilot 1909: 22-23).

Along the Red Sea coast tides are variable, particularly in close proximity to narrow channels (Red Sea Pilot 1909: 21). While tides may not have affected navigation in the Red Sea during antiquity very much, they may well have had an impact on fishing activities.

In general it was probably more convenient to sail in the southern Red Sea, either from south to north, according to the seasonal winds, or from east to west in view of the frequent variability. A Red Sea Pilot published in 1909 states that the Massawa Canal was the best passage for sailing vessels navigating in the southern Red Sea, because dangers due to the coral reefs were reduced in this area (Red Sea 1909: 212-213). In addition, the numerous islands located in this channel may have served for mooring during the night. A series of well-protected bays all along the Eritrean coast may also have provided favourable mooring spots and anchorages.

On the other side, the north-west coast of the Red Sea has a number of underground fresh water sources, not far from the coast, which may have guaranteed water supply for boats and ships navigating along the coast while the southern Red Sea coast is very arid and with few water resources. In this case, wells and cisterns carved in the bedrock all along the south-western shore of the Red Sea and on the islands may have provided the necessary water supply for sailing boats and ships in this region since earlier times (Puglisi 1953; Puglisi 1969).

Compared to the southern sector, the northern coast of Eritrea is short and sandy with very few landmarks; the bays are not well sheltered and the sea bottom is very shallow (Red Sea Pilot 1909: 211-215). This, and the absence of natural resources in inland northern Eritrea, may explain the reduced number of significant archaeological evidence. On the contrary the Eritrean coast south of Massawa is characterised by several protected bays that make for good anchorages. The hinterland is very arid, especially south of the Buri Peninsula in the Danakil depression, a wide volcanic desert region with basalt rocks and sedimentation from alluvial torrents. However in some wadi area soil can be fertile and partially cultivable during the rainy season (Lanzoni 1920: 249-250).

The recent settlers of the Eritrean North and South Red Sea Regions

The recent settlers of the Eritrean coastal region are the Tigré, which is the predominant ethno-linguistic group, the Afar, the Saho, the Tigriyna and a few Arab speaking peoples originating from the Yemen (Department of Statistics and Documentation of Northern Red Sea, 06/09/2008). Cultural groups of the Eritrean coast have different cultural manifestations, religion and dietary habits. The majority of the different cultural groups are Muslim while the minority are Christian. Recent unpublished ethnographic research conducted by the Asmara National Museum reports that the Tigré and Saho peoples depend on agro-pastoralism. The main dish of the Tigré people is meat with milk, while fish is only a recent introduction. The Saho people live on porridge, milk and cereals. Both Tigré and Saho people grow corn, sorghum, water-melon and tomato; sesame and cotton were common during the colonial period. Domesticated animals like oxen and camels are employed for farming, as well as modern means such as tractors. In the Foro region irrigation is widely used since rainfall is rare and seasonal streams are abundant. Due to the high temperatures in summer and in parts of the spring and fall, seasonal movements with the cattle, goats, sheep and camel to the highlands in search of pasture are regular. Fishing is the common livelihood and the daily consumption of Afar people. Tuna and shark are among the fish in common use. Trading of all sorts is a daily activity among the Afar, including fish in exchange for other goods.[1]

The maritime component of Eritrean coastal people

During antiquity, the sea was the main means of subsistence for people inhabiting the Eritrean coast, and it was a better means for communication and transport than traveling across the coastal plains, which are desert and inhospitable. The favorable sailing conditions, the presence of thousands of small islands providing stopping points for navigation, and the proximity of the African and Arabian coasts probably encouraged navigation from an early date, perhaps in order to reach sources of products, such as obsidian, to exchange goods or indeed out of mere curiosity.

Contacts between the northern Horn of Africa and its neighbours across the straits are attested since earlier times. Studies on the distribution of obsidian in the southern Red Sea regions suggest the existence of maritime connections involving both sides of the southern Red Sea from as early as the 7th millennium BC. A certain amount of archaeological evidence attests the existence of genuine maritime exchange networks between the norther Horn of Africa, Southern Arabia and Egypt at least from the 3rd–2nd millennium BC, and these played an important role in the formation and development of state-based

---
[1] This information is gathered from informal interviews and verified using the official statistical report prepared by the Department of statistics, documentation and information of the NRSR (Adulis Fieldwork Report 2011 of the National Museum of Asmara, unpublished).

societies in the southern Red Sea (Zarins 1990; Fattovich 1997). Further historical and archaeological evidence demonstrates the reciprocal cultural influence of proto-Sabean and proto-Aksumite societies which evolved in the Ethio-Sabean kingdom of Da'amat in the 8th-5th century and the pre-Aksumite culture in the 9th-8th / 4th-3rd century BC (Fattovich 1996), again a result of maritime contacts between the opposite coasts.

If the inhabitants of the Eritrean coastal planes developed a maritime component in their culture from earliest times, the people inhabiting the Ethiopian-Eritrean highlands were and remained essentially rural. People on the coast actively participated, with South-Arabian coastal people, in the formation of a "common maritime culture" in the southern Red Sea. The geographical closeness of these societies living on opposite shores might have brought about a common maritime tradition among coastal populations of the southern Red Sea. Evidence of peoples originally from the African shores of the Red Sea who settled in the Arabian Thiamah since pre-Islamic period is still attested in that area (Serjeant 1969: 25-33).

The formation of the Aksumite kingdom on the Ethiopian-Eritrean highland dating from the 2nd century BC / 1st century AD involved the progressive unification of the highland settlements, while the role of the coastal region in this process is not clear from the epigraphical and literary sources. The inscription reported by Cosmas Indicoplustes in 525 AD on the Monumentum Adulitanum mentions the Aksumite defense of the coastal lowland in the 3rd century AD (Wolska-Conus II, 61), a fact that might suggest the important role that the people inhabiting this region had on the subsistence and economy of the Aksumite kingdom. In fact, natural resources available on the coast and in the Eritrean lowlands are always mentioned in classical sources as the main products exported from the Ethiopian and Eritrean regions. Analysis of Adulitan pottery from recent excavations suggests that at least until the 3rd-4th century AD the ancient port town of Adulis and the coastal planes might have maintained a certain independence from the Aksumite kingdom, not surprising if we consider the strong geographical, environmental and cultural differences which still distinguish the region of the coastal lowlands from the highlands. Compared to the coastal areas, the plateau has a temperate climate that allows more vegetation and wet crops. Environmental differences are also reflected in the presence of several distinct ethnic groups in cultural, religious and linguistic traits in the present, as in antiquity.

The inhabitants of the coastal regions mentioned by the Greek geographers and in Latin sources were the nomad populations of Troglodytes, Ikthiophagoi, or Barbaroi, usually relegated to the coast south of Adulis. The maritime component of the Troglodytes and the Ikthiophagoi societies is well attested in classical sources. The Ikthiophagoi were known for their subsistence based on fishing activities, and the Troglodytes as cave dwellers of the coastal Red Sea plains (Manzo 1996). Occasionally the Troglodytes were mentioned together with the Aithiopes, to indicate more in general the people inhabiting the regions south of Egypt, although these latter have to be identified as people different from the Troglodytes in their ethnic and somatic characteristics. They inhabited the inland regions, while the Troglodytes are often mentioned in association with the Ikthiophagoi, people that certainly inhabited the coastal region on both sides of the Red Sea (cf. Pliny the Helder, Natural History ed. Conte 1982: 149-154). It is interesting to note that coastal people on both sides of the southern Red Sea are identified as the same people, with the same name, while people inland are clearly considered apart.

Adulis and the Aksumite maritime hegemony in the Red Sea

Like the Egyptian ports of Berenike and Myos Hormos, Adulis was one of the most important ports in the Red Sea for trade in the Mediterranean and the Indian Ocean during the Roman and Late Roman period. The site is located on the Eritrean coast, in a strategic position between the Mediterranean and the Indian Ocean, in the protected Gulf of Zula, delimited to the north by the Ghedem Mountain, still used today as a landmark by ships navigating in the area (Figures 1 and 2). At present the site is situated some 5 km from the coast, on the north bank of the Haddas River. The Haddas Valley was a caravan trail linking the coast and the Qoḥayto highland where the Aksumite town of Koloe was located, the stopping point for caravans heading to Aksum as final destination. As previously mentioned, the history of Adulis is closely related to the development of the Aksumite kingdom but its foundation was certainly independent.

According to Munro-Hay (1991a: 129), the port of Adulis may date back to the period of the Ethio-Sabean kingdom of D'MT. The Greek geographers do not mention the name of Adulis but a series of ports, possibly of Ptolemaic foundation: Sabat, a base for elephant-hunting, Elea further south, Melinus with another hunting base and finally Antiphilus (Martin 1863: 337). In the first half of the 6th century AD, Cosmas Indicopleustes observed a Greek epigraph, part of the so called Monumentum Adulitanum, celebrating the military expeditions conducted by Ptolemy III Euergetes in Asia in the 3rd century BC at the entrance of the town of Adulis (Wolska-Conus 1968: 372-378). This is further evidence suggests a pre-Aksumite and pre-Roman foundation of Adulis, although many scholars doubt that the Greek stelae was originally placed there; it might have been brought from another place in order to charge the existing monument with ideological and symbolic meaning (Pedroni 2000: 26 and 29, Kirwan 1972: 166-169).

Literary sources testify to the activity of the Adulis port from the 1st century AD onwards, although Pliny suggested the town was founded by escaped Egyptian slaves on the basis of the etymology of the name Adulis, from the Greek a doule (Naturalis Historia VI, 172). This hypothesis has been excluded by almost every subsequent scholar, but

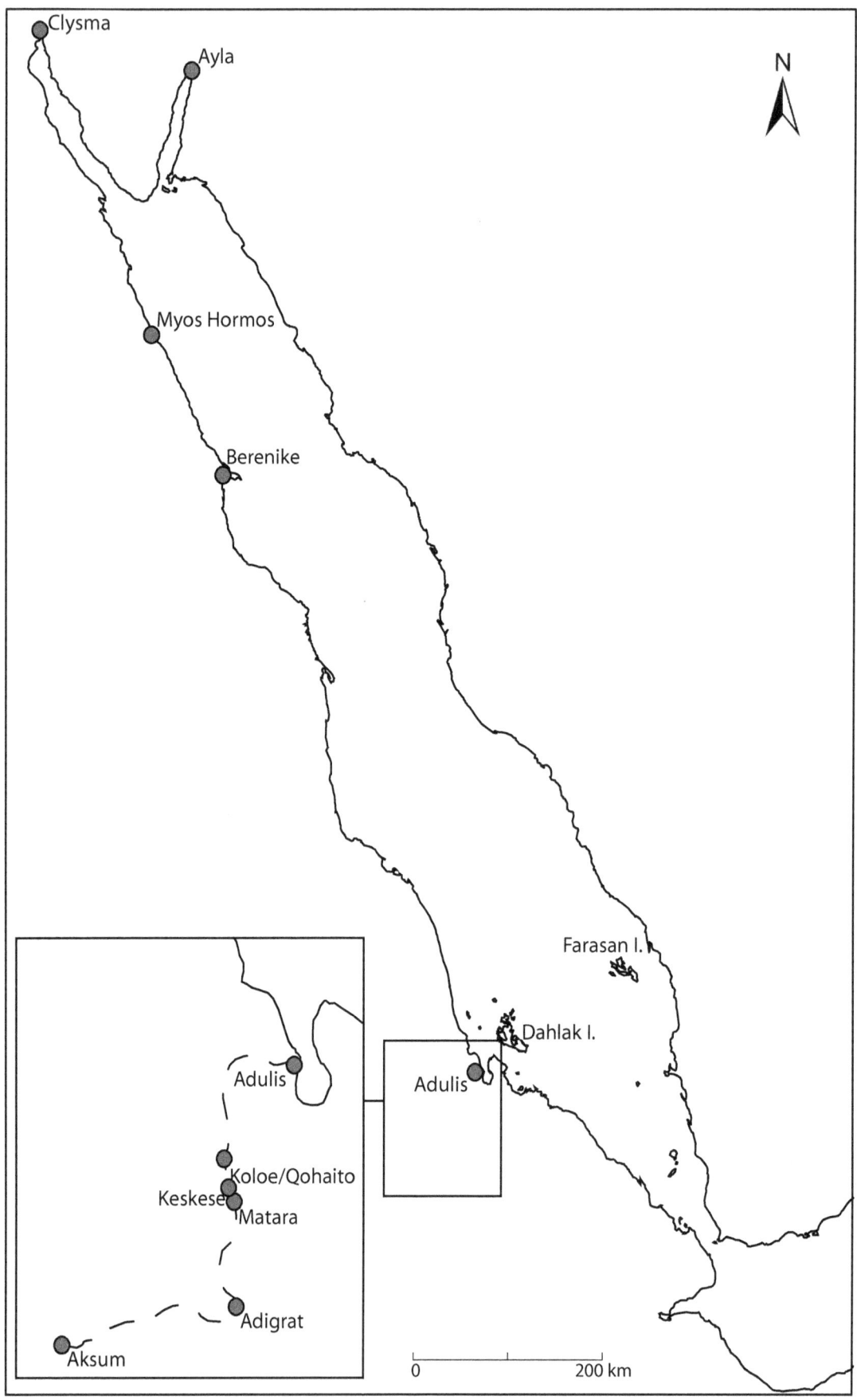

Fig. 1 Map of the Red Sea showing the location of Adulis and of the mainstay ports of the Roman (Myos Hormos and Berenike) and of the Byzantine (Clysma and Ayla) trade in the Red Sea. To the left: the hypothetical caravan route heading to the main urban settlements of the Eritrean-Ethiopian highland.

there may have been previous connections between Egypt and the Eritrean coast. De Romanis suggests an ancient African linguistic origin for the name Adulis, indicating a foundation of the town dating back at least to the early Egyptian navigation in the Red Sea (cf. De Romanis 1996: 152-156).

Only future archaeological excavation will be able to give more detailed information on the origin of Adulis. What we know so far is that in the 1st century AD, Adulis is described as a town (oppidum Aduliton) by Pliny and as a small village and emporion nomimon ruled by a king called Zoskales by the anonymous author of the Periplus (ed. Casson 1989: 45). At this time, Adulis was politically independent from Aksum, but it was the principal port for the products brought in by the inhabitants of the adjacent highland and coastal settlements.

The denomination of Adulis as emporion nomimon is common to two other ports named in the Periplus, Mouza and Apologos. It might refer to the fact that these ports were "legally limited", authorized ports and were safe markets in opposition to the piracy areas in the close vicinity (cf. Bresson 1991 and Casson 1989: 275-276). This might further prove that Adulis played a role of intermediary among the people inhabiting the Barbaria, the territory south of Adulis, or the Troglodytes and the Ethiopians, as mentioned by Pliny (Naturalis Historia VI.172), and the Roman merchants. A role that Adulis seems to have fulfilled also at the time of Cosmas Indicopleustes in the 5th century AD (Topographie Chrétienne II.49.6-8).

Exported products from Adulis mentioned in the 1st century AD sources are: ivory, obsidian, rhinoceros horn, turtle shells and other exotic products, all available in the coastal regions and from the islands. Among imported products, textiles from Egypt and the East, glass from Judea, metals from India, and oil and wine from Italy and Syria are mentioned.

As anticipated, Adulis had a major role in the involvement of the Aksum in the Red Sea trade. Despite its agriculture-based economy, the rise and development of the Aksumite Kingdom during the 1st-4th century AD was strongly stimulated by active participation in the exchange trade networks between East and West in the Red Sea and the Indian Ocean through the port of Adulis (Kobischanov 1966, Munro-Hay 1991a). Epigraphic evidence attests that in the 4th century AD the Aksumite kingdom included other tributary small kingdoms, one of which, Gabaza, might have been located on the coast (Huntingford 1989: 51-52 and 149-150) and might have been a further development of the kingdom ruled by Zoskales mentioned in the Periplus. Archaeological evidence and literary sources both suggest the existence of other coastal settlements or anchorages of Aksumite influence in addition to the main port of Adulis. Architectural constructions in the Aksumite style have been recorded at the island of Dahlak Kebir (Puglisi 1953; Puglisi 1969; Insoll 2001), and Aksumite pottery is attested in the island of Dese (Peacock and Blue 2007: 58). The inscription of the Monumentum Adulitanum also attests that the Aksumite king ordered the Salté population to guard the Red Sea coast on the African and Arabian sides (Wolska-Conus II, 61), a fact that seems to prove the maritime hegemony of Aksum on the Eritrean coast and perhaps on the opposite coast in the 3rd century AD. The title of the king Ezana (ca. 320 – 360 AD) "King of Saba and Himyar" seems also to attest that this sort of hegemony was extended to the Arabian coast (Munro-Hay 1991: 133).

The site of Adulis is known also in Byzantine sources, particularly the History of the Wars I by Procopius and Christian Topography by Cosmas Indicopleustes, as the main port for trade between the Mediterranean and the Indian Ocean on the African coast of the Red Sea (Munro-Hay 1982). Other main ports at that time were Clysma and Ayla (ancient name of Aqaba) in the Gulf of Aqaba. In the same way, Adulis survived the collapse of the Roman trade in the Red Sea and took over the Egyptian ports that, for environmental and political reasons, ceased trading between the 4th and 5th century AD.

In the 5th century AD, Adulis was ruled by Asbas while Ellatzbaas was king of the Aksumite kingdom (Topographie Chrétienne II.56.8) and people from the Barbaria continued to export products like frankincense, cassia and sugar cane through its port (Topographie Chrétienne II.49.6-8). Strong overseas connections might have existed at this time with the Egyptian Christian centers as suggested by the fact that a Bishop of Coptos and Adulis took part in the Council of Chalcedony (Monneret de Villard 1947: 613-623).

At the time of king Kaleb the maritime activities of Aksumites in the Red Sea and Indian Ocean reached their greatest prosperity (Munro-Hay 1982: 114-115). Historical sources related to the expeditions of Christian missionaries in the Red Sea attest the possibility that Aksumites expanded their hegemony on the Farasan Islands where archaeological evidence of Christianity is clearly attested (Baldry 1978: 89). According to Procopius, Adulitan merchants also traded with Indians sailing through the Indian Ocean, using their own ships (Kobischanov 1966: 21). In 531 AD the Aksumite maritime power in the Red Sea and Indian Ocean was so widely recognised that a Byzantine embassy was sent to Aksum in order to convince the Aksumite king to co-operate against the Sassanians and destroy the Sassanian monopoly of the silk trade (Bury 1958: 325).

There is also evidence that Aksumites conducted naval battles in the Martyrium Sancti Arethae, a source reporting the story of the naval expedition of the Aksumite kingdom against the Hymiarites, in South Arabia, in 523-525 AD. Based on this source, Munro-Hay pointed out that Aksum commanded a fleet (Munro-Hay 1991a: 185-186). A shipyard existed in a locality called Gabaza, near Adulis, at least from 525 AD when a fleet including ships from the Farasan Islands, Ayla, Clysma, Berenike and Iotabe were gathered for the naval expedition of the king Kaleb against the Hymiarites (Acta Sanctorum 1869). The Aksumite hegemony in the southern Red Sea seems to have ended when Sassanians took control of the Himyarite territories in 570 AD ca. (Munro-Hay 1991a: 137-138). The Sassanian authority in South Arabia then persisted until the Muslim conquest. In the 8th century AD an Ummayyad Caliph was established on the Island of Dahlak Kebir, later extending its hegemony to Masswa definitively taking over Adulis.

Aksumite coins and pottery found overseas also demonstrate the direct or indirect circulation of the Aksumite culture through maritime trade routes. Aksumite coins have been found at Meroe (Sudan), Antioch on the Orontes (Turkey), Kerala (India), Aqaba (Jordan), Jerusalem (Barkay 1981: 57-59; Arslan 1996: 307-316), Caesarea (Israel) (Meshorer 1965-1966: 76), Bet-Shean, Baalbek (Lebanon) (Bendall 1986-1987: 91); a coin of king Aphilas was found at Berenike (Sidebotham 2002: 41), Aksumite coins associated with Byzantine coins were found at Aden (Munro-Hay 1991a) and more recently on the north coast of Saudi Arabia. Aksumite pottery, particularly jars and bowls dating to the 4th-5th century AD, have been found at Berenike (Tomber 2007: 175-182) and Qāni' (Sedov 1996: 35: III and Salles and Sedov 2010). Strangely, Aksumite pottery found overseas does not include amphoras. The Aksumite power in the Red Sea trade was so strong at that time that it involved also indirect contacts with China, according to literary sources (Munro-Hay 1991a: 139).

The port facilities and the caravan route

The site of Adulis is currently located at a distance of ca. 5 km from the sea. The anonymous author of the Periplus states that the site was located at a distance of 20 stadia from the seashore, which corresponds to ca. 3.6 km, and that the landing place was situated on the island of Didoros (Periplus of the Erythrean Sea 260.5), which has been recently identified with the island of Dissei by Peacock and Blue (2007), an island located immediately outside the Gulf of Zula, not too far from the coast as compared with the other islands of the Dahlak Archipelago. Later sources also mention the fact that Adulis was distant from the sea: Procopius, in the 6th century AD, describes the port of the Adulites as located else where than the town of Adulis, which was 20 stadia inland from the coast (History of the Wars I.xix.22).

Cosmas Indicopleustes states that the town of Adulis was located 4 km from the coast and was used as a port by the Aksumites (Topographie Chrétienne II.54). In the version of the Vatican codex of the Christian Topography by Cosmas, at sheet 15r, the text is interrupted by a drawing featuring the boundary of the kingdom of Aksum and the "Customs of Gabaza" located on the Red Sea shore and not far from Adulis, positioned further inland. This place might be associated with the naval station of Gabaza named in the Martyrium Sancti Arethae (Acta Sanctorum 1869). According to this source the naval station of Gabaza was located within the borders of Adulis town and was big enough to hold thirty-eight ships. Gabaza might also be associated with the coastal region in general if we consider the fact that in the Ge'ez inscription DAE 8, dating to the 4th century AD, a Gabazes king is named and the same name also appears on a coin (Kirwan 1972: 167, Huntingford 1989: 50). The term Gabaza has usually been associated with the Tigriyna and Amaric term meaning "head of a small church, custodian of the treasure and church furniture" (Huntingford 1989: 50), while the first meaning of the word in Ge'ez is "shore", referred to a river (the term gabaz is employed to translate river fluminis in Exodus VII.15). To date archaeological surveys have not been able to identify the location of Gabaza (cf. Sundström 1907: 181-182, Peacock and Blue 2007).

It is not surprising that the port of Adulis was separated from the town, as this was common to other ports in Antiquity both in the Mediterranean and in the Indian Ocean (Ray 1994: 49-50). The process of loading and off-loading commodities was less complicated and safer. The large ocean-going ships could anchor in deep water and in a safe place, also protected from piracy incursions, while small boats were used to transport commodities from the landing place up river to the town, where they were most likely stored in storerooms not far from the river shore as seen at Qāni' (Salles and Sedov 2010).

According to literary sources, most of the imported goods were transported to Aksum. The most suitable way to get to the highlands was the valley of the Haddas river which heads south-west to Addi Kaieh on the highlands where the town of Koloe, mentioned in the sources, is located. According to the Periplus it took three days to get from Adulis to Koloe and from there five days to get to Aksum. Nonnosus mentions the distance between Adulis and Aksum (Photius I.3.6.35-36 ed. and tr. Henry 1959) as fifteen days, while Procopius states twelve days (History of the Wars I.xix.22).

It seems that this caravan route was under Aksumite control: the Ge'ez inscription DAE 10 mentions the fact that the king Ezana sent a punitive expedition against the Sarane that assaulted a caravan while this was passing through their kingdom, the location of which has been tentatively identified by Huntingford in the region between Adulis and Aksum.

Navigational skills, ships and boat technology

In the Yambulo account, reported by Diodorus in the 1st century BC, it is attested that Ethiopian pirates already knew a route to get to India (Diodorus Siculus II.5), perhaps making a single stop in an Indian Ocean island (cf. Kobischanov 1966: 19-20).

According to Munro-Hay (1991: 186) "[…] as a trading nation with a maritime outlet of great importance, and later on an empire to administer overseas, it is certain that Aksum's merchant fleet or navy was a useful, even vital, part of the apparatus of commerce and government." This inspiring sentence reflects an historical reality that unfortunately has not been proved so far by any archaeological evidence of vessel remains. Literary sources are the only evidence giving us information on the nautical devices employed by people in the region.

Pliny the Elder attests that the early navigation of Ethiopians and Troglodytes was conducted in small boats without sails and oars, propelled only by the current (Naturalis Historia XII, 86-88). The anonymous author of the Periplus also attests that the local population in the southern Red Sea used very simple boats (Periplus of the Erythraean Sea, ed. Huntingford 1980: 7, 163). The Periplus also mentions "sewn boats" (Periplus Maris Erytraei, ed. Casson 1989: 9.278.9-10), a tradition which persisted until recently in the Somali, Hadrami, and East African coastal regions. According to Munro-Hay, interpreting Procopius' account, Aksumite ships were made by fastening together wooden planks with rope, instead of using iron nails to fix the hull as in the Mediterranean Roman tradition (Procopius, ed. Dewing 1914: 183-4).

It is interesting to note that the Italian archaeologist who conducted excavations at Adulis in 1906, Roberto Paribeni, found a large industrial area extensively burnt with evidence of oven fragments associated with melted tar (Paribeni 1907: 453). It is possible that the tar was melted to produce pitch for caulking the hull planking of ships. A similar activity might have been connected to ship construction or maintenance performed at the site by specialised craftsmen.

The most important naval expedition of the Aksumites and Adulites is well attested in the Arabic and Ge'ez account of the Martyrium Sancti Arethae (ed. Bausi and Gori 2006). This text also proves the maritime aptitude of people in the southern Red Sea in terms of navigation and naval battle strategies in Antiquity. The Arab version of the account attests that Abyssinians collected their own fleet and ships from their allies in the shipyard of Gabaza. Since the king of the Himyarites did not have a fleet, he employed a stratagem to face Abyssinians. He ordered a floating chain to be made and placed between two islands to stop the Abyssinians from mooring in the bay. The rings of the chain were fitted with dum palm, weighted with lead and dropped into the water. The total length of the chain was presumably 3 miles (Martyrium Sancti Arethae, ed. Bausi and Gori 2006: 73; 29, 15-18). Thanks to the waves that rose above the chain, the nine Abyssinian ships mentioned in the Ge'ez version were able to pass over the chain, after that, the sea turned rough and the chain broke giving the possibility for other ships to enter into the bay (Martyrium Sancti Arethae, ed. Bausi and Gori 2006: 79; 33, 1-8). The account suggests that the first ships to pass over the chain were the smaller ones in the fleet, probably with a little broad keel.

The Ethiopian version adds that, after that, the sea grew calm (Martyrium Sancti Arethae, ed. Bausi and Gori 2006: 279; 33d, 4-6) and the Abyssinian ships remained off the coast where the enemy lay for three days. When the king and the soldiers got out of the ships they were able to stand in the water (Martyrium Sancti Arethae, ed. Bausi and Gori 2006: 81; 35, 11-15). This suggests that the capacity of Ethiopian ships was very small or that these ships were provided with a small keel. It must also be considered that something might have been left out in the account: Abyssinians might have moved from larger boats to smaller boats in order to approach closer to the coast, and to get out in shallow waters.

Another remarkable part of the account mentions the strategy used by the Abyssinians to attack the Himyarites while they were waiting in shallow water with their horses. The large Abyssinian ships were fastened together with rope, masts, oars and other timbers in order to look like a single structure similar to a town. The same was done with the smaller ships in order to build up a sort of wall. In this way the fleet advanced against the Himyarites (Martyrium Sancti Arethae, ed. Bausi and Gori 2006: 83-84; 36, 13-28).

Traces of the maritime aptitude of the Aksumites and their nautical skills can be seen in later sources related to the early Arab navigation in the Red Sea. North Arabs were not originally seafarers and the impulse and the ability to navigate seems to have been imported from southern Red Sea people. This hypothesis is supported by the fact that the Arabic nautical vocabulary has Ethiopian loan-words and that, according to the Arab traveller Ibn Battuta, Ethiopian helmsmen were employed on Arab sanbuqs travelling from Jidda to the southern Red Sea. In his travel account, Ibn Batutta also mentions the capacity of an expert Yemeni helmsman of Ethiopian origins in facing the danger of the navigation in the Red Sea (Dunn 1993: 143). Another source mentions the fact that the ship owners of al-Shu'aybah, a port town in southern Kuwait, might have been Ethiopians (Hourani 1995: 45 note 49).

Subsistence, economy and religious beliefs of ancient Eritrean coastal people

Particular attention is paid by classical sources to the products exported from the Eritrean coast and Adulis during antiquity, which together with some archaeological data gives us a better understanding of the subsistence and economy of ancient Eritrean coastal people.

As previously mentioned, recent research at the Pharaonic harbour of Mersa Gawasis, on the Egyptian coast of the Red Sea, has demonstrated that the Eritrean coast corresponded to the ancient Land of Punt, a region that ancient Egyptians used to reach by sea in the 2nd millennium BC in order to collect exotic products. It is interesting to note that some of the products depicted or mentioned in the relief of queen Hatschepsut's expedition to Punt, in her temple at Deir el-Bahari in the Nile Valley, are the roughly the same as those mentioned in much later sources as products of exportation from Adulis, including apes, animal skins and gold. The particular attention given to the presence of sea turtles in the relief also suggests the fact that these animals were widely diffused and known in the region perhaps also as trade product.

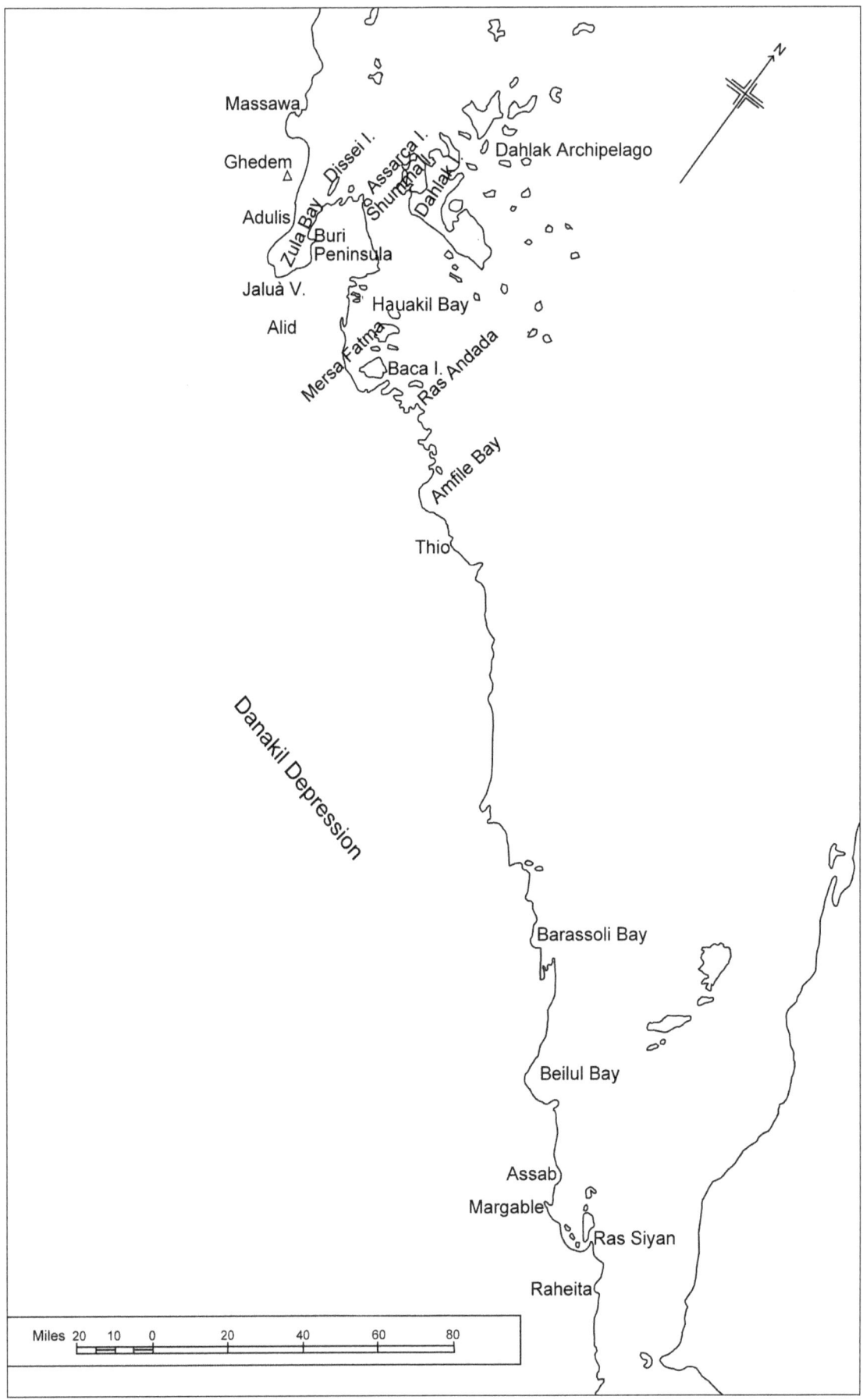

Fig. 2 General map of the Eritrean coast showing the location of bays and islands mentioned in the text.

The sea turtle shell was one of the most cited animal products exported from Adulis and the Eritrean coast in classical sources, in great demand by Greeks and Romans during antiquity. Pliny the Elder mentions that turtle shells were brought to Adulis by the Troglodytes and Ethiopians (Naturalis Historia, ed. Conte 1982: 10). The anonymous author of the Periplus of the Erythraean Sea also mentions turtle shells traded by the Ikthiophagoi at Adulis (Periplus Maris Erythraei, ed. Casson 1989: 52-53). Turtle shells, mentioned in the Periplus, were shipped from the Alalaiou Islands, most likely the Dahalak Islands, and from the coastal region by sea, while Pliny also mentions turtle available in some islands to the south-east of Suakin and, according to Artemidorus, also in one of the islands off the bay of Assab. The current species present in this area is a large sea turtle called Eretmochelys imbricata (Casson 1989: 101).

Sea resources such as shells and turtle shell might have played an important part in the Adulitan and Aksumite economy not only for exported raw materials but also as handcraft products and subsistence for the local population. This is attested by the finding at Adulis of a considerable quantity of shells used both for subsistence and to make ornaments (Paribeni 1907: 561) and by the finding of fish-bones and bronze fish hooks (Paribeni 1907: 483, 540) although Munro-Hay (1991b: 149) pointed out that in later times Christian sources mention both fish and shell-fish as prohibited food.

Apart from sea resources, other products were also available in the coastal regions of the southern Red Sea, such as ivory, rhinoceros horn, hippopotamus skins and apes (Pliny the Elder Naturalis Historia, ed. Conte 1982: VI.173; Periplus Maris Erythraei, ed. Casson 1989: 54-55). The anonymous author of the Periplus mentions obsidian among exported products, and, later in the 6th century AD, Cosmas Indicopleustes also mentions salt (ed. and tr. Wolska-Conus 1968: I. 51).

Hellenistic geographers mentioned elephant hunting stations located along the Eritrean coast. Then Diodorus, Strabo and Pliny mention the presence of people inhabiting the northern Eritrean/southern Sudan and Ethiopian highlands, called Elephantomachoi or Elephantophagoi which used to hunt elephants (Manzo 1996: 28). At the time of the Periplus elephants and rhinoceroses were killed in the interior but occasionally they were still seen near Adulis (Sidebotham 1987: 196). Later on, Nonnosus states that elephants were seen more inland in a plain located half way between Adulis and Aksum (Photius ed. and tr. Henry 1959: VII.250.71). They were hunted for the ivory that was exported but they most probably were also employed for the war in the Aksumite kingdom. The so called sarwe dakwe mentioned in the Ge'ez inscription DAE 10 might, according to Littmann, be the elephant troupes of the Aksumite kingdom (Littmann 1906). Elephants were still seen along the Eritrean coast near Massawa at the end of the 19th century (Paribeni 1907: 561, note 1).[2]

The main sources for obsidian were located at the Amoerale and Alid volcanoes (Franchini 1957: 47; Anfray 1965: 13; Zarins 1990), and in the region of Assab (De Amezaga 1880). Evidence of obsidian flakes and tools also associated with remains of shells is attested at Ras Siyan (Desanges-Reddé 1994), in the Hayachil Bay (Salt 1814: 192; Sapeto 1857: 147), at Margeblà (Franchini 1953: 26-27; Anfray 1966: 5-15), Gurgussum (Roubet 1970: 13-20) and at the island of Dahlak Kebir, but coming from coastal sources (Blanc 1952: 355-357) (Figure 2).

Salt sources were available in the Dankalia plain (Figure 2). Cosmas Indicopleustes states that salt ingots were traded by Aksumites, also with iron, since the 6th century AD in exchange for gold from Sasu (Topographie Chrétienne ed. and tr. Wolska-Conus 1968: I 51.). The trade of salt probably started much earlier and possible ancient sources of salt have been localised at Arohò (O'Mahoney 1970: 147-148) and near the bay of Anfile where evidence of Byzantine amphoras was also found. Ancient internal trade routes of salt were attested at Aiumàn and at Asgara (Shiferaou 1955: 15), also associated with archaeological evidence.

Concerning the religious beliefs, in general very little is known of cults performed by the Aksumites and Adulitan or coastal people before Christianity. One source attests that the Adulitan religion was closer to the Greek tradition than to South-Arabian religious traditions, a fact that might be due to sea trade. Another source refers to Christian beliefs.

At the end of the inscription of the Monumentum Adulitanum it is mentioned that the Aksumite king Aphilas went to Adulis to make an offer to Zeus and Ares and also to Poseidon to ask him to protect the sailors (Topographie Chrétienne ed. and tr. Wolska-Conus 1968: II 63). Poseidon is the Greek god of the sea presumably invoked by king to protect their sailors before converting to Christianity in the 4th century AD. In the account of the Marthyrium Sancti Arethae, mentioning the Abyssinian expedition against Hymiar, the Abyssinian king Kaleb addressed a prayer to the Christian God as soon as he and his troupes had got onto the ships (ed. Bausi and Gori 2006: 273; 32, 5-6; 77; 32, 5).

Starting from the 5th century AD, Christian symbols are very common in architecture, pottery and jewellery found at Adulis. As was also common in the Byzantine world, Christian symbols are widely present in the context of trading activities seen on archaeological finds found at Adulis such as the impressions and incisions of the cross on pottery and the cross or other Christian symbols on amphora lids (Paribeni 1907: 454). The presence of these amphora lids and fragments of Saint Menas ampullae, suggests that a close connection with the north Egyptian monasteries might have existed in the 5th-7th century AD. This aspect will be discussed in the conclusions, after the examination of museum collections of archaeological finds from Adulis.

---

[2] A place north of the modern village of Afta, ca. 50 km south of Massawa, still bears the name Hand of Elephant. According to local informants this was an area were elephants used to gather to get water in the past.

The Eritrean coast in Italian and other European travellers' accounts and previous investigations

In classical literary sources, the Red Sea coast between Ptolemais Theron, presumably located in southern Sudan, and the strait of Bab el Mandeb, down the present Somali coast – the so called Country of Species in the source – was called Troglodytiké. In this region, Strabo mentions the presence of at least six coastal settlements, each with a different function: elephant-hunting stations, watchtowers, fortifications, harbours, and an altar (Strabo, tr. and ed. Jones 1960). Although it is difficult to locate place-names mentioned in the ancient sources, on the Eritrean coast south of Massawa at least six bays might have been suitable anchorages during antiquity.

Apart from the archaeological site of Adulis and the evidence of ancient settlements on the Dahlak Islands, very little is known about the archaeology of the Eritrean coast. After a meticulous observation of nautical charts, Red Sea Pilots, ancient and modern cartography and 19th – early 20th century travellers' account, the author realised that a lot of archaeological evidence in the coastal region did exist and was referred to in the above mentioned sources.

This study has been associated with the study of more recent sources and of the modern topography of the area to corroborate hypotheses and better identify the places of archaeological interest. Unfortunately recent topographic information on the Eritrean territory is still scarce because no recent cartography of the country has been produced. Some aerial photos and satellite images are often available but the cartography produced in the colonial period is still one of the main sources of information. For example, colonial maps and the guide of the Africa Orientale Italiana indicate several ancient ruins, usually identified on the basis of what cartographers were told by the local population. Colonial cartography has also been very useful for locating places that are mentioned in the colonial literature and that may not correspond to today's place names.

The Istituto Geografico Militare produced the complete cartography of Eritrea at the turn of the 20th century.

The maps examined for this study are:

Zula in scale 1:50000, this is the smallest scale existing map for this area, part of an edition of Eritrean cartography issued in 1909-38 in 26 sheets and incomplete. This cartography was created on the basis of an aerial survey conducted in 1885-1891 and it comprises the central part of the colony between Zula, Emberèmi, Giangheren and Himberti. Single sheets are 0.40 x 0.40 m corresponding to 20 km on the ground. The publication started in 1890 with a polychrome edition (black for the nomenclature, roads, sand dunes, blue for hydrography; bistro for ground and red for trigonometric share) for the first sheet and then was continued in black. In 1909 a new edition was prepared in black contours with equidistance of 50 m. Relative trigonometric points were fixed using flat coordinates and straight lines indicating the distance from the meridian and the perpendicular. The system of projection was the one adopted by Cassini, the coordinate (meeting point of the meridian and the perpendicular) was located on the axis of the dome of the Massawa Military Command, whose geographical position was determined astronomically since 1885 by R. Marina and with the azimuth in Dese Island.

The maps for Dese Island, Shumma Island, the Bay of Hauachil (or Bay of Araberta in Italian records), Archico Bay, Gulf of Zula (Zula and Arafali) are in scale 1:100000. These maps are part of the 1909-34 edition in 36 sheets. This cartography is based on routine survey carried out in 1891 in scale 1:25000 and then resumed at 1:100000, considering that the scale at 1:50000 was too big for the whole country. The projection used was polycentric, similar to that used for the contemporary map of Italy, replacing the system prior used by Cassini. Integrating the new survey with the previous cartography in scale 1:50000 was thus prepared the topographic map of Eritrea in scale 1:100.000 in 36 sheets, each corresponding to a trapezoid of 20' lat. To 20' long. The area represented extends north to the parallel 15°53' as in the map in scale 1:50000, south to the southern border Mareb-Belesa-Endeli, and west to the 37°45' long. east Greenwich and east to the Gulf of Zula and the peninsula of Buri. The map was printed in color lithography by adopting the black for the text, railways, housing and borders, the blue for water, the bistro for the contour lines (drawn with a solid line from 100 to 100 m and dotted every 50 m), red for the road network. To make more evident the plastic representation of the terrain, a pastel shadow was added to the curves.

The maps of Emberemi, Massawa, Zula, Gruta, Harena and Assa are in scale 1:400000. These maps are part of the 1934 edition in 12 sheets.

A map of Assab in scale 1:174000 was produced during the exploration of the Assab Bay lead by Amezaga (De Amezaga 1880).

A map of Adulis in scale 1:4000 was produced by the colonial officier Michele Checchi during the archaeological excavations directed by Paribeni (1907: 439, pl. 1).

The other reliable alternative to the Istituto Geografico Militare cartography is the Russian cartography produced on the basis of aerial photos taken in the 1960s-1970s. This cartography covers the whole country and the islands and it is now kept in Addis Abeba.

24 aerial photos, taken in the 1960-70s and covering the territory from Zula to Arafali from 15°N to 15°20'N and from 39°30'E to 39°45'E, were donated to the University of Asmara and a copy of them was given to the author. These photos show sparse bush vegetation and darker marks indicating the presence of stone buildings where the water stagnated. The 24 aerial photos were stitched together by the author using ErMapper (Figure 3) and single photos overlapped to the cartography for study purpose.

The University of Asmara also owned QuickBird images of the Zula region, taken on 24th October 2003, with a resolution of 60 cm, this was also overlapped to the aerial photos for research purpose.

The coast and the islands

Massawa Bay (Figure 7)

The bay of Massawa offers a number of convenient landing places which are easily recognizable for the presence of several landmarks represented by islands and coastal reliefs. The present port of Massawa is located between two islands and two peninsulas and is protected by two reliefs, Ras Mundur and Abd el-Cader. Today it is considered one of the best and safest ports in the Red Sea. The best landing places are located on the north side of the island of Khor Dakhiliya and in the Massawa port that can be safely reached passing between Massawa town and the Island of Taualud, a flat coral island, ca. 350m long, attached to the coast. Wind conditions in this area depend on land and sea breezes that are continuous during the whole year (Red Sea Pilot 1909: 214-217).

The date of the town's foundation is still obscure, with some archaeological evidence found on the island of Taualud pointing to a period between Late Antiquity and early Islamic. The travellers Rüppel (1830-1840: 211) and Heuglin (1877: 219-220) mention the presence of an ancient building on the peninsula of el-Gerar, characterised by square volcanic stone columns which might have been a Christian church. This statement might be true if we consider that monumental building and Christian churches at Adulis are all characterised by squared basaltic columns. According to oral traditions, the mosque of Sheikh al-Hammal, near the cemetery on the island, was built above the remains of a church consecrated to the Virgin Mary and founded by the Syrian monk Frumentius (D'Abbadie 1868). In fact, according to the 4th century AD historian Rufinus, who cites Frumentius' brother Edesius as his authority, as children (ca. 316 AD) Frumentius and Edesius accompanied their uncle Meropius on a voyage to Ethiopia and their ship stopped at one of the harbours on the Red Sea coast which could have either been Massawa or Adulis.

Lord Valentia identified Massawa with the ancient town of Sabat mentioned in Hellenistic sources. In the past Massawa has also been seen as the ancient Adulis by Casson (1984) and Sleeswyk (1983) who, referring to the Ptolemy map, suggested an identification of the Diodorus Island with the island of Sheikh Said rather than with the island of Dilemmi as suggested by others (Sleeswyk 1983: 279-291).

Earlier archaeological evidence recorded in this region was found by Trucca in the 1970s in an area called Gurgussum, at Khor Dakhiliya, north of Massawa. In his unpublished Diario Archeologico (Archaeological Diary) kept in the library of the Centre of African Studies in Asmara, the following finds are mentioned: small amount of nucleolus south of the Ramadan hotel, a nucleolus north-west of the Nuovo Albergo Paoli, and some scattered evidence of potsherds and stone flakes (Trucca 1971). At the same time Roubet (1970:13-20) also found obsidian tools and potsherds with comb decoration, suggesting that the site could be dated to the Neolithic.

Archaeological evidence in the area of Massawa includes two fragments of twisted columns, the original provenance of which is uncertain (Puglisi 1969: 38-39; Manzo 1996: 116). One of the two columns measures 70 cm in height and 105 cm in diameter and it has been observed more recently by Manzo near the stairs of the Palace of the Governor at Massawa. This column is very similar to the column found at Adulis and kept in the National Museum of Asmara (Manzo 1995: 116). It is difficult to date this type of column only on stylistic grounds, the provenance is also difficult to establish without petrographic analysis; it is possible that they could also have been carried on the boats as ballast.

The English traveller Salt mentions the finding of an Egyptian style column in an unidentified place on the coast off Massawa which, according to the local inhabitants, was brought from the Zula bay (perhaps from Adulis?) (Salt 1814: 145).

Local traditions also mention the presence of ancient cisterns in Massawa, attributed to the Furs – presumably the Persians. Conti Rossini states that in the 16th circa 49 cisterns were located on the island and one of those was located at Ras Mudur on the Taulud Island, underneath the Hospital Umberto I (Conti Rossini 1944-1945).

In addition to this, it is worth mentioning the presence of a shipwreck recently discovered in the bay of Massawa near the coral reef at 20 m depth. This shipwreck has only been partially investigated by Pedersen (2000). He conducted a much more detailed investigation of the Assarca shipwreck that will be mentioned later in this section. The two shipwrecks seem to be contemporary and dating to the Byzantine era, as suggested by the presence of globular ribbed amphoras (Pedersen 2008) one of which might be the one observed by the author in the storeroom of the National Museum of Eritrea.

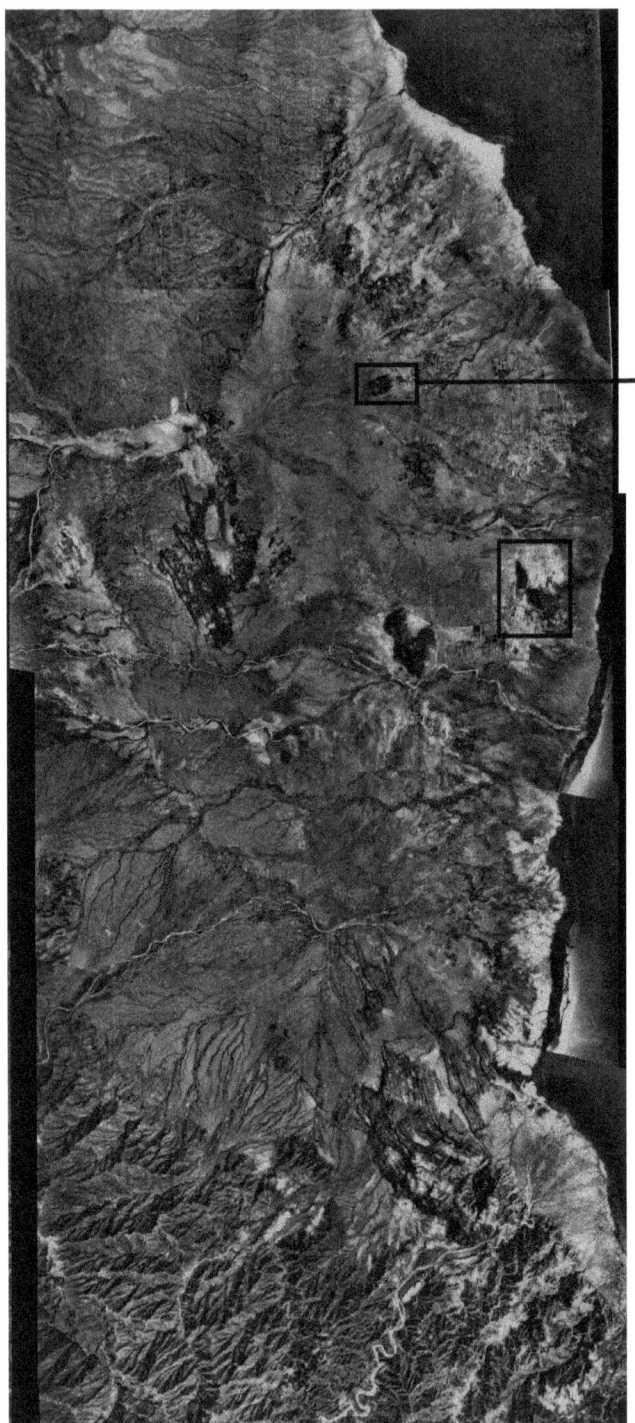

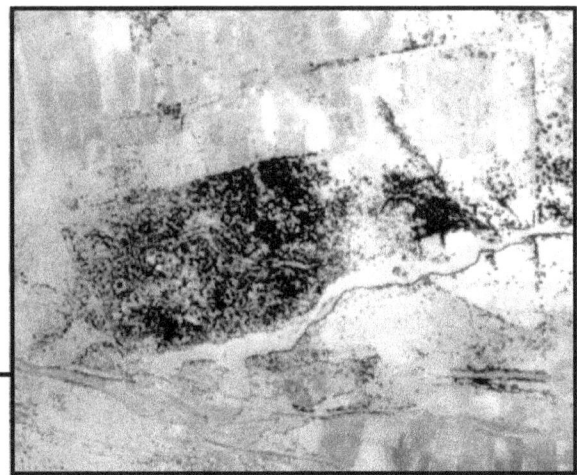

Fig. 3 Mosaic of aerial photos, taken in the 1960-70s and covering the territory from Zula to Arafali from 15°N to 15°20'N and from 39°30'E to 39°45'E.

The site of Adulis is located 56 km south of Massawa, currently 5 km inland from the coast, delimited to the south by the dry bed of the river Haddas, which is periodically filled by water during the raining season.

The town of Adulis appears in its actual location in the bay of Zula, starting from 16th century maps of the world of Contarini (1506), Waldseemuller (1516) and Schoener (1523-124) (Sauter 1957-1961, unpublished). This does not mean that these maps reflect a real knowledge of the geographical location of Adulis at that time; it is more likely that they reflect the identification of the area after the description of the Ptolemy's Geography and other classical authors like Pliny who mentions the location of Adulis at five days navigation from Ptolemais Theron (Pliny the Elder Naturalis Historia VI.173) and the anonymous author of the Periplus who mentions a distance of three thousand stadia south of Ptolemais Theron (Periplus Maris Erythraei 4.259.19-20).

Zula Bay and the archaeological site of Adulis (Figures 2 and 3)

The Gulf of Zula is a well protected bay south of Massawa, delimited by Ras Amas and Corali, to the north of the Buri Peninsula, extending for 48 km north-south and ca. 22 km east-west. The coral reef extends for 1.6 km but the seabed near the coast is deep enough for the boats and anchoring is easy everywhere in the bay (Red Sea Pilot 1997: 63). To the north the bay is delimited by the Ghedem Massif, a mountain that is still used today as a landmark by ships navigating in the Red Sea and is even visible from Port Sudan.

The identification of the actual location of Adulis is due to the pre-colonial and colonial explorations of the African continent by European travellers. The earliest British and French modern sources mentioning the location of Adulis are described in detail in a recent book by Peacock and Blue (2007). The present author will briefly summarize these earliest explorations and then examine more in detail investigations conducted by Italian scholars.

The location of Adulis was established by the English traveler Henry Salt, who mentions the site in his account published in 1814 (Salt 1814: 451-453). Initially Salt identified Adulis with the modern village of Zula on the basis of the geographical location, the similarity of the name and the finding of a column. Later Salt interviewed people from the Assaorta tribe who told him about the presence of an ancient town called Azoole, situated near Zula and characterised by the presence of houses, cisterns and columns. According to the local inhabitants this ancient town was more prosperous than Massawa during the past and was destroyed by a river flood. In fact, the local inhabitants found several metal objects and a stone vessel in the river bed (Salt 1814: 408-409, fig. 15). Unfortunately Salt never managed to visit the site.

After a few years the geographer and naturalist Eduard Rüppel visited the site and noticed the presence of a large building with square pillars and capitals with a basilica-like groundplan (Rüppel 1830-1840, I: 226).

Subsequently the French scientists Vignaud and Petit visited Adulis as part of the Lefebvre expedition. They identified three "temples" and twisted columns and produced a map of the area with drawings of two pillars and a twisted column (Lefebvre 1845). It is interesting to note that the hexagonal pillar drawn by them represents one of the rare items of South Arabian evidence on the site (Manzo 2002).

During the British military expedition, conducted under the auspices of the Brtish Museum in 1867, new observations and the first excavations were carried out. Clement Markham, in his account of the British expedition, mentions the name of Dr. Lumsclaine who conducted a short excavation and found a bronze scale and chains (Markham 1869: 155, note 1). He also mentions that before the end of the British expedition, Capitan William West Goodfellow was in charge of conducting an archaeological excavation for about two weeks. He uncovered a church with an apsidal plan and square pillars, perhaps built on an earlier building (Figure 4). Inside he found a coin of the king Kaleb (c. 520 AD) and some marble fragments. Unfortunately the plan of the church has never been published, but the area is currently under investigations. Holland and Hozier reproduced drawings of the findings and further information about the excavation of the British military expedition and so did Acton (Holland and Hozier 1870: 398-399; Acton 1868). Holmes also mentions the finding of a church with the apse oriented to the east, square pillars similar to those in the church of Dongola and Agula and marble slabs with incisions of crosses.

The Italian interest in the site of Adulis and the archaeology of the region in general, was significant during the colonial period. The fact that the Italian government strongly encouraged archaeological excavations and surveys in Eritrea has an ideological explanation. The predominant opinion among scholars at that time was that the South Arabian civilization first and the Roman Empire later were responsible for the spreading of early civilisation in the Horn of Africa (cf. Conti Rossini 1928: 91-108). As a result, the common perception was that Adulis and the region around flourished during the Greco-Roman hegemony of the Red Sea, and that Adulis itself was originally founded by the Romans. This manipulated vision of the past was obviously intended to justify the colonial politics in the country, meaning the Italian nation had the right to retrieve a territory that once belonged to the Roman Empire, and the Africans had to be grateful for the bringing of civilisation. Excavation reports and travellers' accounts of the colonial times referred to Adulis, often in similar words: "and now the New Rome, the reborn Italy, reviving the tradition of Ancient Rome, will start a new flourishing era for trade among West and East" (Reinisch 1885: 587). Paribeni states at the end of his report: "There is no to despair for the future of the Italian colony. The ancient inhabitants of the Zula plain managed to reach a great level of prosperity yet the present inhabitants, despite 20 years of Italian colony, are still far from this. The restitution of their past might be helpful for the future glory of the Italian nation." (Paribeni 1907: 572).

Although the colonial approach tends to attribute the origin of civilization in this part of Africa to the Romans, it is a fact that people in the coastal regions of Eritrea traditionally give the name of Rom, Romi or Rumanion to the people who inhabited these areas during the past, before their arrival. An ethnographic research conducted in the villages of Afta and Zula, near Adulis, by the team of the National Museum of Asmara revealed that local elders interviewed agreed in stating that "the civilization of Adulis was long established and ceased to exist long before their arrival in the area and their ancestors had no connection with the society responsible for this civilization. They however, have stories passed through generations that Adulis was known by the name of Azulia or Azuli, deriving its name from Greek language. It had a trade contact with Rumanion, probably Romans, and Aksumites although the inhabitants of Adulis are referred as Aksumite by some of the informants." (Adulis Project Fieldwork Report 2011, unpublished).

The tradition of the Rom or Romi does rather suggest the existence of strong relationships between Adulis and Roman merchants and between the Aksumite and the Roman Empires with the emerging of Red Sea trade.

The first Italian to report information about Adulis was a missionary, traveller and diplomatic agent, Giuseppe Sapeto, who visited Adulis in 1869 as part of the French diplomatic expedition to Ethiopia.

Sapeto located the site in between two rivers, and stated that it was delimited by a city wall. It is interesting to note that Sapeto is the only visitor of Adulis who clearly mentions having seen parts of the city walls. He believed he had identified the eastern access to the town in correspondence with a mound of columns, pedestals and capitals; he also observed an area intended for the market and the storerooms, in the north-west sector; a building east-west oriented c. 7 m long and c. 5 m large and several pillars and tombstones in white marble. Other archaeological remains were scattered in the neighbourhood, especially on the sides of the Haddas up to the Taranta, which might have been the start of the caravan trail (Sapeto 1871: 22-71). This area seems to correspond to an area that today looks

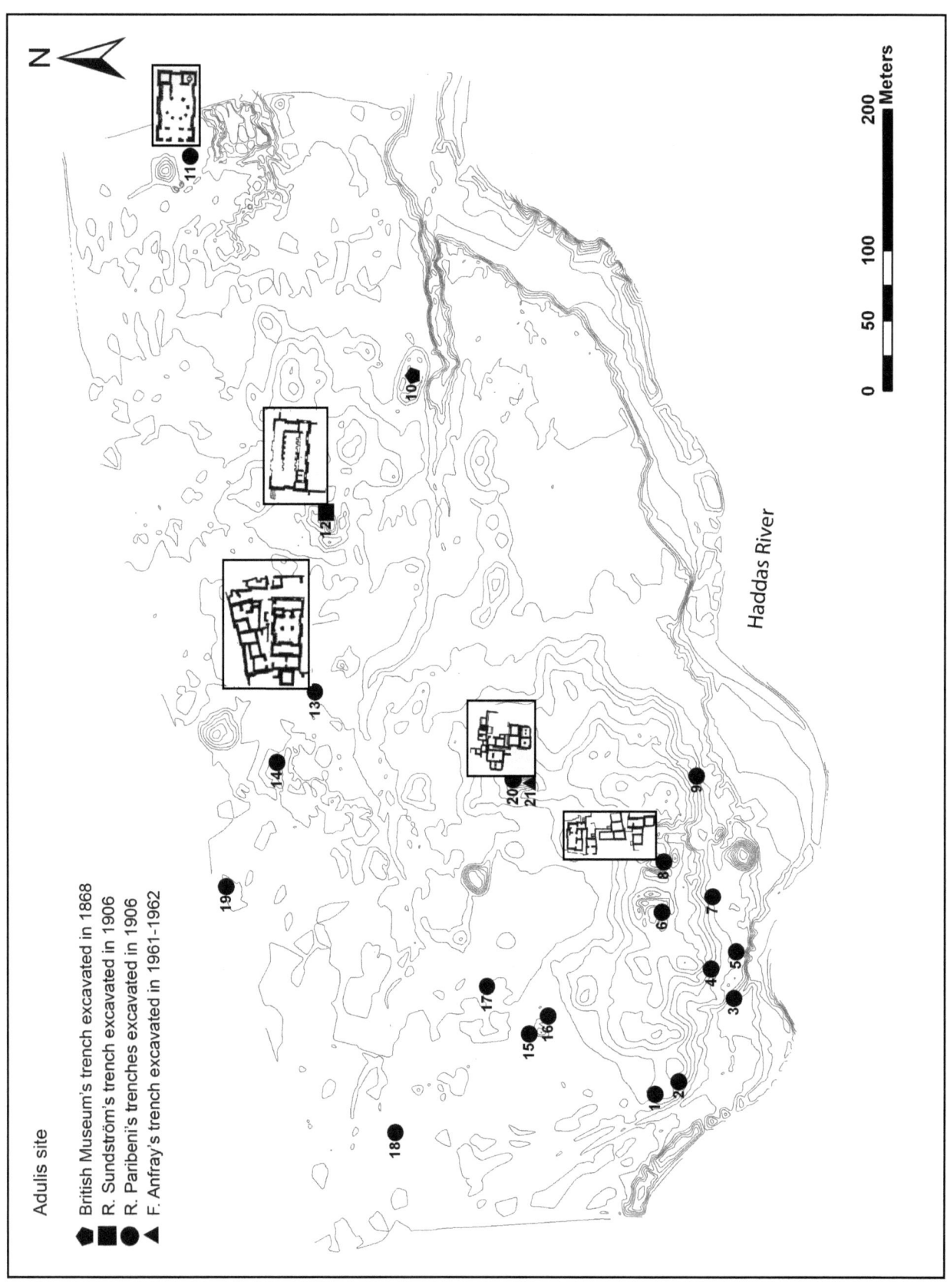

Fig. 4 Topographic map of Adulis showing the location of excavated trenches (modified from Bigliardi, Cappelli, Cocca 2013).

like a flat and wide plane with concentrations of imported amphora fragments on the surface.

According to Sapeto a French mission lead by captain Russel excavated some trenches in Adulis in 1859, later identified by Pribeni in some areas of the site (1907: 440).

Among the travellers who visited Adulis at that time, it is worth to mentioning Luisa Reinisch, wife of the philosopher Leone Reinisch. In her account she describes the region around Adulis mentioning, in particular, the presence of ancient stone houses for several kilometres near the Ghedem mountain, the above mentioned highest mountain in the region located half way between Massawa and Adulis. Then Reinisch mentions the Haddas river and the Islamic cemetery with its tombs decorated with ribbed amphora fragments, large marble slabs and other worked stone blocks. Next to the cemetery she found the remains of an ancient "temple" with a rectangular plan and eight octagonal columns on each side, with a "porch" and the shrine and the foundations made from large squared stone blocks. She noticed that the building masonry included volcanic stone blocks and also bricks measuring 16 cm x 9 cm x 5 cm (Reinisch 1885: 584-587). This structure seems to correspond to the church identified by the British military expedition. In fact, eed bricks are still visible on the surface today, as well as part of the masonry.

Later on Carlo Conti Rossini was charged by the director of the Colonial Office to conduct research in Eritrea in order to find possible archaeological evidence in the area. His visit to Adulis was not very successful, for he found very little in the way of archaeological remains: the ruins of a "temple", some capitals, some column fragments and broken obelisks, perhaps the result of what was found during the excavation of the British expedition. After his visit to Adulis, Conti Rossini focused his investigations on the ancient caravan trail connecting Adulis to Aksum (Conti Rossini 1900: 114).

In 1906 Adulis was briefly excavated by Richard Sundström, as part of the Enno Littman's Princeton expedition to Abyssinia. Sundström partially uncovered the remains of a large building, a palace or a church (Figure 4), but he did not obtain the permit by the colonial government to continue the excavation. The building was characterised by the typical wall architectural style of the contemporary highland settlements, recessed at intervals on the straight alignment and stepped back with increased height (Phillipson 1998: 84) with stairs on the west side. According to Sundström the building was perhaps originally characterised by two stairs, only two rooms were excavated and the central area of the building with square pillars and a fragment of spiral column. Sundström also surveyed the area south of Adulis and first suggested a possible identification of the hills called Gamez or Galala with the Adulis harbour of Gabaza named in the Christian Topography (Wolska-Conus 1968). After few months Roberto Paribeni, a notable Italian archaeologist, superintendent to the Roma and Lazio antiquities, professor at the Cattolica University of Milan, and Francesco Gallina, professor of Ethio-Semitic languages at the University of Naples "L'Orientale", resumed the excavation at Adulis on request by the governor of the colony Ferdinando Martini. Gallina was in charge of studying the coins and assisting Paribeni in the direction of the excavation.

The work conducted by Paribeni and Gallina at Adulis was the most extensive conducted so far on the site and it served as reference for all the other excavations conducted there. The results of the excavation are collected in a complete report (Paribeni 1907) and a brief account is given in the Bollettino Ufficiale della Colonia Eritrea (Gallina and Paribeni 1907). An article written by Mancini (1908: 207) in the newspaper called Illustrazione Italiana clear shows the political colonial propaganda intent, already mentioned elsewhere, behind the excavation project.

At first, the aims of the Paribeni's and Gallina's investigations was to understand the topography of the town and to find the city wall. The wall was not found or, more likely, it did not exist. During the survey Paribeni identified the two buildings previously excavated by the British expedition and by Sundström and two Islamic cemeteries one located in the south-east area of the site near the British excavation, called Sheik Mohammed and the other in the central part of the site, Biet Khalif, in the area where Anfray will excavate a trench in the 1960s (Figure 4). This latter is now abandoned, while the first is still now visited by the local people who gather there in special ceremonial occasions to celebrate next to the Sheik's grave and to perform rituals[3]. Paribeni recorded several square pillars, columns and marble or alabaster slabs from the site reused as decorative elements in these burials. The areas excavated by the British expedition were still visible at the time of Paribeni who recognised excavated trenches in the southern part of the site and the remains of the main building consisting in basalt slabs and in 16 octagonal pillars.

The maximum extension of the archaeological area identified by Paribeni was ca. 20 hectares while more recent investigations raised the area extension to over 30 hectares.

Twenty trenches were excavated in different sectors of the site. Over 10 trenches were opened in the south-west area, one of which was excavated in depth up to 12 metres and revealed the presence of earliest levels of occupation consisting in remains of fireplaces, huts, black burnished pottery and obsidian (Paribeni 1907: 446-453).

Around this area Paribeni noticed the remains of wall alignments related to an intense occupation phase very distinctive from the most recent one visible on the surface, dating to the Byzantine and Christian era, and characterised by massive stone structures including large basalt and pebble stones roughly shaped.

The trenches opened along the river Haddas revealed the presence of an housing quarter of the last occupation period (Paribeni 1907: 457-462).

---

[3] The presence of the two Islamic cemetery is very interesting: it testifies the local people's perception of the area as an ancient and sacred place.

To the north and to the east of the town Paribeni uncovered the remains of two churches showing the classic plan of a early Christian basilica with narthex, the choir and the presbyter and fences on both sides. The apse is usually small and located to the east (Paribeni 1907: 463-511 and 529-540). The church located to the north was most likely built on the top of a previous monumental building characterised by the typical step masonry of the highland settlements of the first half of the 1st millennium AD. Paribeni called this monumental podium 3 metres high "Ara del Sole". The findings of the Paribeni excavations are discussed in the second part of this book.

Further mentions of Adulis are by Dainelli and Marinelli, two geologist-geographers who contributed excellent work to the knowledge of the Eritrean environment during the colonial period. In one of their main essays there is a short mention of Adulis and the previous investigations conducted there (Dainelli and Marinelli 1912), including the investigation conducted by a school professor, Brunetti, in 1924 which is only mentioned elsewhere by Anzani (1928-1929: 6). According to these authors, Brunetti conducted an archaeological excavation but no record of it survived and apparently he did not make any significant finds.

Very little is known about an underwater survey conducted in 1957 by the Institute of Ethiopia Studies in the Bay of Zula, directed by Roger Sauter, even before Francis Anfray's excavation at Adulis. The only written record on this survey consists in an unpublished field report found in the Centre for African Studies in Asmara. The manuscript bears the French title "Section d'Archéologie. Rapport de l'Expédition du Moana (avril 1957)". The Moana was the boat employed for conducting the survey. The manuscript consists in a few notebook pages describing the project, the results of the underwater survey, a map sketched in pen showing the surveying area and notes on the history and archaeology of Adulis from previous excavations. Sauter and his team conducted the survey in six places in the area indicated in the map, exactly in the area where the British expedition landed in 1868 and built a dock, at Ras Malkatto (Sauter 1957-1961, unpublished manuscript kept at the Centre for African Studies in Asmara) (Figure 5). They found only a few lithic instruments, potsherds and jar fragments, brought to the National Museum of Addis Ababa. The contribution of this investigation is very limited since neither the identification nor the dating of the finds have ever been further discussed.

In 1961 and 1962 the French archaeologist Francis Anfray, already involved in the direction of excavations and survey of other important highland settlements, including Maṭarā, conducted archaeological excavations at Adulis with the Institute for Ethiopian Studies of Addis Ababa. At this time Eritrea was once again part of Ethiopia. Anfray investigated the remains of a housing quarter located near the Islamic cemetery of Biet Khalif (Anfray 1974: 745-765) (Figure 4). The excavated area was characterised by the remains of several buildings one close to the other and including two or three rooms, the walls sometimes show evidence of re-building and may perhaps be referred to different building phases. The use of bricks was attested as well as the use of large pillar perhaps to sustain the roof. Detail on the excavations are currently in course of publication in collaboration with the author. The Anfray excavation produced a large quantity of archaeological materials, especially domestic type of pottery, now in the National Museum of Addis Ababa, examined in detail in the second part of this book.

In 2004 and 2005 the University of Southampton, the Asmara University and the National Museum of Eritrea conducted a topographic and geophysical survey on the site with the aim of producing a topographic map showing the presence of structures on the site of Adulis. A surface pottery collection was also conducted, as well as a systematic study of decorative stones. The site was studied in the context of the environment and the coastal region; a regional and geomorphological survey was also conducted along the coast from Massawa to the Bay of Zula and on the Island of Dese and the western coast of the Buri peninsula (Peacock and Blue 2007).

In January 2011 the National Museum of Asmara, the CeRDO (Eastern Desert Research Center), the Museum of Rovereto and the CGT (Centre of Geological Technologies) of the University of Siena resumed archaeological excavations in Adulis. The project aimed to expose monumental buildings excavated in the past and to excavate a deep trench to better understand the stratigraphic sequence.

During the 2011, 2012 and 2013 field seasons three sectors of excavation have been investigated, and plans of structures and the topography of the site have also been produced using differential GPS and photogrammetry. One sector of excavation was located in the centre of the town where Paribeni found the Christian church in the central area of the site (Figure 4). The church is today in a state of decay but the rectangular plan and an apse flanked by two rooms called pastophoria were identified. The masonry is typical of the region, called "graduated" or "step masonry". The church can be dated, according to associated materials, to the 6th-7th century AD. Two other excavation sectors were opened to the southwest and southeast. The deep trench in the southwest sector of the site is designed to investigate the stratigraphic sequence of the site; the most outstanding results of excavations conducted here so far show the presence of an earlier building phase and a domestic space dating to the 2nd- 4th century AD. Excavations in the southeast sector revealed the presence of a complex building dating to the latest phase of the town and corresponding to the building annex to the church investigated by the British Army (Figure 4). A small trench was also opened in 2011 in the Haddas River and it delivered potsherds probably dating to the earliest period of occupation.

Arafali Bay (Figure 7)

The Bay of Arafali, in the southern Gulf of Zula, is an open bay enclosed by the coral reef and marked by the presence of the Dola Vulcan. The area is rich in hot water springs and there are many nearby wells (Red Sea Pilot 1909: 231). In the second half of the 19th century, Sapeto recorded the remains of fence enclosures and a large wall, perhaps 3 m long, in a unidentified place called Gobetli, considered ancient by local people (Sapeto 1871: 22-71). No other archaeological evidence has been recorded in this area, apart from evidence of obsidian lithic tools collected by Franchini on the nearby volcano Amba Jaluà (Franchini 1957: 47; Anfray 1965: 5-15). Other lithic tools found by Franchini, without any reference concerning provenance, were kept in the old museum "La Salle" of Asmara (cf. Tringali 1985-1986).

Dese Island (Figure 7)

The Island of Dese is located at the entrance of the Zula Gulf. Dese is a volcanic island and the hilliest of the archipelago. The coral reef extends for 4 miles to the north and almost connects this island to Madote Island. The best anchorage is a bay to the south-east characterised by a sandy bottom, where there is also a village and wells (Red Sea Pilot 1909: 233-234). According to De Rivoire, who visited the island in 1864 when it belonged to France, the bay was a stopping place for local and foreign vessels; he noticed in fact the presence of fresh drinkable water near the main village (De Rivoire 1867: 252-253). Visiting the island at the beginning of the 20th century, Angelo Marini noted ancient structures and a monolith that he says was taken off the island by the crew of a French ship (Marini 1909: 379). Another Italian scholar, Puglisi, mentions cisterns on the island that he attributed to the Furs (Puglisi 1953: 69).

Peacock and Blue recently published new archaeological data from Dese Island (Peacock & Blue 2007: 57-64), which they identified with the Oreinê Island of the Periplus. Interestingly the island was already identified as Oreinê Island in the Renaissance maps based on the Geography of Ptolemy (Sleeswyk 1983: 279-291).

Peacock and Blue found evidence of shell middens associated to the Aksumites and Mediterranean imported pottery. Next to the village they found an abandoned village with glazed pottery sherds on the surface that could be dated to the medieval period (Peacock & Blue 2007: 57).

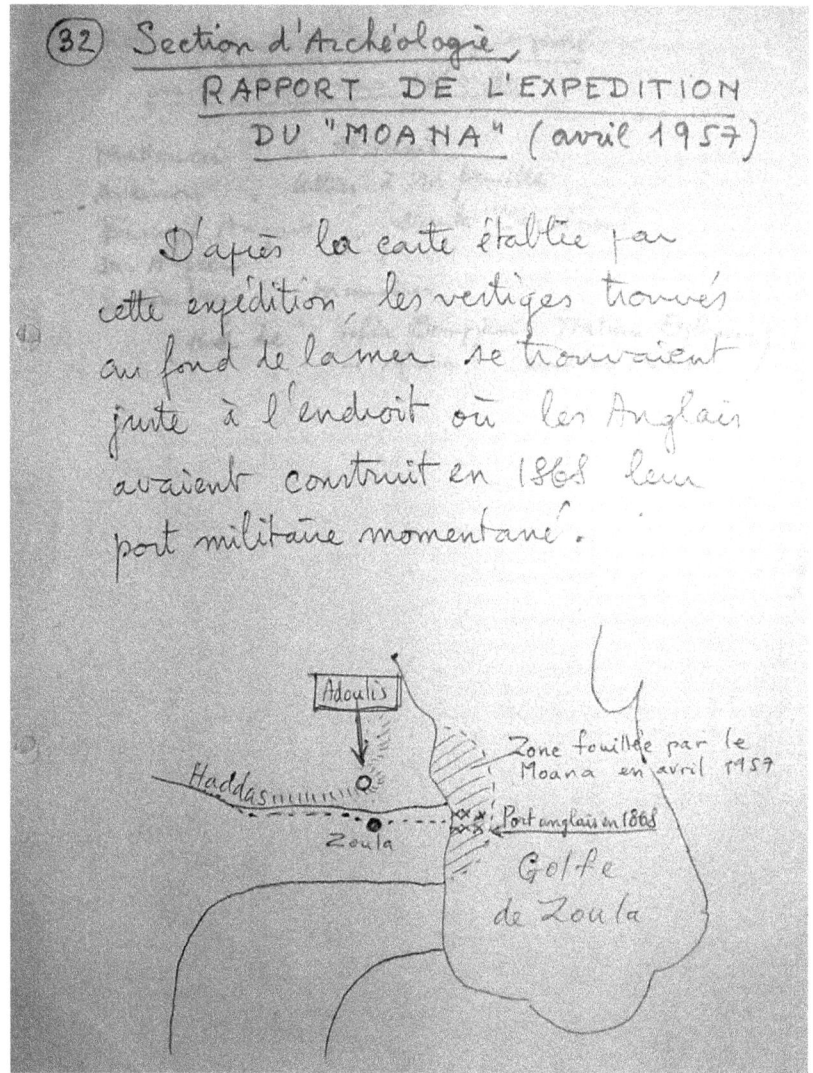

FIG. 5 MANUSCRIPT PAGE FROM SAUTER 1957-1961 (UNPUBLISHED) SHOWING THE AREA IN THE GULF OF ZULA SURVEYED UNDERWATER BY A FRENCH TEAM IN 1957.

Assarca Islands (Figure 7)

Assarca and Black Assarca islands are about one mile apart; they are located south-west of the Massawa Canal, between the Buri Peninsula and Dahlak Islands. The name Assarca means "guardian" (Pedersen 2000: 5) perhaps referring to their central position in between the north and the south part of the Massawa Canal. Despite the presence of archaeological evidence, these two islands do not seem to have been mentioned in classical sources. Both islands are deserted although the south-easternmost, Assarca, is regularly visited by people from the nearby islands to water their cattle.

Black Assarca is characterised by black coral rocks, the bottom is shallow and rocky, while the other Assarca is sandy and covered with euphorbia, there is also a cistern 8.5 m deep (Red Sea Pilot 1997: 64). The anchorage in this area is not recommended, most likely because of the strong currents and winds that canalize in the passage (Red Sea Pilot 1909: 236).

In the 1990s a member of the Eritrean Ministry of Marine Resources found a Byzantine shipwreck near Assarca, and in 1995 the Institute of Nautical Archaeology recorded the site (Pedersen 2000: 5). The most outstanding result of the excavation is the finding of four different types of amphoras including the Ayla/Aksum type, a jar fragment with filter, dating to the 5th-7th century AD and a lead counter-weight (Pedersen 2000: 3-13). The shipwreck might suggest that during antiquity vessels crossed the Masswa Canal in this area between Dahalk Island and Assarca Island. This passage is still used today.

During a visit to this island this author identified several potsherds on the shore and, partly buried under sand (Figure 5), an almost complete globular pot with a cylindrical neck, which recalls proto-Aksumite types in shape (Rodolfo Fattovich and Andrea Manzo, personal communication). The decoration of incised geometric lines on the body seems to be rather unusual.

Shumma Island (Figure 7)

The island of Shumma, in the strait between the Buri Peninsula and the Dahlak Archipelago, is about 2.5 miles in length and 1 mile wide, it has vegetation and a good anchorage for large boats south-east of where the coral reef is interrupted. According to the Red Sea Pilot, sanbuqs and small vessels can land on the north-west side of the island (Red Sea Pilot 1909: 237).

The Italian geologist Marini, during a scientific exploration of the island at the beginning of the 20th century, noted ancient structures, potsherds, tombs and stone enclosures (Marini 1909: 375-400). A few decades later Puglisi also visited the area and suggested that this enclosure might have been fulla, the stone enclosures typical of the islands employed to collect rain water using natural slopes (Puglisi 1953: 56).

Dur Gaam and Dur Ghella (Figure 7)

These two islands are located north of Dahlak Kebir, they are small and relatively rich in vegetation (Red Sea Pilot 1997: 61). Alfredo Coppa, University of Rome "La Sapienza," recorded the presence of burials associated with potsherds, perhaps amphoras and mounds of Lambis lambis shell type. The potsherds were collected and stored at the National Museum of Asmara.

Dahlak Island (Figure 7)

Scholars usually identify the Dahlak Archipelago with the islands that classical sources say exported turtle shells to Adulis.

Dahlak Kebir is the main island of the archipelago, it measures 760 square metres and rises from a coral formation, and the ground is convenient for the pasture of sheep and gazelles thanks to the rich vegetation of acacia and dum palm that spread over the island after the raining season, in December-March.

Until now, archaeological research on the island have been very limited if we consider the potential of the monuments identified for cultural heritage. These include cisterns, an early-Islamic cemetery, tombs attributed to the Furs, remains of a building similar to Adulis' buildings, near the village of Gim'hile, a marble column, and several surface sherds (Puglisi 1969: 35-47). More recent research has been conducted only by Insoll (2001).

Concerning earlier evidence, in the 1930s an Italian engineer collected some obsidian microlithic tools on the island that were successively studied by Blanc. He distinguished fourteen different types including blades, small blades, retouched flakes and nucleolus which he compared with similar tools attributed to the Wiltonian culture in East Africa. Blanc also suggested that the source for the obsidian was located between the bay of Meder and the bay of Assab (Blanc 1952: 355-357). The island is also characterised by several shell middens that cannot be dated but might be contemporary to some of these tools.

Today there are no convenient anchorages for large boats around the island; usually even sanbuqs use small boats to approach the shore. Near the village of the Dhalak people south-east of the island there is a small harbour area for the local fishermen with a hut and a small boatyard area. The island is poorly inhabited, with few villages and houses made using small coral blocks as in some other sudanese and yemenite modern coastal villages of the Red Sea.

The main village of the island is inhabited by the two groups of Dahlak-Afar people and Arab-Afar mixed people. Next to this latter is located the modern cemetery made with slabs inserted vertically and horizontally into the ground in the same style as the nearby ancient cemetery. The cemetery extending for 230 m from north to south and 400 m from east to west is traditionally attributed by the local people to the Furs, maybe the Persians, who might have started visiting the island in the 6th century AD (Tedeschi 1969). The burials are gathered around the remains of tall mausoleums called qubba in the Islamic tradition which can be compared to those found in the necropolis of Gebel

FIG. 6 A GLOBULAR VESSEL FOUND ON THE ISLAND OF ASSARCA DURING A VISIT BY THE AUTHOR IN 2004.

Mamam in south Sudan (Rodolfo Fattovich, personal communication). The surface area is covered with Islamic or other undated potsherds. The tombs attributed to the Furs are characterised by four large slabs and sometimes inscribed tombstones in kufic characters dating from between 1040 and 1100 AD (Oman 1976, Schneider 1983). Most of these tombstones are now kept in the Civic museum of Modena, in the Museum of Treviso, at Bar-el-Duc in Lorena, in private collections and in the Museum of Asmara (Cerulli 1933: 152-156). Other possible ancient burials were recorded in the village area of Assaghe and Nocra, on the highest point of the island near a signal for navigation (Puglisi 1953 and 1969).

To the west of the Dahlak Kebir village, Puglisi found the remains of a building on the top of a mound surrounded by an Islamic cemetery on the west side. The building includes a "podium", arches, a ramp and a marble column with spiral grooves (Puglisi 1969: 38-39, 41 figs. 6 and 7; Insoll 2001: 45). The building was interpreted as a Christian church with Syrian influence, dating perhaps to the 4th-5th century AD. The column can be compared to Late Roman or Late Antiquity period, similar to columns found in the portico of Apamea in Syria and in other eastern Roman towns. According to Insoll the building is now in a bad state of conservation but has apparently been rebuilt and reused several times (Insoll 1997: 382-388 and Insoll 2001).

In the north-east corner of the island, at Gim'hile (or Gium Helli), 100 m south-west of Dassho, a former village of pearl divers, near the well called Ela Camarani, Puglisi found a building called by local people the Persian church, these ruins are also mentioned in the guide book of the Italian colony (Guida A.O.I. 1938: 183). The building photographed by Puglisi is characterised by the typical step-masonry, a four stairs square capitals and a square pillar with bevelled corners that can be compared to similar elements characteristic of the monumental architecture in Adulis and other highland settlements such as Tokonda and Qoḥayto (Puglisi 1969). The building might date to the 2nd-3rd century AD or later (cf. also Insoll 2011: 45-46).

Other related archaeological surface evidence includes potsherds of red ware amphorae with yellow slip that can be compared to the Byzantine amphoras.

Howakil Bay (Figure 7)

The Bay of Howakil has characteristic landmarks represented by a hill called Barn, 1575 m high, and the Ras Andada, a headland which delimits the bay from south-east. There are also good anchorages in the bay, and navigable channels around it (Red Sea Pilot 1909: 265) which make it a good landing.

At the beginning of the 19th century, Henry Salt and later Sapeto (Sapeto 1857: 147) noted several polished obsidian fragments on the beach near the village of Arena (Salt 1814: 192). Salt noticed the presence of stone tools some kilometres inland, possibly indicating the presence of nucleolus production for the sea trade rather than the source of obsidian itself which, according to Sapeto, might be located near the volcano Amoer-Ale (or Jalua), near Arafali or at the volcano Alid (Zarins 1990: 507-541 and Franchini 1953: 25-30). According to Anfray, the obsidian collected by Salt was kept in the National Museum of Eritrea for a certain period (Anfray 1966: 13), although this has not been seen by the author in the present collection.

This bay has frequently been identified with the ancient source of obsidian, particularly the one mentioned in the Periplus (2.261.16-19) as located 800 stadia (ca. 142 km) south of Adulis.

Baca Island (Figure 7)

The island of Baca is located in front of Howakil Bay and it is easily recognisable for the large mountain of Baca. A coral reef extends from the northern limit of the island for

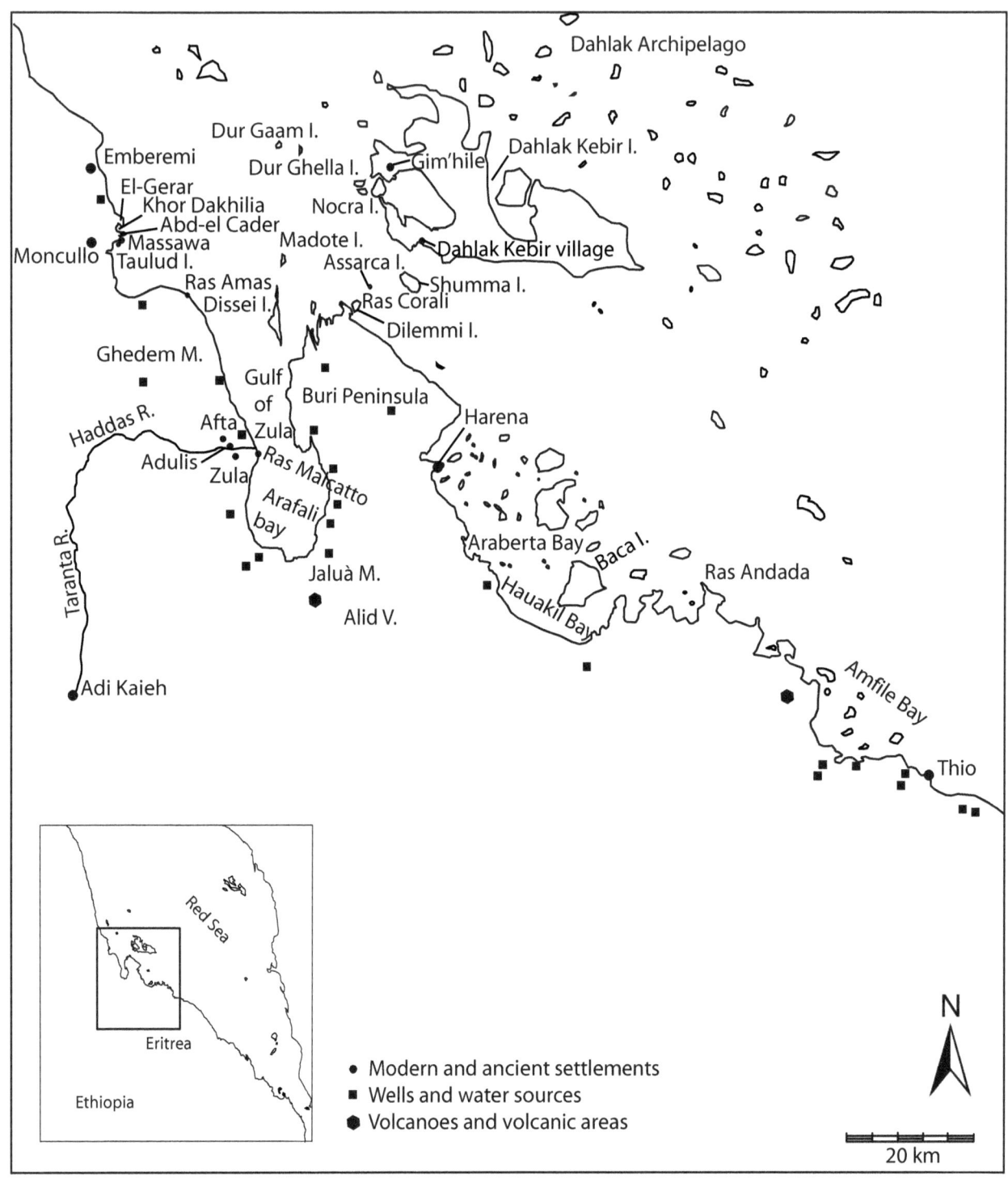

FIG. 7 MAP OF THE ERITREAN COAST, CENTRAL SECTOR, SHOWING THE LOCATION OF MODERN AND ANCIENT PLACES AND RUINS, WELLS AND WATER SOURCES, VOLCANIC AREAS AND SALINES MENTIONED IN THE SOURCES AND ON THE COLONIAL MAPS.

5 miles and constitutes the southern limit of a navigable channel between Baca and Howakil Bay. The island also provides a good anchorage with a sandy bottom on its north-west side (Red Sea Pilot 1909: 240-241).

Puglisi suggested that Baca was used in the past as a source of the green-diorite lithic tools found at Dahlak Kebir. Puglisi also mentions having seen large grinding stones on the highest part of this island (Puglisi 1969: 40, see also note 10).

Anfile Bay and Mersa Fatma (Figure 7)

The bay of Anfile is characterised by several inlets, the coast line appears flat and sandy from the sea apart from Ras Anrata, a coral relief which looks like an island. The bay is well connected to the Massawa Canal, north of Ras Shaks. A convenient landing place is Mersa Fatma, which was used as a harbour in colonial times. It was the last stop on the road leading to the so-called 'Piana del sale', or Salt Plain which was also in the past the main source of salt (Guida AOI 1938: 337). South of this bay, near Ras Anrata, is a village called Thio (Red Sea Pilot 1909: 273 and Guida AOI 1938: 334) where Anfray recorded evidence of Ayla-Aksum amphoras (Franchini 1953: 25-30; Anfray 1966: 11).

Huntingford suggests identifying Anfile Bay with the ancient port of Antiphilos described by Strabo. This identification was suggested only on the basis of the linguistic similarity between the ancient and modern names (Huntingford 1976: 170).

Bahar Assoli Bay (Figure 8)

The bay of Bahar Assoli and the adjacent beach called Bolugaba extend for 6 miles until the island of Rahmat. The bay is characterised by rocks and small islands, the sea bottom is suitable for the landing of boats (Red Sea Pilot 1909: 334) especially at Rakhmat; not far from here wells are indicated on the IGM map. Related information about the presence of ancient remains in this area seems to be contradictory.

At Undulli, near the Bolugaba beach, De Amezaga recorded evidence of stone tombs and was told by local Dancali people that they belong to an ancient Muslim town rich in treasures. The tombs are described as lozenge shaped limestone dug into the ground (De Amezaga 1880: 34). Conti Rossini mentions hearing about the remains of an ancient town in this area (Conti Rossini 1900: 114-115) and the 1938 IGM map indicates remains of ancient ruins near the Cabya Point. On the contrary, the guide book of the Italian colony states that there were no ancient remains of a Sabean or Persian town in Undulli, as suggested by some travellers who visited the area, but only natural mounds of basalt and coral blocks (Guida A.O.I. 1938: 337).

Beilul Bay (Figure 8)

South of Ras Rahmat, a main landmark in the southern sector of the Eritrean coast, starts the bay of Beilul, well protected from the winds from the south east in winter. The best anchorage is in the eastern part of the bay which is quite deep, while the western part was usually employed for the anchorage of sanbuqs (Red Sea Pilot 1909: 268). On this beach Puglisi (1969: 40, note 10) found a large volcanic grinding stone without giving further details. The author believe that this volcanic grinding stone might be similar to the volcanic circular grinding stones found by Anfray at Raheita (see below), which were perhaps transported by boat as ballast or employed for grinding on the shore of imported cereals. Some more recent ruins attributed to the Galla people were noted here by the authors of the Red Sea Pilot (1909: 268).

Assab Bay and Raheita (Figures 8 and 9)

The Bay of Assab and the coastal area that stretches north and south of the bay is characterized by the presence of various archaeological evidence.

The bay stretches for about 16 miles, the entrance located between Ras Luma west and the islands that stretch north-west of Ras Sintiyan, the entrance to the north is an excellent anchorage for all types of vessels and sheltered from all winds (Red Sea Pilot 1909: 269). Nevertheless, the Bay of Assab is characterized by a strong wind that makes landing problematic in the period between October and March. In the Italian colonial era the area was considered strategic because it represented a passage for the caravans that connected the Ethiopian plateau to the sea.

At the end of the 19th century, De Amezaga noted a hill at the entry of the Bay of Assab on which was an enclosure or military station with basalt walls and red bricks alongside ancient paths (De Amezaga 1880: 50-55). Franchini in the 1950s noted obsidian associated with decorated and coloured glass fragments and ancient remains on the wadi terrace of the Arsilé stream near Assab, between the Ado Ali volcano and the oasis of Margable, on the coast (Franchini 1953: 26-27; Anfray 1966: 5-15).

Exploring the area around Raheita, Conti Rossini and later Francis Anfray found ancient ruins at Eilù, including potsherds, pits excavated in the soil and large grinding stones made of volcanic material (Anfray 1970: 41-42, Pl. XX-XI). As suggested by Anfray, the pits excavated in the soil may have been horrea employed for the storage of traded commodities and particularly cereals which might have been grounded at the seashore or elsewhere.

Conti Rossini (1920: 291-298) suggested that the Raheita archaeological evidence should be identified with the ancient town of Deirè named by Strabo. The pottery collected by Anfray at Raheita is now kept in the storeroom of the Addis Ababa National Museum and was analysed by the author. Some of the sherds were also included in Anfray's publication of his survey (Figure 9 cf. Anfray 1970 Pl. XXIIb). Unfortunately the level of conservation of the sherd is very poor which prevented the identification of the fragments. The author can only suggest some possible identifications: a painted fine ware potsherd showing the characteristic brown bands alternating with a yellow surface might be compared with Late Aksumite painted ware (Figure 9, bottom); glazed pottery sherds might be dated to the late Sassanian or early Islamic period (Figure 9, centre) and testify to early Islamic navigation in the area, four fragments of orange ware vessel (jar?) with incised narrow straight and wavy lines forming a net seen elsewhere in the Red Sea area and on the surface layer at Qane (Salles and Sedov 2010: 155 and pl. 80 cat. 617), while a potsherd of blue and white porcelain can certainly be identified as modern pottery from China. Other pottery fragments are more difficult to identify but the collection in general seems to suggest that the harbour area at Raheita might have been employed over a long period. A basalt grinding stone, two plaster fragments identifiable as two fragmentary jar stoppers, and three glass fragments are also part of the collection.

The eastern lowlands and the Danakil depression

The area of the eastern lowlands, the Semhar, is an intermediate zone of great importance, located between the coast and the highland plateau where the shepherds

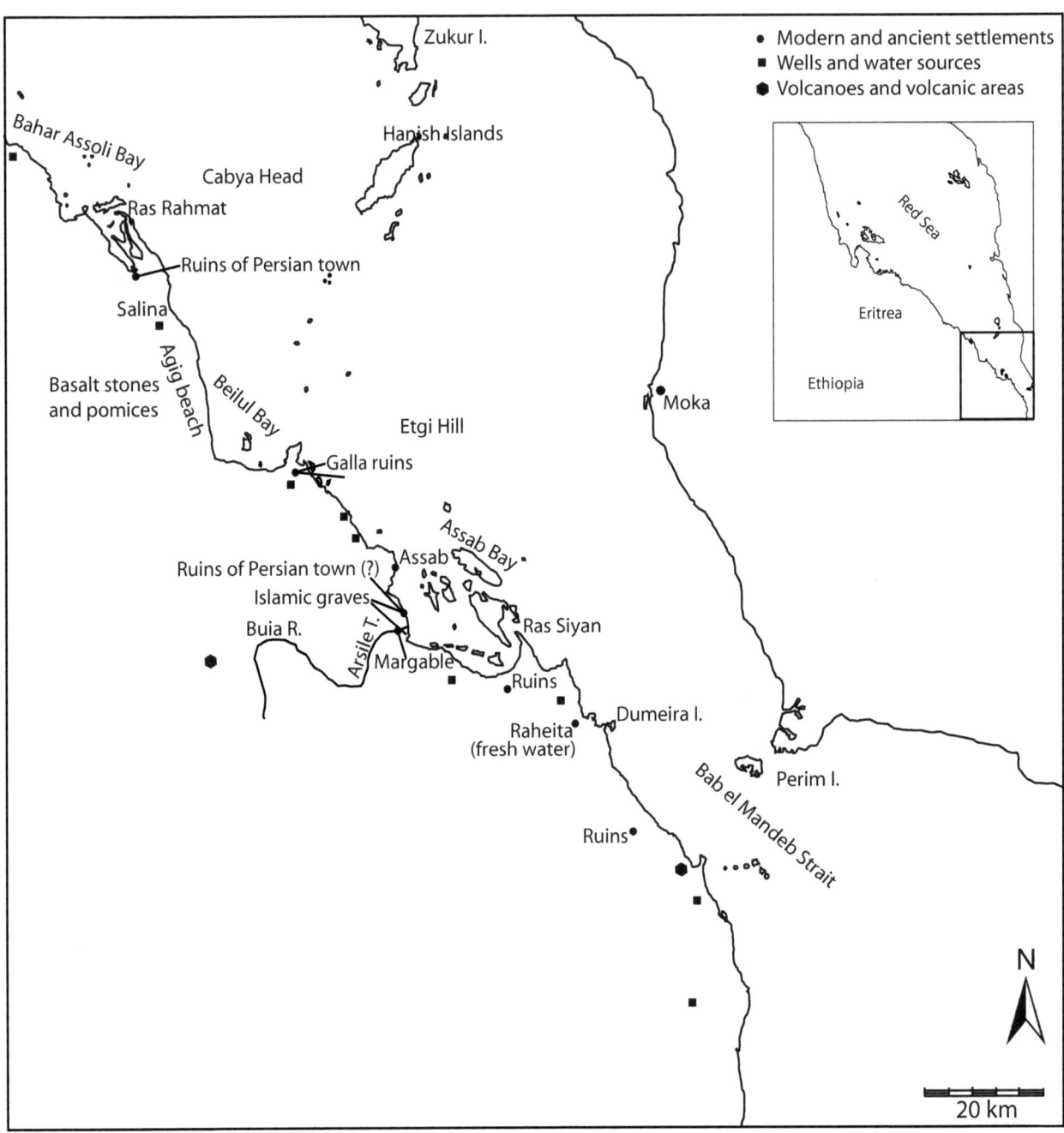

Fig. 8 Map of the Eritrean coast, southern sector, showing the location of modern and ancient place and ruins, wells and water sources, volcanic areas and salines mentioned in the sources and on the colonial maps.

go in winter in search of pastures and warmer climate. In the past the nomadic people moved seasonally between highlands and lowlands in search of pasture and hunting, as demonstrated by the numerous rock paintings on the theme of hunting seen in shelters located in the eastern walls of the Eritrean highlands overlooking the river valleys (Franchini 1957: 1-12). Culturally the eastern lowlands are also a link between the rore, an area between the eastern lowlands and the highlands, and the coast. This was probably also a strategic area of control ensuring safe access to the highlands. Although the eastern Eritrean lowlands have never been subjected to systematic archaeological surveys, some possible archaeological evidence was described by scholars and explorers during 19th and 20th century.

Conti Rossini has suggested the possibility of a geographical and cultural continuity among the Aksumites of the highlands and nomad people inhabiting the valleys between the Lebca and Massawa and between the Anseba and Barca valleys (Conti Rossini 1922: 266-270). Geographically the eastern lowlands extend into Sudan where ancient archaeological evidence observed at Aqiq and Kasalā dates mainly to the Islamic period (Dainelli and Marinelli 1912: 525, cf. Crowfoot 1911: 549-550, Manzo 2005).

The Eritrean coast in Italian and other European travellers' accounts and previous investigations

Fig. 9 Materials collected on the surface at Raheita by Francis Anfray in 1965, now kept in the National Museum of Addis Abeba.

The Danakil desert is a volcanic region stretching to the south of Massawa, along the Eritrean coast, in the north-eastern part of Ethiopia and north-western region of Djibouti. It is a very hot and inhospitable place located below sea level. In the northern part of this region is the broad basin called the Salt Plain in Italian colonial literature, located 120 meters below the sea level. In this area the salt deposit covers an area of about 8000 square km (AOI Guide 1938: 38). The geology of the Danakil depression consists of two main types: volcanic rocks composed mainly of basalt and sedimentary rocks composed of marl, sandstone, gypsum, conglomerates and limestones. The sedimentary alluvial soils are suitable for cultivation during the seasonal rains (Lanzoni 1920: 250), and in these areas cultivated oases can be found, as for example at Margheblà. The Danakil region is currently inhabited by the Muslim Cushitic Afar who are partly nomadic, partly farmers growing tobacco, cotton and corn (see Fattovich 1992: 74). Thus oases and farmlands developed near the river beds and especially in the coastal area, while the inner Danakil region is desert. The historical and archaeological interest of the Danakil depression derives from the presence of abundant obsidian sources sometimes associated with stone tools, and the presence of saline deposits associated with ancient caravan routes for the transport of salt from there to the highlands. These two areas, the Danakil and the Eastern Lowland, represent an important cultural interface between the coast and the highlands, essential to understand the dynamics of trade and contacts over a long period of time.

Elghena-Falcàt (Figure 10)

Carlo Conti Rossini refers to some finds described by Talamonti a mile from Elghena on the right bank of the river Falcàt located in the eastern lowlands, not far from the rore (Conti Rossini 1922: 266-270). These are stone mounds believed to be contemporary to the kingdom of Aksum, and some fragments of atypical pottery associated with them. The piles of stones were identified as burials for the presence of human bones and badly preserved camels bones and a type of ceramic which is comparable, according to Conti Rossini, to Aksumite pottery. He describes, in particular, a type of amphora made with non-purified ware, well cooked and about 1 cm in thickness, red brick color on the external surface, grayish inside and with horizontal parallel deep grooves, similar to pottery fragments observed at Tokonda and Adulis. Other fragments are described as belonging to big vessels with diameters of 35 cm, another fragment refers to an amphora of about 23 cm in diameter, made with fine ware, well cooked and dark, the outer surface is smooth, red brick color and incision of horizontal rows comprising large impressed dots. Other scholars mention the presence of vessels with thinner walls including a rim 14 cm in diameter, non-purified, reddish yellow ware and outer surface crossed by longitudinal deep grooves, and a fragment of an amphora with reddish brown surfaces decorated with vertical and horizontal bands (Fattovich 1995: 168).

Lebca (Figure 10)

In the last century, scholars such as Heuglin, Sapeto, Munzinger and Issel noted ancient ruins in the area of the river Lebca along a road that leads from Massawa to the valleys of Anseba and Barca (Dainelli and Marinelli 1912). Unfortunately, no further deatils on the characteristics of these ruins is given.

Desset-Moncullo (Figure 10)

The site of Moncullo, named in several literary sources of the last century, is located between Kanfer and Massawa along the stream of Desset, in the eastern lowlands. This region is potentially fertile and suited to the establishment of ancient settlements, considering that in this area cultivation downstream of the bridge Dogali was possible until recent times thanks to the presence of the Desset. The archaeological area consists of stone mounds traditionally identified as burials and attributed to an ancient population called Rom by local inhabitants. The pre-colonial and colonial literature identified the name of this people with the Romans. Another suggestion is that the descendants of the Rom are the current Irob-Saho people (see Reinisch 1885, p. 587). The tradition of people called Rom, in the Eritrean coastal area, is usually employed to indicate people coming from another place, non-local people. Sapeto reports in the south of Desset there are the ruins of an Abyssinian city with six hundred houses, some with foundations measuring one meter in diameter. Large square buildings are also described, and houses built with limestone and pebbles. On the south west of the river stands an Islamic shrine in the shape of a square tower made of overlapping stones plastered with lime. According to Sapeto, this was the tomb of Marabut, a Dervish or guru, although the inhabitants of Massawa believed this was the monumental building of a king of Samahr. At the time of Sapeto, the ruins comprised merely piles of stone 2-5 meters high (Sapeto 1857, pp. 258-260). Lejean William (1828-1871) also observed archaeological evidence in the area of Desset and he also related it to the Rom on the basis of ethnographic interviews he conducted with the local inhabitants. He describes a wide flat rectangular plane occupied in the south-west and south-east by two distinct groups of mounds dominated in the center by a structure called the "Koubet es-sultan", the tomb of the king. Lejean also explored the interior region, without however finding any archaeological evidence that could suggest the presence of an ancient settlement associated to the burials area. Among the many legends related to Rom and the mysterious ruins, the author reports that, according to the natives, spending the night near the tombs provided poetic inspiration (Lejean 1865: 742-763).

Lejean William (1828-1871) also observed archaeological evidence in the area of Desset and he also related it to the Rom on the basis of interviews he conducted with the local inhabitants. He describes a wide flat rectangular plane occupied in the south-west and south-east by two distinct groups of mounds dominated in the center by a

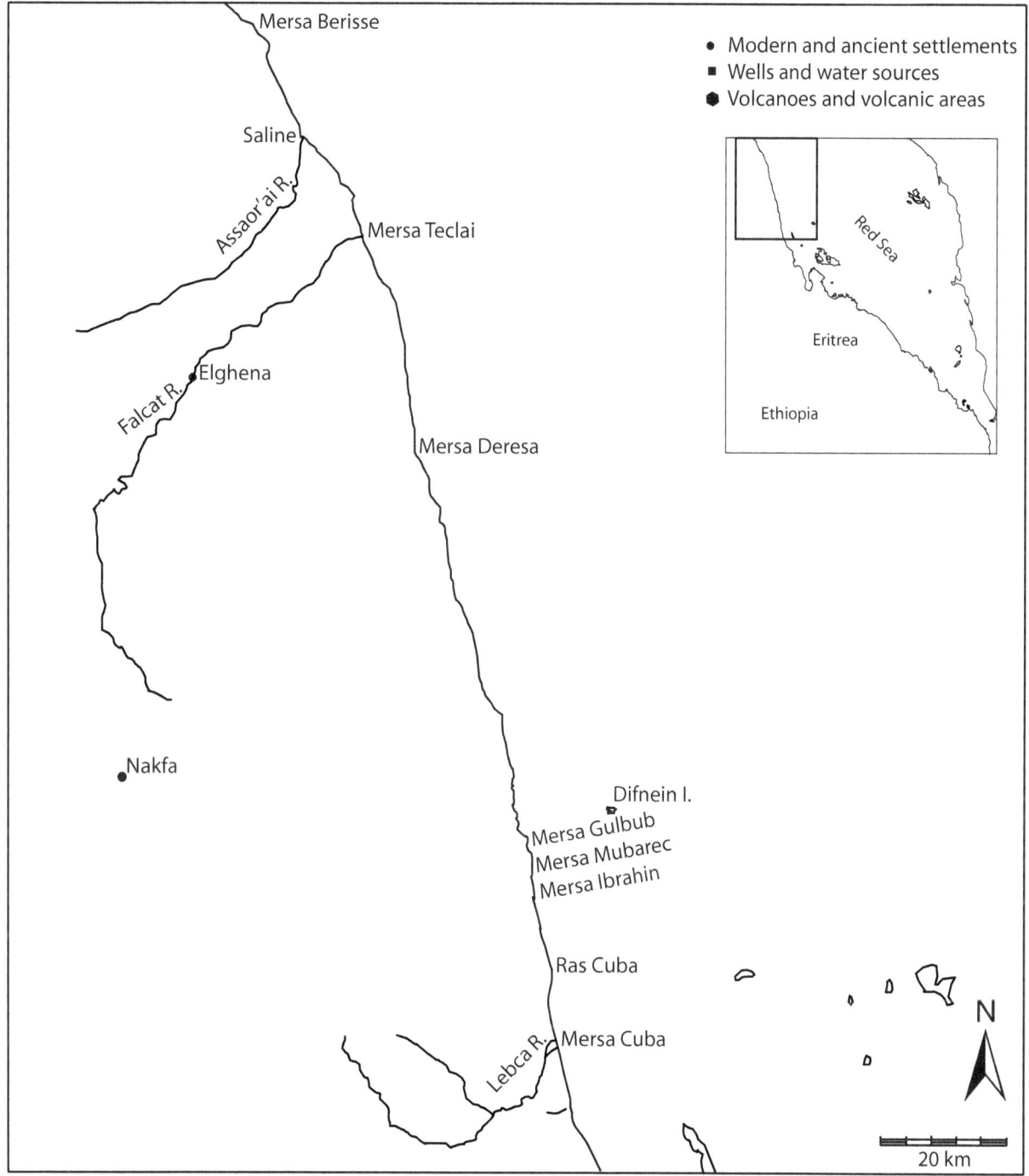

Fig. 10 Map of the Eritrean coast, northern sector, showing the location of modern and ancient place and ruins, wells and water sources, volcanic areas and salines mentioned in the sources and on the colonial maps.

structure called the "Koubet es-sultan", the tomb of the king. Lejean also explored the interior region, without however finding any archaeological evidence that could suggest the presence of an ancient settlement associated to the burials area. Among the many legends related to Rom and the mysterious ruins, the author reports that, according to the natives, spending the night near the tombs provided poetic inspiration (Lejean 1865: 742-763).

De Rivoire (1867, p. 247-248) describes two groups of twenty ancient burial mounds located just north of Massawa, presumably at Muncullo, not far from each other and varying in size. The mounds he describes resembled stone mounds showing the base of partly sunk walls. At the center of these structures, De Rivoire also noticed a square tower or truncated pyramid built of stacked flat rocks, most likely the Koubet es-Sultan described by Lejean. De Rivoire also confirms that according to local tradition the mounds were attributed to the population of Rom. Despite the devotion of the local population towards these tombs, De Rivoire managed to investigate one of these tombs recovering a human skeleton but nothing that could clarify the identification of the people who built them.

Later on Conti Rossini in his Storia d'Etiopia refers to these features as the Tombs of Rom Habi Mentel, Salabat to Carcabat (Conti Rossini 1928, pl. LXV n. 208-211). Issel in his account mentions more generally Islamic tombs identified near Massawa and at Moncullo (Issel 1885: 61-64, 77-83), while Orazio Antinori shows a striking image from the road near the Desset showing on the right many mounds interpreted as a village consisting of round huts and domes (Antinori and Bonati 2000: 60-61). The area was later reported in a list of the monumental buildings by the Ministry of Education ("Desset: tumuli and tombs of uncertain age" MPI 1912: 88-89). One of the most detailed descriptions of the mounds is given by Puglisi. He visited the place as he was intrigued by the information shown on the maps of the IGM mentioning remains of buildings. Puglisi gathered information from oral traditions reported by local informants which differed from those mentioned by previous visitors. Local informants reported to him that in this area the population of Degdeghè had lived up to 150-200 years before, when a conflict with the population of the Taura wiped them out. The population of the Degdeghè, of which a few descendants seem to survive, was said to be originally from Arabia, and occupied the region from Suakin to Jeddah until they settled in the area of Desset (Puglisi 1958: 13-21). Other informants reported that these structures were often traditionally interpreted as the ruins of an ancient city but, according to Puglisi, this was in fact a necropolis consisting of tombs of different types and shapes. The subdivision proposed by Puglisi is based on the location of clusters and on the typological distinction of the different mounds. The group A is located a kilometer east of the main mausoleum and consists of about thirty tall piles of stones of two types: one type shows a perfect cone, well preserved, consisting of large rust-colored pebbles piled up to form a cone. The top looks flat and is covered with sand. Another type is much more damaged but might show a square shape or roughly like a truncated pyramid, with some traces of broad strokes one meter high for two or three rows of stones with possible overlapping edges and corners, and perhaps a monumental door. The top is flat, covered with sand and gravel and measuring 2 by 2 meters. The group B is located west of the main mausoleum and 250 meters from group A. This group consists of six smaller clusters of less than a meter high mounds and one measuring 1.60 m, with three neighboring clusters with a north-south orientation.

The group C is about 350 meters from group B and consists of about 60 mounds of the same type as the preceding; it extends for 180 meters in an east-west direction. The tombs are once again cone-shaped with dark reddish pebbles and truncated pyramids made of stones of various shapes.

Another group is perhaps of more modern graves and it lies in the vicinity of the main mausoleum. These mounds are as high as a man and it has two forms: some are in the shape of cones with pebbles piled up and a bed formed of pebbles of quartz at the base, while others show a circular plan made of overlapped slabs and a tower filled of dark blocks.

The mausoleum is labelled in the IGM map as "Tower Desset" but it is also referred to as "Cubbet es-Saladin." It is located in the center of a group of burials, circular overlapping or shale with a few stones and gravel inside. It is a structure with a square plan of stone slabs held together by mortar of earth, with traces of lime plaster visible on the outside, each side measuring 3.50 meters wide and 4.45 meters in height. The structure was topped by a pile of stones, the base consists of a platform, on the north side there is a 3 m wide pavement.

Andrea Manzo proposed distinguishing the entire site, which is spread over an area of about 4 km, in ten different groups of mounds and mounds of stones.

These mounds can be compared with the traditional Muslim graves in qubba, known along the coast and in southern Sudan and attributable to early stages of penetration of Muslim people in Africa (Crowfoot 1911: 550 and 535), dating from between 1100 and 1500. The geographical distribution of these burials would extend to the borders Sudan and Kasalā, since similar tombs have been observed at Jebel Maman (see also Conti Rossini 1928, pl. LXV n. 208-211).

Water storage installations in the wider context of the south-central and southern Red Sea

A number of ancient water storage installations and cisterns are located along the southern and south-central Red Sea coast and islands. The date and origin of these stone structures are unknown: local informants report legends and traditions ascribing their construction to the Furs, presumably the Persians according to the Arabic translation (Arab: al-Furs = Persians) (Conti Rossini 1928: 295-296; Puglisi 1969: 41-43; Tedeschi 1966: 51). Systematic archaeological investigations of these structures and their context have not been conducted yet and our knowledge is mostly limited to travel accounts and short surveys of the last two centuries.

A re-consideration of these cisterns and local oral traditions related to them can help to understand some aspects of navigation in the Red Sea and the dynamics of maritime contacts in this area during the antiquity and the early medieval period. This may also help to better understand dynamics of human adaptation to the local environment. Water resources were in fact of vital importance for seafaring people and for people inhabiting the Red Sea coasts. Even now most of the cisterns represent the only means to keep water for the sustenance of people and their cattle.

While the north-west coast of the Red Sea has a number of underground fresh water sources not far from the coast and along the routes of the desert, on the contrary, in the southern Red Sea, fresh water is scarce. Except for the western Yemeni coast which is relatively rich in underwater sources, the southern coast in the Gulf of Aden is rather arid, like the opposite coast on the African side and the islands.

The most common system adopted during antiquity, and still today, to meet the need for water storage in this area is to collect rainwater which, in the southern Red Sea, falls in the period from December to March and especially from February to March, in a large enough quantity to fill water storage installations and supply water for the rest of the year (Puglisi 1953: 53).

The formation of the Red Sea shore and islands is the result of "emergent" reef limestone frequently composed of coral rocks, commonly referred to as "madrepore", a kind of rock which is very porous (Seeger, Sidebotham, Harrell, Pons 2006: 10). Due to the porosity of the soil rainwater is easily absorbed into the soil, flows away after the rain and turns salty. The digging of water storage installations during antiquity must have been problematic because of the hardness of the bedrock, but, where suitable, artificial cisterns were carved. The internal surface of the rock was usually mortared in order to store drinkable water until the following raining season.

On some islands like Dahlak Kebir, Nokra and Norah, the soil upheaval generated internal water pools in which the rainwater stagnated without turning salty (Puglisi 1953: 53), so people obtained water also from these natural features. Probably some of them were, at least in part, artificially modified or adapted in order to keep the water longer.

The location of ancient settlements in this part of the Red Sea most likely depended on the availability of water: the suitability of the soil to dig cisterns and wells and the accessibility of natural water pools were essential conditions. The availability of water might have strongly influenced not only ancient settlements but also maritime trade routes.

The islands of the southern Red Sea, with their natural and artificial water resources, might have represented an important element of connection for ships and boats. Most likely some islands were linked with a main port on the coast, providing watering and support facilities as suggested by archaeological and environmental data from Bahdur Island and Adobana, on the coast (Seeger, Sidebotham, Harrell, Pons 2006: 16), and as in the case of Dese Island and Adulis (Peacock and Blue 2007: 126-127). The functional interaction between the islands and the coast is also mentioned in classical sources. Islands were also important sources for exotic products.

As a result of the major role played by the islands of the southern Red Sea during antiquity, the most interesting and well preserved evidence of ancient water storage installations is located on the islands of El-Rih and Bahdur (Crowfoot 1911; Seeger, Sidebotham, Harrell, Pons 2006), in Sudan, and on the islands of the Dahlak archipelago, at Dahlak Kebir, Nokra and Norah (Puglisi 1953 and 1969, Insoll 1997 and 2001), at Black Assarca (Red Sea Pilot 1997: 64), Dese, Baca, Hababarre' (Abu Berri) and Mandola (Puglisi 1953: 69-70).

Water storage installations recorded along the coast are located at Suakin (Chittick 1981), Aydhab (Murray 1926: 235-240, Peacock & Peacock 2007), Adobana, Aqiq, in Sudan, and at Massawa (Conti Rossini 1944-1945), along the Danakil coastal plain, on the peninsula of Buri, in Eritrea. Ancient cisterns are also attested in Djibouti, at Wadi Eygu, near Godoria (Barthoux 2002: 75-77); in Somalia at Hafun and Daamo (Chittick 1979); in Yemen at Aden and Qāni' and on the islands of Zukur and Camaran (Puglisi 1953; Puglisi 1969).

Suakin (Sudan)

In the 1980s Chittick recorded a cistern on the Island of Condenser, at Suakin[4]. This cistern was cut in the coral rock, the ground plan was roughly circular, c. 6 meters in diameter and the roof was slightly domed, supported by four circular columns of bricks. The entrance was probably located in the roof. The sides of the cistern were also lined with similar bricks, red or yellow-green in colour. The cistern was coated with two layers of plaster: the lower was grey in colour, scored with a criss-cross pattern to take the upper rendering, which was pink. These two types of plaster were described as very hard. Chittick suggests a pre-Islamic dating on the basis of the type of bricks and for the mortar which could be Roman (Chittick 1981:181-183). According to Bloss, this cistern was different from those recorded on the islands near Aqiq (presumably El-Rih and Bahdur) and at Aidhab, which probably dated from the Islamic period (Bloss 1936: 277).

Unfortunately, no evidence of this cistern has recently been found during recent investigations conducted at Suakin (Mallinson 2004: 92).

Bahdur Island (Sudan)

Bahdur is a Sudanese Island located close to the mainland in the region of Aqiq. It is possible that this island was originally part of the mainland and would have formed a long peninsula. According to a team which recently surveyed the area, this would have created a very large and well protected harbour for the ancient port of Adobana, providing water and other support facilities for ships anchored in the area (Seeger, Sidebotham, Harrell, Pons 2006: 16).

In 1911, Crowfoot published a report on the cisterns he recorded on this island. At the end of a natural wadi, he noticed a squared pit cut in the natural rock ca. 3-3.5 metres in depth and 7-9 metres across in which wells were carved. He also counted 60 circular openings of wells, ca. 60 cm in diameter which extended beneath into a cistern, supported by pillars. According to local people these cisterns were not coated; at the end of the raining season they were covered with wood and stones in order

---

[4] Bloss (1936: 277) previously described this cistern. He mentioned a Roman thank, oval in shape with brick and a roof supported by three central pillars. According to Bloss this thanks was also used during the 1885 campaigns.

to prevent evaporation. Crowfoot (1911: 540-541) argues that even if most of them were still in use, those that were not coated must become useless since the water seeps away or turns salty.

During a short recent survey, nine stone structures, Muslim graves and cisterns were recorded on the island. Cisterns are described as cut either vertically or horizontally into the limestone bedrock, originating from natural cavities. Horizontal cisterns are characterised by an open basin which is carved at the base of a small mound giving access to the cistern through five arches. Vertical cisterns are also carved at the base of small hills or mounds and characterised by circular openings on the surface, surrounded with a sort of ring shaped wall (Seeger, Sidebotham, Harrell, Pons 2006: 14-15). One of the cisterns recorded by Crowfoot had five arches and can be perhaps identified with the one recorded during the recent archaeological survey (Seeger, Sidebotham, Harrell, Pons 2006). As also noticed by Crowfoot, the interior of some of these structures seems not to be plastered. The surface collection of pottery and glass has been generally attributed to the Islamic period (Seeger, Sidebotham, Harrell, Pons 2006: 17).

El-Rih (or Airi or Iri) Island (Sudan)

The island of El-Rih (or Airi) is located north of Ras Cosar, south of Bahdur Island. Both Crowfoot (1911) and Hebbert (1936) recorded cisterns on this island in the first half of the 20th century. Crowfoot identified the island with Badi, a harbour described in Islamic sources dating to the 650-1170 AD. It has also been suggested that this site replaced Ptolemais of the Hunts in the early Islamic period. Hebbert identified buildings and cisterns on this island, suggesting they were built before the 7th century AD. More recent research there has been conducted by Kawatoko (1993).

Crowfoot remarked a series of levelled basins, east and north of the main village of the island, each containing one or more covered cisterns. In all he counted 100 cisterns but he believes that there were many more elsewhere on the island. Among those cisterns he mentions a small "domestic" cistern (Crowfoot 1911: 543), probably associated with a house. Another cistern was lying in a 2000 square metres basin with an oblong plan (Crowfoot 1911: 544). This cistern was partially cut in the coral rock and partially built up with coral blocks and roofed with a flat arch in order to prevent evaporation. Inside, the cistern was coated with hard lime-plaster. The water was received on all sides from the banks, and two inlet channels were recorded on one of the long sides. He also noticed a small platform on which the buckets or skins for the water were rested. In the middle of this platform there was a shallow hole, 10 cm in diameter, in which, according to the locals, people put money to pay for the water.

Hebbert counted more than forty cisterns, dating, according to him, to the 7th century AD. He described cisterns of different shapes and sizes: the circular cisterns were cut in the natural coral rock and were generally bottle-shaped, in section, with the neck about 1 meter wide and up to five metres in length. Cisterns with a rectangular groundplan were carved in the coral rock and some of them were vaulted. The original bottom of the cisterns was not found because most of them were silted up. According to Hebbert, the water was drawn up through a hole in the roof of the cistern and emptied into a vessel (Hebbert 1936: 312-313). The estimated depth of some cisterns was about 5 meters. Hebbert noticed that the cisterns were still in use at his time since local people used to go there during the winter and draw their water from wells and cisterns.

Some vaulted structures, carved in the side of small hills with a build up vault made with coral blocks, were also recently recorded on the island. It is in doubt if these are cisterns or ancient excavated galleries (Michel Pons Pers. Comm.).

Khor Taggut/Adobana (Sudan)

At Khor Taggut, near Adobana, Crowfoot mentions finding red bricks in the wadi bed, apparently forming the foundation of a circular pier about 1.5 m in diameter, probably the remains of a cistern connected to ancient cultivations, as suggested by local people (Crowfoot 1911: 539).

Massawa (Eritrea)

Conti Rossini attests that at Massawa there were 49 cisterns in the 16th century attributed to the Furs, presumably the Persians, by local people, although, he does not mention his source. The only ascertained cistern was originally located at Ras Mudur, now lying below the former Hospital Umberto 1st (Conti-Rossini 1944-1945: 34).

Dahlak Kebir Island (Eritrea)

In the 18th century, Bruce affirmed he had seen 360 cisterns at Dahlak Kebir (Bruce 1790). In 1946, Puglisi recorded 70 cisterns in the village of Dahlak Kebir and 30 in the village of Adal. In 2003 I briefly visited the Island of Dahlak Kebir. At first it was difficult to identify the cisterns, some of them were buried and others were completely covered by the vegetation, only visible for their small openings to the surface. I could not estimate the total number of cisterns, but I could notice that some of them were still in use by local people.

The work conducted by Puglisi still remains the most exhaustive investigation, but unfortunately it is only published in the Bolletino di Asmara (Puglisi 1953). According to Puglisi, some cisterns are better manufactured than others, carved in a compact coral rock, sometimes roofed with a vault and with pillars; in some cases the vault is built up on the surface with coral blocks, in other cases it is carved in the rock. The inner parts of the cistern are plastered with strong gray-pink in color mortar. The rainwater entered naturally from the area around, sometimes channels carved in the rock facilitated the passage of the water. The opening is usually oval and one meter wide, sometimes enclosed by a ring shaped wall, with lateral openings, usually from 90 cm to 1.30 m in diameter. Cisterns are usually between 2 m and 4 m in depth, but most of them are partially silted up. Cisterns with an oval plan measure up to 8 m in diameter; those with rectangular plans 9 m x 3 m or 8 m x 4 m.

The largest oval cistern is 17 m x 12 m with two pillars inside, the largest rectangular one is 16 m x 5 m in plan. Long channels measuring up to 46 m long are also attested.

One cistern shows three different strata of cement, testifying that some of them were maintained or reemployed during the past. Another cistern has a rectangular basin with an additional opening at the bottom giving access to another basin with two openings.

Puglisi also recorded fulla (Arabic transl. pools) that he describes as large natural pools, surrounded with semicircular arrangements of large stones, vertically fixed in the soil. According to local people, fulla can keep the water for two or three months after the rainy season using the slope of the ground. The deepest part of this kind of barrages usually can reach 1 metre in depth. The procedures of management of those basins consist in digging into the soil until reaching the coral rock strata, which withholds water. The barrage is subsequently surrounded with a mound of soil for waterproofing (Puglisi 1953: 55-57). These barrages are attested at Gim'hile' and Das-Go, at Saleeit, Dubhello, Derbuscet, at Adalè near Amrac and at Dargaba at Adal in Dahlak Kebir and also on the islands of Arue' and Shumma (Puglisi 1953: 55).

According to Puglisi, the Dahlak cisterns were built in the 7th-8th century AD during the maritime expansions of Persians from Siraf to provide water for African slaves traded in Egypt, in the Arabian Peninsula, in the Gulf, in India and China.

Timothy Insoll recently visited the island of Dahlak Kebir and also recorded cisterns. In contrast with the oral tradition attributing the construction of the cisterns to the Furs, he found no evidence of Sassanian or Islamic-Sassanian pottery, or later pottery from the Gulf (Insoll 2001: 48), although he admits not being a specialist in these materials.

Wadi 'Aygu (Djibouti)

In the 1960s Barthoux recorded a cistern built with cut stones joined with a mortar of sand and lime at Wadi 'Aygu, 8 kilometres from the coast, near the bay of Godoria (Labrousse 1978: 76). Most likely, this cistern was originally filled with the water of the wadi (Labrousse 1978: 75; Desanges-Reddé 1994). The cistern consisted in two perpendicular basins (21 m long, 3.40 m wide and 2 m deep) with a small channel for the water which might originally fall from 2 metres into the basin 7 m long (Barthoux 2007: 75-76). The capacity of this cistern was 350 cubic metres.

The last part of the small basin had projecting stones to assist in dredging it to the bottom, the corners of the cistern were smoothed, the surfaces were covered with a thick rendering for waterproofing. The cistern is now silted up and difficult to find (Labrousse 1978: 76).

In 2009, the author conducted an archaeological with Dr. John Cooper as part of the MARES Project, based at the University of Exeter (Agius, Cooper and Zazzaro 2009). Unfortunately, due to tension at the border between Eritrea and Djibouti, the team could go no further north than Godoria. The archaeological survey was therefore limited to locating the cistern found in the 1970s by Bartheaux (2007: 75-77). The wadi has now silted up the cistern, but fragmentary remains of its coating were still visible on the surface. The coating consists in a thick layer of mortar covered with plaster, a technique recorded both in pre-medieval and medieval cisterns along the Red Sea coast.

Daamo (Somalia)

Chittick attested at Hafun and Daamo (Somalia) a number of wall-like features cut out of the coral rock interpreted as remains of buildings (Chittick 1979: 273-277 esp. 275). The author believes that these kinds of structures could also be interpreted as fulla or large water pools like those found at Dahlak Kebir.

Water storage installations and the "Furs" tradition

At this stage the research is limited to comparing the typology of different water installations of the southern Red Sea on the basis of indirect sources, but a systematic archaeological study of the cisterns will be essential for future investigations.

According to our sources, water storage installations in the southern Red Sea consist in diffcrent type of cisterns, pits, wells and rainwater pools (fulla) carved in the limestone and in the coral rock.

Rainwater pools were designed to capture rainwater on rocky plains and slopes; these were usually natural pools improved with artificial barriers.

Concerning the cisterns, some received water coming from natural aquifers, others from rainwater. Cisterns are excavated both horizontally and vertically in the rock without roof and with a small circular opening, and usually coated inside. Other cisterns are roofed, sometimes with a built up vault to avoid the evaporation of the water and pillars to sustain the roof.

TThere is a large variation in types and several components need to be analysed in order to properly investigate these cisterns and determine the manufacture and date. Some variations are probably due to different environmental contexts in which cisterns have been built, others to different traditions of construction and coating techniques, which could date back to the 1st century AD.

Comparisons are recognised among cisterns found on the islands of El-Rih, Bahdur and Dahlak Kebir. In both cases cisterns have openings characterised by ring-shaped walls, a thick coating, oval and rectangular plans. Furthermore, both islands have epigraphic evidence dating back to the 10th-11th century. These inscriptions demonstrate the important role that the two islands played at the beginning of the Arab navigation in the Red Sea and of the Arab expansion in Sudan and Ethiopia.

On the other hand, some cisterns found at Dahlak Kebir, which are characterised by a system of channels with different openings, could be compared with similar technologies adopted in the Arab/Perisan Gulf area (Cressey 1958), but this needs to be proved by systematic archaeological investigations.

In the 6th-10th century AD regular contacts between the Gulf and the western Indian Ocean also extended to Africa. Monneret de Villard analysed trade movements of Persians which departed from the port of Siraf, at first, and then from the port of Qais to Africa (Monneret de Villard 1937-38). Archaeological evidence of this trade network is attested on the East African coast, mainly at Ras Hafun (Somalia) but also further south along the coasts of Kenya and Zanzibar. Literary sources also attest that the southern Red Sea was included in the Sassanian maritime hegemony during the 6th-7th century AD. The Persian presence in the Red Sea was discontinuous and, to some extent, related to the struggle with Byzantines for the control of trade with the East. The kingdom of Aksum, ally of the Byzantine Empire, controlled most of the maritime trade network between the Indian Ocean and the Mediterranean in the Horn of Africa during the late 4th-6th century AD. Starting from the 6th century, the maritime hegemony in the southern Red Sea shifted from the Aksumites to the Persians, ruled by king Khosrow I. Their supremacy in the Red Sea, particularly in South Arabia, lasted for a brief period (572-597 to 628) while the Persian trade ended definitively with the Arab expansion in the Red Sea during the 9th-10th century AD.

However, while historical evidence of people from the Gulf on the African coast of the Indian Ocean is corroborated also by archaeological evidence, there is a lack of archaeological information for the southern and central Red Sea.

Puglisi attempted to trace the history of the Persian presence in the southern and central Red Sea on the basis of the cisterns, supported by ethnographical sources. Several scholars and travellers visiting that area attested that local people inhabiting the coast from Suakin to Aden and on the islands of the southern Red Sea, tended to attribute the construction of stone structures to the Furs. Bruce was the first to mention this tradition related to the attribution of the construction of the cisterns at Dahlak Kebir (Bruce 1790: 401-402), followed by Issel (1872: 70 note 2), Munzinger, Odorizzi (Odorizzi 1911: 255) and Pollera (Puglisi 1969: 41).

According to Conti Rossini, cisterns, wells and remains of towns attributed to the Furs were located at Gammela (near Edd), Barassoli, Beilul, Alale', Marghebla, Raheita in Eritrea, at Siyan, Gebel Gen (Tadjoura) in Djibouti, and in Somalia (Conti Rossini 1928: 295). The main town of the Furs, called Adga, may have been located in the bay of Amfila; Assab was another important centre of the Furs, its harbour located in Raheita (Conti Rossini 1928: 295).

In the 1940s Puglisi recorded cisterns attributed to the Furs on the Island of Dese, on the Island of Baca, on the peninsula of Buri, on the Island of Hababarre' (Abu Berri), on the Island of Mandola and Aiuman, near an ancient salt trade path; and in Yemen on the Islands of Zukur and Camaran (Puglisi 1953: 53-70, esp. 69). During the author's short visit to Dahlak Kebir in 2003, local people interviewed still attributed the construction of the Dahlak cisterns to the Furs.

Some Islamic sources corroborate the relation between water storage installations and Persians. Ibn al-Mujāwir attributes the original construction of the Aden water tanks to the "people of Sīrāf" (Margariti 2002: 71). A local tradition attributing the construction of cisterns to the Persians in Aden was also attested by Pulgisi, presumably a reminiscence of the Persian presence in South Arabia in the 6th century AD (see also Puglisi 1969: 43).

Puglisi's suggestion to look at the cisterns to trace the history of the Persian presence in the southern and central Red Sea (Puglisi 1969: 41-43) is a very interesting point in order to conduct a comparative study of the Red Sea and the Gulf. However, the problem of the interpretation of the cisterns seem to be more complex and needs a more detailed analysis. Puglisi's research fieldwork was in fact limited to a preliminary survey of the cisterns in Dahlak Kebir. It must also be considered that water storage installations in the Red Sea may have existed since the beginning of long navigations. Cisterns might have been built since earliest times and been reemployed, improved, modified or increased in the following centuries. Already Pliny the Elder (1st century AD) in fact mentioned cisterns probably in the area of the Sudanese coast (ed. Conte 1982: VI, 189), and Diodorus, Photius and Strabo mentioned cisterns in the southern part of the Red Sea (Desanges-Reddé 1994).

The museum collections of Adulitan materials

History of the museum collections

The history of museum collections of finds from Adulis is interesting because it had different phases and it involves museums of various countries and continents. Materials from Adulis are today kept in five different museums: at the British Museum (London, UK), at the National Museum of Eritrea (Asmara), at the National Museum of Addis Abeba (Ethiopia), at the former African Museum in Rome (Italy) and in the Museum of Ethnography in Stockholm (Sweden).

Some of the collections, like the one now kept in the National Museum of Eritrea, moved from one location to another over a few years and survived the war with few losses, while some precious objects such as gold chains, coins and cornelian beads disappeared in the course of the time. Apart from six objects exhibited in the National Museum of Addis Abeba, all the finds are currently located in the storerooms of the museums, which is why very little is known to date about these materials.

In the collections of the Department of Prehistory and Europe in the British Museum are currently kept five marble fragments from the excavation conducted by the British Army, under the auspices of the British Museum in 1868. According to Munro-Hay the collection included – in addition to two marble fragments with cross decorated in relief, most likely the chancel panel typical of Early Byzantine churches, an octagonal alabaster column and a Corinthian capital – also a coin, some pottery fragments, metal objects and a ribbed amphora (Munro-Hay 1989: 44, Pl. IV and V) that can be easily identified with the Ayla-Aqaba type. The column and the Corinthian capital are also illustrated in the volume of the French scientific mission led by Teophile Lefebvre in 1845 and they may be the same objects (Peacock and Blue 2007: 121, fig. 9.11). In an account of the British Army excavation at Adulis a copper pair of scale and chains are also mentioned (Markham 1869: 155 note 1). An attempt to identify additional objects was made in 1987 by Munro-Hay and the curators of the British Museum but without positive results a part for the five marble fragments. The author was able to examine the British Museum collection from Adulis in 2012 and to identify and photograph the five marble fragments.

In the National Museum of Addis Abeba the materials from the Adulis excavation of the Institut éthiopien d'archéologie lead by Francis Anfray in 1961 and 1962 are kept. The collection has been examined by the author and her colleague Luisa Sernicola in 2004. It consists in over four hundred potsherds, ca. ten glass fragments, coins, metal and few stone objects. Only five pots and a copper pair of scale are displayed in the Museum, all the other materials are kept in cardboard boxes in the storeroom of the Museum. Each box bears an inventory number and a tag inside indicating the place and date of finding. Unfortunately the original inventory numbers have been replaced with new inventory numbers that cannot be related to Anfray's notes anymore, preventing any clear context information. Despite the lack of chronological data, these materials are still interesting for an understanding of ceramic typology and traditions in Adulis, considering that most of them come from the same context of excavation of an housing quarter. The imported sherds can also tell us a lot about trade contacts.

Some of the findings listed by Anfray are absent in the present collection: 142 Aksumite coins, including 3 golden coins and 1 foreign coin, 3 small bronze weights, marble and glass fragments and a carnelian gem with a lion incised (Anfray 1974: 745-765). Anfray suggested that the gem with the lion incision could be Sassanian in origin or even Indian as the representation of a lion is very common on gems associated with figures symbolising Buddha in Gandhara art (Glover 1996: 140, 155, tab. 5). In an anonymous inventory of Adulis' finds kept in this Museum, the following items are listed: ribbed amphoras sealed with schist (?) stoppers, small lamps, grinding stones for wheat, a golden coin from Israel, 152 Aksumite coins in gold, silver and copper and one from Syria, potsherds, glass fragments, Byzantine oil lamps, large marble fragments, a copper pair of scale and the already mentioned gem. As previously said, most of these items were not observed in the present collection.

At the National Museum of Asmara most of the materials found by Paribeni in 1907 are kept today in the storeroom and only a few marble architectural elements and pots are on display. The history of the Paribeni collection is interesting because it follows the various vicissitudes of the museum over many years. The first location of the collection was temporarily in the former Asmara Police Station and it included 1600 objects (Gallina and Paribeni 1907: 90-92). Subsequently the collection was moved into the Liceo Ferdinando Martini and the Institute "Vittorio Bottino", then to the Museum of the Italian Library in Asmara, and then, from the 1950s, finally into the National Museum of Asmara (Gabriel 1953: 13-16). In the 1960s the Adulitan materials on display included: small marble pillars, capitals, grinding stones, amphorae, glass and ceramic fragments, lamps, small female figurines, clay discs, metal objects, ornamental objects in ivory, bone, mother of pearl and shells (Anfray 1965 and Franchini 1963: 67). In the 1980s, according to Ricci (1983), the collection included: a granite mortar found by Paribeni, a fragment of twisted column in marble found by Lefebvre (1845), a fragment of a doorpost or pillar in limestone with vine-stock motifs, four small pillars and three marble slabs found by Paribeni, ten pots, three gypsum lids with impressed seals, three miniature amphorae, two small copper cross, three lamps, two female figurines (one in stone and one in ceramic), a small red ware pot with polished surface, a jar, a Saint Menas flask, a lamp with Greek inscription, a stone mould, sixteen architectural elements, two in alabaster, the others in marble, several copper, bronze and iron objects, ceramic objects including a bird figurine, cylindrical dish with incised concentric circles, and black and red ware sherds from the lower strata excavated by Paribeni including a globular pot with moulded arms forming a zigzag motif. According to Ricci, the twisted column, characterised by green veins, was found by Lord Valentia. This column can be compared with another fragment of column kept in the Palace of the Governor in Massawa (Manzo 1995: 116) and today in the Northern Red Sea Regional Museum. In the 1990s the collection of the National Museum of Asmara was hosted in the Presidential Palace (Andrea Manzo, *pers. comm.*). After the war with Ethiopia the collection was moved back to the National Museum. It seems that on this occasion some of the objects included in the Adulis collection were lost. At present some of the objects displayed in the Museum bear wrong labels, stating for example that fragments of South Arabian inscriptions and statues are from Adulis (Manzo 1996: 121 and Ricci 1983: 11-13). Among the objects on display today those that are most likely to come from Adulis are: a small female statue, a marble capital, an architectural fragment in limestone and another in marble, two ribbed amphoras, two marble pillars (see Paribeni 1907, figs. 15, 17, 27, 34, 36, 58) and a twisted column (Seguid 2005: 13, fig. 2). More recently, a marble fragment from Adulis bearing the end of a cross (cf. Paribeni 1907: 466, fig. 9) was noticed on display in the Northern Red Sea Regional Museum. The rest of the collection is currently kept in the storeroom of the National Museum of Eritrea and it represents the most interesting documentation on the site of Adulis. The actual collection examined in September 2005 and in January 2011 in collaboration with Andrea Manzo and with the assistance of Amaha Segid and Tseaga Habtay, features about 400 findings including potsherds and complete vessels, glass, vessel stoppers, stone vessels, metal, ivory, shells and bone artefacts all dating to different periods, probably from the 1st millennium BC to the 6th-7th century AD. Part of the collection is probably lost since some objects described and illustrated in the Paribeni excavation report are absent. All the finds are located on shelves with other finds from other unknown locations; some pottery fragments and the obsidian flakes were stored in plastic bags with an indication of Adulis provenance. Among all the finds kept in the storeroom, the Paribeni collection was identified due to the presence of small stamps with serial inventory numbers that had been pasted on the finds during or just after excavation by Paribeni. Other objects bear a newer paper tag pasted on them which might correspond to a recent reorganization of the collection, although some of the objects bearing the tag do not seem to have been originally part of the collection. The tag reads E.R.M.ADU. followed by an inventory number. No catalogue was shown to the author in the course of her fieldwork at the museum.

Part of the Paribeni collection, including metal finds, has been recently kept in the storerooms of the Italian Institute for African and East (IsIAO) in Rome but it was originally on display in the former Colonial Museum inaugurated in 1923 (see Illustrazione Italiana 1923: 640-641). Those finds also showed the same method of labelling with stamps noticed in the Asmara collection. The metal objects are displayed on wooden panels and bear three different inventory numbers which correspond perhaps to three different phases of arrangement of the collection. The present inventory includes heighten numbers, corresponding to sixteen panels and two isolated objects. There is no trace of the collection of coins found by Paribeni (cf. Paribeni 1907: 569) which was supposed to be in Rome (Munro-Hay and Yuel-Jensen 1995). According to Mancini the collection included 260 gr. of gold constituting 42 golden coins and 390 copper coins (Mancini 1908: 207 see also Gallina and Paribeni 1907: 90-92). The collection included coins of kings Endubis, Ezanas, Ezana, Almiryis, Ella Gabaz and Ioel; on the bronze coins the names mentioned are Gersem, two anonymous kings, Kaleb, Ouzebas, Wazena, Ioel, Armah and Hataz (Munro-Hay and Yuel-Jensen 1995). According to Paribeni a small treasure of Arab coins mixed to ashes, was also found to the west of the modern village of Zula (Paribeni 1907: 571). Unfortunately, there is no trace of this collection in any of the museum collections examined.

More recently an archive document mentioning the collection of materials from the 1906 Adulis excavation lead by Richard Sundström, as part of the Enno Littman's Princeton expedition to Abyssinia, has been identified in the Museum of Ethnography in Stockholm. As reported in the digital archive, the collection includes: 1907.59.0001 Floor tiles, from the Adulis digs (in the attic); 1907.59.0002 Various pieces of glass, bronze object[s?] etc., Adulis; 1907.59.0003 Lod(?) Adulis (Azmara Nigusse, Stockholm, personal communication); the two gold coins are no mentioned (Paribeni 1907: 569). Unfortunately, the collection has not been identified yet, consequently the author has not examined it.

Ceramic artefacts

The study of the Adulitan ceramic artefacts kept in the museum collections started in 2003 as part of the author's PhD thesis. The collections examined were those of the National Museum of Asmara and the Museum of Addis Ababa respectively including over 500 complete and fragmentary vessels and clay objects from the Paribeni and Anfray's excavations.

Unfortunately, no reliable stratigraphic information accompanied the record of the pottery from both collections, although in some cases, Paribeni reports the find context of certain pottery artefacts which are easily recognizable in the collection and are also illustrated or described in detail in his report. Excavations conducted by Anfray were limited to a restricted area, an housing quarter, which represents a close and coherent context most likely dating to the last occupation phase, to the 6th-7th century AD. In view of this, for determining the possible date of local pottery, Paribeni and Anfray's excavation notes were taken into consideration together with close comparisons with pottery fragments from different cultural neighbors and more recent data from ongoing excavations at Adulis.[1] The imported pottery collection is in general comparable to Hellenistic and Roman - Byzantine types from the Mediterranean area, especially the Near East and North Africa, also recently found in other sites of the Red Sea, especially at Quseir al Qadim and Berenike. In general, the re-examination of Paribeni and Anfray's collections was aimed to distinguish local pottery traditions from the pottery production typical of the highland settlements and to identify the different provenance and date, when it was possible, of imported pottery.

The ceramic material collected by Paribeni is, in some respects, more varied in function and date, since he investigated different areas of the site and dug deep excavation pits, up to 12 m below the surface. Therefore, the ceramic classification proposed by Paribeni is based on a morphological description of the fragments which does not necessarily reflect the chronological phases of different contexts in which they have been found. This typological distinction includes five different groups:

1. Friable "glossy" black ware with incised decoration of geometric patterns on the surface. This type of pottery has been found in abundance in association with charcoal, bones, copper, glass and obsidian fragments in a pit excavated in the south-west sector of the site, in the lower layers from -5 to -10 meters below the surface. Paribeni suggested that this pottery dates back to the earlier Ptolemaic age (Paribeni 1907: 446-451).
2. Coarse friable ware with dark and smoothed surfaces using a spatula and decorated with incised geometric patterns. Most representative fragments belonged to globular forms with handles or grips with holes for the passage of a string.
3. Ribbed vessels jars, most likely used as containers, characterized by pale pink sandy ware with creamy surfaces. The forms vary from amphora shape to globular flasks with rounded bottom, with short neck and two handles, globular jars with three-lobed lip with perforated septum and conical vessels with flat base.
4. Fine red ware characterized by red slip cover on the surface often decorated with incised or impressed crosses. Forms correspond to small cups, dish, bowl, globular vessels with spout sideways and "little pots" with a small vertical handle.
5. Red slip pottery usually found in association with painted vessels. This type is characterized by fine buff ware with yellow slip and painted decoration of purple and black lines, including herringbone bands, punctuation and netting.

In the light of more recent studies on pottery found in other contemporary sites from the highlands, it is possible to compare and better identify these ceramic types. The first and the second group seem to correspond to a local pottery tradition now named "Adulitan" and dating most likely from the end of the 1st millennium BC (Zazzaro and Manzo 2012). The third type clearly refers to Ayla/Aqaba and Late Roman amphoras from the Eastern Mediterranean, North Africa and Egypt dating roughly from the 4th to the 7th century AD. The fourth and the fifth type may refer to the Aksumite fine pottery tradition typical of the highland settlements. The fourth type showing decoration of incised crosses can be likely dated to the second half of the 6th-7th century AD (Fattovich, Bard *et al.* 2000: 25), painted vessels are also usually found in contexts dating to the Aksumite 4 (ca. 550-700 AD) or Late Aksumite (cf. Phillipson 2000: 330).

Francis Anfray's pottery collection was collected during excavations conducted in 1961 and 1962 in a housing quarter located in the southern and western sectors of the site (Anfray 1974: 752). In the excavation report, Anfray distinguished two main ceramic groups, one of red ware Aksumite tradition pottery characterized by incised or painted crosses, dating to the 6th-8th centuries AD, and the other of imported pottery. Anfray also mentioned the presence of some pottery fragments possibly dating to the pre-Aksumite period but without providing any further description. According to him, the imported pottery assemblage included ribbed amphoras and *terra sigillata* from the Mediterranean area. Among the amphoras he distinguished ribbed amphoras with a thick and uniform body and amphoras with thin, irregular body and rounded in shape.

Some of these ceramic fragments were selected and submitted for laboratory analysis. The samples chosen included: a fragment of African red slip ware, a fragment of red slip ware, a fragment of pink ware, smoothed and with an incised cross, a fragment of red pottery polished internally and externally, thin-walled, a fragment of polished red pottery with incised decoration, a fragment of red-brown ware pottery comparable to types found in the upper levels of Maṭarā, on the highland, and a fragment of red pottery blackened outside. The results of the analysis revealed that a constant component of Adulis pottery fabrics is biotite (brown or mica) and green hornblende (Gautier 1976: 57-69) which is absent in the samples selected from the other highland settlements. The result of the analysis suggests that a local tradition did exist. The re-examination of the Anfray collection discussed here will illustrate that actually most of the potsherds in the

---
[1] The project is led by the National Museum of Asmara, the Northern Red Sea Regional Museum in collaboration with the Ce.RDO and other Italian institutions among which the University of Naples "L'Orientale"

collection are of local manufacture, well distinguished, not only in the ware, but also in the forms from common pottery productions of the highland settlements.

The criteria that Anfray and Paribeni adopted to select the sherds to be kept in the collections, has also to be considered. Presumably all the diagnostic fragments that the French archaeologist collected during the excavation are included in the collection. Diagnostic fragments of local pottery are mainly related to cooking vessels and storage vessels, in fact this pottery was found in a housing quarter. Fragments of fine red slip small pottery, decorated with crosses and grooves similar to the pottery production of the highlands are also present but in smaller quantity. The cooking and storage vessels seen in Anfray's collection are absent in the Paribeni collection, although he also did excavate an housing quarter in the southern sector of the site. The author hypothesis is that either Paribeni selected only fine ware and decorated vessels to be preserved in the museum collection or that part of the collection might have been lost and only the finds from his excavations of monumental contexts was preserved. In fact, although the most common diagnostic types in the Paribeni collection are fragments of fine red slip pottery, he did mention the presence of utilitarian pottery of rough manufacture in the excavation report.

In general, most of the fragments from the Paribeni collection can be compared with similar pottery from the highland settlements dating mainly to Aksumite 3-4 (ca. 400 AD – 450/550 AD / 550 AD–700 AD), only few sherds can be dated from the beginning of Aksumite 1 and 2 (ca. 150–400/450 AD). These data are obviously conditioned by the fact that the lower levels of the site have not been adequately investigated. Rare specimens are to be placed in a post-Adulitan or unknown phase.

The local ceramic artefacts in the National Museum of Eritrea

A preliminary definition of the Adulitan pottery tradition

The Adulitan tradition of pottery production has been preliminary defined by combining the study of recent finds from the Adulis Project 2011-2012 (Adulis Fieldwork Report 2011 and Adulis Fieldwork Report 2012, unpublished) with the results of the study of museum collections conducted in 2003-2004 (Zazzaro and Manzo 2012).

The pottery has been studied at first using a portable microscope and a geological lens, then petrological analysis has been conducted by the Department of Geology of the University of Naples Federico II. The preliminary analysis of the fabrics immediately suggested that some of the pottery assemblage was locally produced, while other ware might have been brought to the site from the nearby regions.

The preliminary typological and chronological analysis had to rely for comparisons and association on the dated materials from the highland settlements of Aksum and Adigrat, from Yēhā and Maṭarā, and from the Onà sites in the Asmara area, as well as from other sites on the Red Sea coastal region.

In the earlier phases, the Adulitan ceramic tradition was characterized by a grey-black to grey-brown micaceous ware, a very typical mineral fabric which may result from the use of the local sand as a temper, perhaps confirmed by the rounded shape of the mineral inclusions. A fabric characterized by the association between the mineral micaceous temper and the organic inclusions was recorded as well. Concerning the surface treatments, this pottery is characterised by the occurrence of smoothed/burnished, well defined horizontal, diagonal or vertical lines on the external surface and also on the internal surface in the unrestricted shapes. For the decorations, incised and impressed patterns on the external surface are typical. Grey and black polished bowls or cups are often characterised by rim bands while brown or grey ware flat and triangular in section rims are often associated with oblique incisions. Sometimes the impressions are characterized by a wavy outline, possibly obtained by impressing the edge of a shell on the wet paste. From a technological point of view, all these Adulitan vessels were hand made. The recorded shapes were all characterized by a rounded bottom. Cups, bowls, carinated bowls and basins could have alternatively restricted or unrestricted rims.

As previously mentioned, this type of pottery was first identified by Paribeni. It was found in the lower layers of the pit no. 1, between 5 and 10 meters below the surface. The collected fragments were easily recognised in the collection of the National Museum of Eritrea, thanks to the drawings published in the report (Paribeni 1907 Tav. III-VI).

Recent excavations have only yielded a few scattered small fragments suggesting that their original stratigraphic context has not yet been reached. Consequently the dating for this pottery type is currently under discussion. Although typical of Adulis, the wavy-shaped impressions possibly produced by the edges of shells occurring in these assemblages were also recorded in assemblages dating to the 2nd millennium BC in sites close to Djibouti (Gutherz et al. 1996, 273–79) and even on the Egyptian Red Sea coast, in an Egyptian Middle Kingdom assemblage, where they are considered as imports from the southern Red Sea (Manzo 2012). The use of burnished lines as a decoration is also widespread in the Yemeni Tihama (Buffa 2007, 34–35) and recorded in some materials imported from the southern Red Sea on the Egyptian Red Sea coast (Manzo 2012). On the other hand, similar pottery types have also been found in small numbers in the lower layers of occupation at Maṭarā (Anfray 1967 Tav. XLIX, fig. 7) and Haoulti (de Contenson 1963a: 51), with associated materials dating to the 3rd-1st century BC. Further, according to Paribeni, this pottery cannot be "too old" having been found in association with glass and metal fragments (Paribeni 1907: 547-548). Unfortunately, a firmer dating cannot be provided until stratigraphic excavation reaches levels similar to those excavated by Paribeni in 1907, down to 10-12 metres below the surface.

Apart from the black-gray ware fragments, the rest of the Paribeni collection does not include types that can be considered typical of the Adulitan tradition although Paribeni (1907: 447) does mention the existence of pottery types that this author has recognized as typical of the Adulitan tradition after having analyzed the recent finds and the Anfray collection. This Adulitan pottery tradition shows the same micaceous paste as the black-gray ware and is characterized by a red to brown color. Very typical of these phases were bag shaped jars or bottles with cylindrical neck and a moulded ledge between neck and shoulder. The ledge is very often characterized by a decoration of cross incisions. These Adulitan ceramic types are prevalently for domestic use and it seems to be dating from the 3rd century AD (Zazzaro and Manzo 2012). The pottery that can be ascribed to the widespread Aksumite tradition could have been brought from the highlands rather than locally produced, although this might depend on the different phases and is still far from being demonstrated. In the present work, this pottery has been dated on the basis of comparisons with dated assemblages excavated in the highland settlements and preliminarily named as "Aksumite".

Adulitan black-grey ware

The thirteen samples kept in the museum and described below seem to be representative of the typological range of rim also found in recent excavations, providing a preliminary typology. The different types have been grouped on the basis of similar fabric, form, decoration and size.

Class I: Restricted Bowls and Jars

Type 1. Black-gray or black-brown ware, medium density mineral inclusions up to 1 mm, comprising mica. Globular restricted bowls, rounded profile, 12 to 22 cm in diameter characterized by recurved narrowing rim. The external surface is burnished, especially from right to left on the body surface, the internal surface is wiped. The decoration consists in geometries of semicircles and triangles and patterns of incised straight lines and/or impressed discontinuous wavy lines; in some cases traces of white paste are present in the incisions (Figure 11.1a).

Type 2. Black-gray ware, medium density mineral inclusions up to 1 mm, comprising mica. Restricted bowls with round profile and vertical semicircular handle below the rim, 18 cm rim diameter, flat narrowing rim, rounded profile. Surfaces are burnished.

The decoration is geometric with patterns of incised straight lines and/or impressed discontinuous wavy lines (cf. Paribeni inventory number 68) (Figure 11.2).

Type 3. Black-brown ware, medium density mineral inclusions up to 1 mm, comprising mica. Restricted bowls with vertical profile, flat flaring rim, 10 cm rim diameter. Surfaces are burnished and the decoration is geometric with patterns of incised straight lines (Adulis Fieldwork Report 2012, unpublished, Table 3).

Type 4. Black-brown ware, medium density mineral inclusions up to 1 mm, comprising mica. Restricted bowls with vertical profile, rounded narrowing rim, 14 cm in diameter. Surfaces are smoothed and burnished. The decoration is geometric with patterns of incised straight lines (Adulis Fieldwork Report 2012, unpublished, Table 3).

Class II: Unrestricted Bowls

Type 1. Black-grey ware, medium density mineral inclusions up to 1 mm, comprising mica. Small bowls or beakers with pointed straight rim, 20 cm in diameter. Surfaces are burnished. The decoration is geometric with patterns of incised straight lines and/or impressed discontinuous wavy lines (Paribeni inventory number 89 112) (Figure 11.1d).

Type 2. Black-brown ware, medium density mineral inclusions up to 1 mm, comprising mica. Bowls with slightly rounded profile and flat straight thickened rim, 16 up to 32 cm in diameter. Surfaces are burnished. The decoration is geometric with patterns of incised straight lines (Figure 11.3a).

Type 3. Black-brown ware, medium density mineral inclusions up to 1 mm, comprising mica. Bowls with slightly rounded profile and recurved rim, 10 cm in diameter. Surfaces are burnished. The decoration is geometric with patterns of incised straight lines (Paribeni inventory number 8950) (Figure 11.3b).

Type 4. Black-grey ware, medium density mineral inclusions up to 1 mm, comprising mica. Bowls with rounded profile, rounded rim, 28 cm in diameter. The external surface is burnished, the internal surface is smoothed. The decoration consists in patterns of impressed semicircles and wavy discontinued lines or dots (Adulis Fieldwork Report 2012, unpublished).

Type 5. Black-grey ware, medium density mineral inclusions up to 1 mm, comprising mica. Bowls with rounded flaring rim, 24 cm in diameter. Surfaces are burnished. The decoration consists in patterns of incised lines (cf. Paribeni inventory number 88a) (Figure 11.4).

Class III: Carenated Bowls

Type 1. Black-grey ware, medium density mineral inclusions up to 1mm, comprising mica. Carenated bowls with vertical rim, 17 cm rim diameter, vertical profile above the carena which becomes rounded below the carena and at the base. Surfaces are burnished especially from right to left. The decoration consists in impressed discontinuous wavy lines possibly obtained using a shell edge (Figure 11.5).

Fig. 11.1-7 Ceramic artefacts in the National Museum of Eritrea.

Fig. 11.8-14 Ceramic artefacts in the National Museum of Eritrea.

Fig. 11.15-22 Ceramic artefacts in the National Museum of Eritrea.

Type 2. Black-grey ware, medium density mineral inclusions up to 1mm, comprising mica. Carenated bowls with pointed flaring rim, 13 cm rim diameter, vertical profile above the carena which becomes rounded below the carena and at the base. Surfaces are burnished especially from right to left. The decoration is geometric with patterns of incised straight lines and/or impressed discontinuous wavy lines (Figure 11.6 and 11.7). Similar pottery fragments have also been found in the lower layers at Maṭarā (cf. Anfray 1963b: 105, pl. LXXXVI, fig. 5, pl. XCIX, fig. 37, pl. XCIX, fig. 38).

Proto-Aksumite (ca. 400 – 50/40 BC)

Five pottery sherds can be ascribed to a proto-Adulis tradition if compared with similar types found in proto-Aksumite contexts in the highland settlements. The collection includes globular jars with cylindrical neck, a cup and a bowl.

Globular jar, short cylindrical neck, straight rim with rounded lip, 16 cm in diameter, rounded profile and base, vertical ring handles on the shoulder, half-moon moulded decoration between the two handles and moulded boss on the opposite side. The ware is red-orange, mineral tempered with quartz inclusions, internal and external orange slip, burning marks on the external surface (ER.M.ADU3.10) (Figure 11.8). This type is similar in style to other proto-Aksumite vessels but the author could not find any close comparison with published proto-Aksumite pottery forms.

Globular jar, medium cylindrical neck, straight rim with rounded lip, 8 cm in diameter, rounded profile and base, vertical ring handles on the shoulder, decoration of a moulded ledge with incised lines on the shoulder. The ware is red-orange, mineral tempered with external red-orange slip (Figure 11.9). This type is stylistically similar to proto-Aksumite vessels found on the highlands (Manzo 2003a: Tav. VI, fig. 6.a and tav. III, fig. 3.l and m).

Open bowl, rounded everted rim, 12 cm in diameter, rounded profile, discontinuous ring base with footrest, decoration of a moulded ledge on the shoulder. Red-orange ware, red-orange internal and external surface (Figure 11.12). This type is stylistically similar to proto-Aksumite vessels found on the highlands (Manzo 2003a: Tav. IV, fig. 4. a)

Two proto-Aksumite vessels are considered part of the collection with some reserve because they do not bear the tag with the inventory number given by Paribeni.

An orange-red ware globular jar with cylindrical neck, a moulded ledge on the shoulder and a vertical handle between the neck and the shoulder (Figure 11.10); a red-brown ware globular jar with cylindrical neck, incised lines below the rim, a moulded ledge on the shoulder and a vertical handle between the neck and the shoulder (Figure 11.11). These types are stylistically similar to proto-Aksumite vessels found on the highlands (Manzo 2003a: Tav. I, fig. 1.d and tav. III, fig. 3g and i).

Adulitan/Aksumite 1-2 (ca. 150 BC – 400/450 AD)

Bowl fragment, base diameter 9.5 cm, similar to Perlingieri (1999) Type 2/d, the decoration consists in shallow vertical grooves, mineral fine orange ware with quartz inclusions, external and internal red slip (Figure 11.13 cf. Wilding 1989 Fig. 16.88).

Bowl fragment, 8 cm rim diameter, straight rim, continuous profile with rounded base, vertical handle, the decoration consists in three shallow horizontal grooves below the rim and shallow vertical grooves, mineral fine tempered red-orange ware, external red slip, internal smoothing. This type of bowl is typical of the early Aksumite pottery production (Wilding 1989 Fig. 16.39; Perlingieri 1999: Type 2/b) (Figure 11.14).

Adulitan/Aksumite 3-4 (ca. 400/450-700 AD)

Very typical of the Aksumite 3 and 4 tradition are bowls with rounded profile, ca. 13 cm rim diameter, straight rim, with decoration of shallow diagonal grooves on the body, mineral fine tempered orange-red ware, external red slip, internal smoothing. This type of bowl is found at Maṭarā (Anfray 1967 Pl. III, IV and IX) and in several other Aksumite contexts often showing decoration of incised cross (cf. de Contenson 1961 Pl. XVII) (Figure 11.15).

Other bowl and cup fragments ranging from 6 to 13 cm rim diameter include types of bowls with rounded profile and base. The decoration consists in shallow diagonal or vertical grooves (Figure 11.16 h cf. Anfray 1967 Pl. III), sometimes associated with other incised decorative patterns and crosses (Figures 11.16 a, b, d, h, l, n and 11.17 a, d, e, f, g) or circles (Figure 11.16 g and m) or a moulded ledge shaped like a human arm (Figures 11.16 c and 11.19, cf. Anfray 1967 Pl. XL 144; Wilding 1989 Fig. 16.125, 16.148, 16.150; Perlingieri 1999 Type 4/h) (Paribeni inventory number 124). Other bowls, 18-19 cm in rim diameter, are characterized by a flaring flat rim (Figures 11.16 e, f and 11.20) sometimes shaped in a zigzag form (Figure 11.16 i) (Paribeni inventory number 16[..]93), with a stylized cross motif (Figure 11.23 and 11.24 cf. Perlingieri 1999 Type 12a) sometimes filled with white paste (Figure 11.22) or with incised words in Ge'ez characters on the ledge (Figure 11.21 cf. Perlingieri 1999 Type 4/s) meaning "[...] wash with clean [...]"[2] (E.R.M.ADU.3-41).

Bowls with ring shaped base and elaborate incised decoration of a cross on the internal surface are also typical of this tradition (Figures 11.25, 11.26 and 11.27, cf. Anfray 1967 Pl. XXXIV n. 174) and perhaps develop in similar forms in a later period (Figure 11.28). The type featured in Figure 11.27 might correspond to the description by Paribeni of a similar vessel base found in room H of the

---

[2] The author acknowledges the assistance of professor Yaqob Beyene (University of Naples "L'Orientale") and Mr. Amaha Seguid for the translation.

Fig. 11.23-32 Ceramic artefacts in the National Museum of Eritrea.

THE MUSEUM COLLECTIONS OF ADULITAN MATERIALS

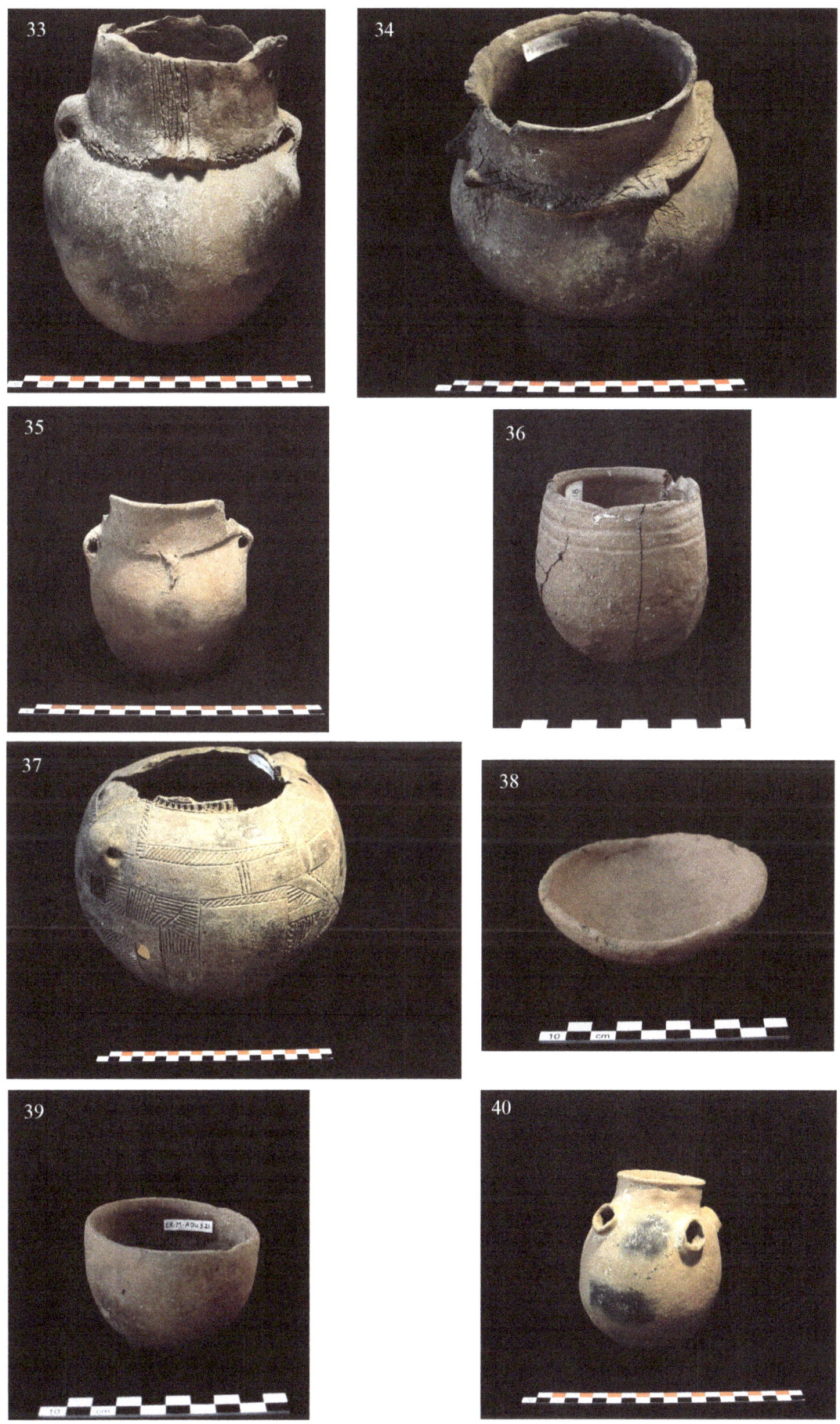

FIG. 11.33-40 CERAMIC ARTEFACTS IN THE NATIONAL MUSEUM OF ERITREA.

Fig. 11.41-49 Ceramic artefacts in the National Museum of Eritrea.

buildings excavated north of the site dating to the last phase of occupation of the town (Paribeni 1907: 487).

Within the same pottery tradition of orange-red ware vessels with red slip is a dove-tail shaped grip with an incised cross (Figure 11.29) and beakers with a diameter of ca. 8 cm are also common. They are usually characterized by straight rim, vertical profile, rounded flat bottom, a groove below the rim and sometime the incision of a cross (Figure 11.30).

An orange-pink ware cauldron with flaring rim and lateral grips perhaps dating to the same period (Figure 11.31) (cf. Wilding 1989: 269, fig. 16. 227).

Six fragments of buff fine mineral tempered ware bowls, ca. 0.5 to 0.8 cm in thickness, straight rim, characterized by a creamy slip on both surfaces with decoration of purple bands and lines incised below the rim (Figure 11.17 b and c). Similar vessels were found in other Aksumite contexts dating to the 5th-6th century AD (cf. Wilding 1989: 311, fig. 16.456, 457 and 458) and are considered of elite use (Phillips 2000: 330 and 396). According to Paribeni, pottery painted with purple bands was found associated with pottery bearing incisions of crosses especially in the north-east and north-west part of the basilica named "Altar of the Sun" (Paribeni 1907: 496 and 557).

An uncommon red micaceous ware spouted stainer that could be tentatively ascribed to a local contemporary tradition (Figure 11.32).

An elongated globular jar with cylindrical neck showing a moulded ledge between the body and the neck, with incised crossed lines and moulded grips and small vertical handles (Figure 11.33). This type can be tentatively ascribed to a middle-late local pottery tradition on the basis of comparisons with types found during recent excavation conducted at Adulis (Adulis Fieldwork Report 2011 and 2012, unpublished) and decoration style attested in the Anfray collection (see below).

A globular jar with cylindrical neck and incised moulded ledge between its globular body and the neck, grips and decoration of incised crossed lines (Figure 11.34).

This type can be tentatively ascribed to the late periods on the basis of stylistic comparisons with similar vessels found in late Aksumite contexts at Aksum (cf. Phillips 200: 318, fig. 275 d, e and f).

A small jar with cylindrical neck, rounded flaring rim, 10 cm in diameter, rounded base, vertical ring handles below the neck, moulded ledge decoration between the neck and the shoulder. The ware is dark-grey with mineral tempered and large vegetal inclusions, orange external and internal surface with traces of burning (ER.M.ADU3.12) (Figure 11.35).

A bowl with rounded rim, 4 cm in diameter, rounded base. The decoration consists of three rows of incised lines below the rim. The ware is red-orange with red-orange internal and external surfaces (Figure 11.36).

Unidentified, undetermined vessels

The pottery described below consists in other orange and black ware vessels which are difficult to ascribe to any known pottery tradition in the area and types which seem to be inconsistent with the dating of the rest of the findings examined in the collection and that could have been accidentally mixed up with the Paribeni collection.

Globular jar lacking neck and rim and characterized by geometric patterns of lines impressed on the body surface perhaps using a shell, two small vertical handles (Figure 12.37). This jar was found in the upper layer and almost at floor level next to the door of the room "X" in the group of buildings north of the town (Paribeni 1907: 521, fig. 4). This jar is different in decoration style from other known types in the coastal region and on the highlands. A small orange ware dish and a bowl (Figures 11.38 and 11.39), a jar with four spouts (Figure 11.40), a small black ware restricted bowl (Figure 11.41), an orange-red ware unrestricted bowl with flaring rim and two moulded grips (Figure 11.42).

It is worth mentioning the presence of four small orange-red ware vessels that could be ascribed to the pre-Aksumite tradition typical of the highlands, one black topped bowl (Figures 11.43), a bag shaped globular jar (Figure 11.44) (cf. Manzo 2003a: Tav. I fig. 1.t), a cup with grips and decoration of incised zigzag line below the rim (Figure 11.45) and a "tulip" vessel (Figure 11.46) resembling types found on the highlands and dating to the pre-Aksumite period (cf. Anfray 1967: 14, fig. 2).

Miniature ceramic, lamps, lids, figurines and other miscellaneous clay objects

The collection also includes miniature vessels like an orange mineral tempered flat bottomed beaker, 3 cm in diameter, with vertical and horizontal grooves and showing a small hole (Figure 11.47). This object was found by Paribeni in the upper layers of the street identified in the area of the group of buildings north of the town, associated with an alabaster container (Paribeni 1907: 495).

A small unrestricted bowl with rounded bottom (Figure 11.48) and a cup with elevated ring base and open spout, which might be identified as a lamp (Figure 11.49). Five other orange mineral tempered flat bottomed beakers or bowls similar to the one featured in figure 11.47, some also showing the same vertical and horizontal grooves (Figure 11.50).

Three buff ware small amphoras with rhomboidal shape which seem to imitate Eastern Mediterranean amphora types and could be imported (Figure 11.51). According to Paribeni, miniature amphoras were discovered in the upper layers of excavation at the site (Paribeni 1907: 520).

Only one lamp seems to have been locally produced on the basis of the examination of the red and micaceous tempered ware, the typical red slip and a shape which is uncommon for the Mediterranean area, which seems to account for all the other lamps in the collection. This lamp has an open globular body with open spout and traces of burning on it and measures 0.8 cm in thickness (Figure 11.52).

A light orange ware lid, pendant or sealing, 7 cm in diameter, slightly domed in shape and not perfectly modeled, with incised decoration of a cross filled with cross lines and pierced grip (Figure 11.53). Similar objects, in clay or stone, are rare in Aksumite context: one has been found in Aksum in contexts dating from the classic to the middle Aksumite, a larger number of samples have been found in the most recent layer of occupation at Maṭarā and they have been interpreted as possible sealings (Anfray 1967: 43, fig. 6).

Several small fragmentary objects, one (Figure 11.54, above on the right) could be a fragment of a lamp while all can be the applied leg fragments of vessels (Figure 11.54 cf. Wilding 1989: 283). They are made in a light pink ware mineral tempered with possible traces of outer red slip and they measure ca. 4-5 cm in length, 1.2 cm in thickness. Similar objects were found by Paribeni in the 12 meter deep pit No. 1 (Paribeni 1907: 447).

FIG. 11.50-57 CERAMIC ARTEFACTS IN THE NATIONAL MUSEUM OF ERITREA.

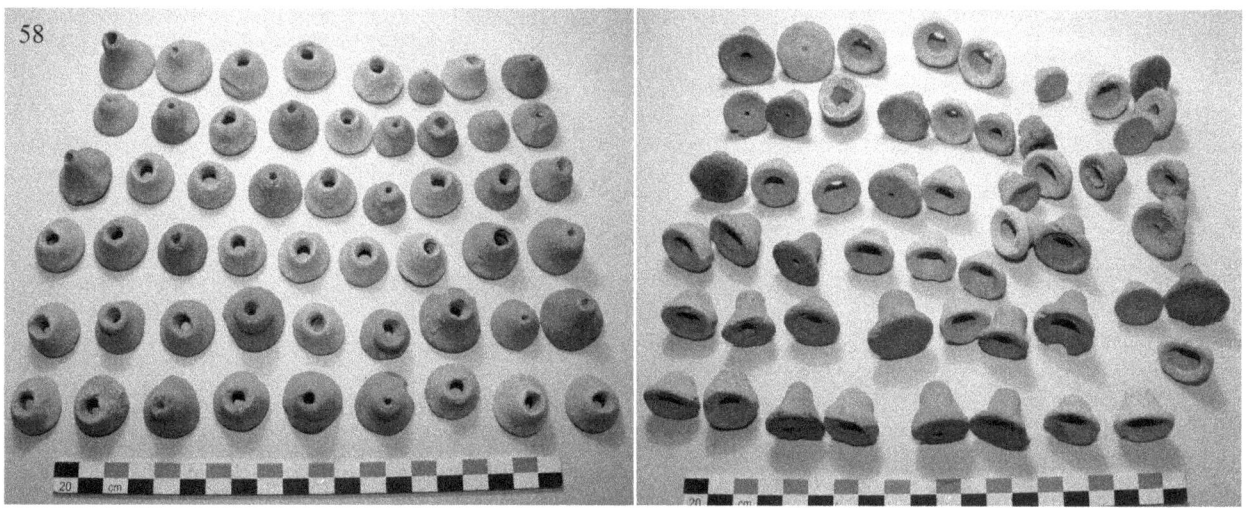

FIG. 11.58 CERAMIC ARTEFACTS IN THE NATIONAL MUSEUM OF ERITREA.

Orange-red ware discs with one or two holes 2-3 cm in diameter and ca. 0.5 cm in thickness (Figures 11.55 and 11.57).

Orange-red ware discs with lateral groove, 2-3 cm in diameter and ca. 2 cm in thickness (Figure 11.56). These objects are common to other Aksumite contexts but their interpretation is still not certain. Similar larger objects, found at Aksum, have been interpreted as possible loom weights or spindle whorls (Phillips 2000: 290 j). Pierced discs of smaller size, also found in Nubian contexts (Adams 2002 Tav. 35 c, 36 a, c, d), have been interpreted as earrings (Tringali 1984: 93-95).

Eighty-four perforated cones, about 3 cm long, with concave or flat profile at the wider end (Figure 11.58). Similar objects found at Aksum provide a close comparison with these elements with either a concave (Munro-Hay 1989 Fig. 16.466 and pl. 16.1; Phillips 2000: 334-335, fig. 290 f, g) or flat base profile (Phillips 2000: 399, fig. 347 b). These objects have been found in several Aksumite contexts but their function is still unknown and they have been variously interpreted. Paribeni (1907: 494) described the finding of these objects in one of the room in the north building of the town and he interpreted them as small lids. The most plausible interpretation is as possible necklace beads or equipment for a game as they are too light to be employed as loom weights.

A fragment of an orange mineral tempered ware dove-shaped figurine with decoration of an incised cross on the tail, measuring about 6 by 5 cm (Figure 11.59). A graphic representation of this figurine features in Paribeni's report (1907: 528; fig. 48).

A fragment of a Roman style human figurine, holding a stick, is also part of the collection but as no mention is made by Paribeni of this object, it is likely that this figurine has been accidentally included in the Paribeni collection; it might come from the coastal region (Figure 11.60).

The imported ceramic artefacts in the National Museum of Eritrea

Most of the imported pottery present in the Paribeni collection comes from the Mediterranean area, especially from the Eastern Mediterranean but also from North Africa, dating mainly from the 4th to the 7th century AD. Only an *unguentarium* may suggest an earlier date, perhaps 3rd-2nd century BC, on the basis of Egyptian Hellenistic comparisons. Fragments of Sassanian glazed ware, also found at Aksum, confirm the existence of trade relations with the Arab/Persian Gulf area. The collection of imported materials includes dishes in *sigillata* ware, amphorae, filtered jars, lamps, pilgrim flasks, glazed ware and the above mentioned *unguentarium*.

Hellenistic Pottery

Two fragments of buff silty ware small vessels, one certainly is an *unguentarium* of a type widespread in the Hellenistic Egypt on a long period, the other, with only part of the fusiform body, could also correspond to the same type (Figure 11.61). The best preserved fragment has a rounded flaring rim and a ledge between the neck and the shoulder. Both fragments are of fine well manufactured ware with evident signs of manufacture using a wheel. These two fragments can be compared with types dating to the 3rd-2nd century BC (Rodziewicz 1976 Fig. 4; Ballet 2001: 23). Paribeni (1907: 523) described the finding of a typical Hellenistic - Roman fusiform vessel widely circulating throughout the empire, often interpreted also as tears-bottle (*lacrymatoria*). The *unguentarium* was found in the small corridor "S" of the group of houses on the Haddas, in the third level of occupation, which could confirm an earlier date for this object.

Terra Sigillata

Cups, bowls, dishes and basins in *sigillata* ware are mentioned by Paribeni (1907: 552) as a common find in various areas of the site, although the present collection includes only a few fragmentary samples of dishes and lamps which will be described in the lamp section. A rim fragment of an open bowl, 10 cm in diameter, with foot ring, flat ledge rim and two decorative notches (Figure 11.62). This fragment is comparable to the form Hayes 72 dating to the early 5th century AD (Hayes 1972: 122, fig. 21).

Large dish, almost complete form, characterized by a rounded recurved rim, 30 cm in diameter with central impressed decoration of a lion biting a sheep (Figure 11.63), the impression is very light and is better visible in the drawing published by Paribeni (1907: 525, fig. 44). The dish is comparable to the form 104 (ii) associated with the stylistic decorative motif characterized by the presence of animals and humans in the middle of dish E (ii) of the *Atlante delle Forme Ceramiche* (E.A.A. 1985) and it can be placed in a span of time ranging from the second half of the 6th to the early 7th century AD. The dish was found in the house "Z" of the group of buildings north of the town, in the upper level of the excavation, confirming a dating to the 6th-7th century AD (Paribeni 1907: 525).

Two fragments of dishes in African s*igillata* ware (Late Roman B), one shows burnt surfaces, perhaps due to the fire elsewhere mentioned by Paribeni and it presents a pattern of concentric circles alternating palmettos arranged radially toward the center of the plate (Paribeni inventory number 138; ERM.ADU.6.51, Figure 11.64). The decoration is in Hayes style A (ii) (1972) and is often found on forms of dishes of the type Hayes (1972) 59 AB, dated between the second half of the 4th and early 5th century AD. This fragment was probably found in room "N" of the group of houses on the banks of the Haddas, which suggests a dating for the second level of occupation of the settlement, mentioned by Paribeni, to the 4th-5th century AD (Paribeni 1907: 514, fig. 37 and 517). The other fragment (Figure 11.65) is decorated with concentric circles surrounded by a pattern of small indentations (style A (ii) - (iii) of Hayes) dating from the second quarter of the fourth and early 5th century AD. Similar dish fragments are usually found in North Africa and especially in Egypt (Egloff 1977: 67-89, tav. 11, nos. 4 and 9 and tav. 9, nos. 1 and 2).

Two body fragments are certainly to be identified as imported for the type of ware: one bears an unusual decoration of pointed studs while the lower part is characterized by a thick red slip (Figure 11.66), the other is characterized by a moulded decoration of encircled flowers (Figure11.67).

Jars and Amphoras

A very common find at Adulis are fragmentary and complete ribbed amphoras and jars (Paribeni 1907: 549, fig. 58; Anfray 1974; Peacock and Blue 2007), although very few are preserved in the present collection and only one complete Ayla-Aksum ribbed amphora is on display in the museum. This type of amphora has also been found at Aksum (Phillipson 2000: 395, fig. 343), in several other Aksumite settlements, in the Island of Assarca (Eritrea) shipwreck (Pedersen 2000), in Yemen, Turkey (Alpozen, Ozdas and Berkaya 1995: 101) and at Ayla/Aqaba where also a center of production has been identified (Withcomb 1994: 23-25). According to recent excavations conducted in the Red Sea area, these amphoras are found in contexts dating to the 4th-5th century AD (Hayes 1996: 159-161) and the 5th-7th century AD (Kuzmanov 1973). An accurate petrographic analysis will help in better distinguishing the different productions of this widespread type of amphora in terms of time and place.

The collection includes:

One handle fragment of an Ayla-Aksum amphora, dark orange ware, creamy slip on the surfaces (Figure 11.68).

Two fragments of amphoras, still with their lids in place, characterized by a typical funnel shaped neck, short and narrow, to which the handles are attached, can be compared with similar amphoras from the Mediterranean dating to the 6th-7th centuries AD (Figures 13.1-3) like for example the LR2, already identified at Adulis by Peacock (Peacock and Blue 2007: 97, fig. 8.16.8; see also Kuzmanov 1973 type XIX and Alpozen, Ozdas and Berkaya 1995: 49, fig. 42 and 111).

A complete globular amphora with concentric ribs observed on the shelves of the storeroom turned out to belong to the collection of finds from the Assarca Island shipwreck or from another shipwreck observed in the bay of Massawa (Pedersen 2000: 10).

A fragment of a double handled filtered jar is certainly part of the Paribeni collection. The rim, 5 cm in diameter, is pointed and straight, the neck is short, narrow and ribbed, the handle attaches to the neck and the shoulder, the filter, made before the firing, is located at the bottom of the neck, the preserved part of the body shows horizontal ribs (Figure 11.69).

A fragment of a pink ware filtered jar with flat flaring rim and creamy slip (Figure 11.70).

Glazed pottery

The collection also includes some 20 fragments of glazed Sassanian bowls and jars.

Twelve mineral calcareous buff ware open bowl fragments with profiled rims, varying from 8 to 23 cm in diameter; the glaze colour varies from green to yellow and blue (Figures 11.71, 11.72 and 11.73).

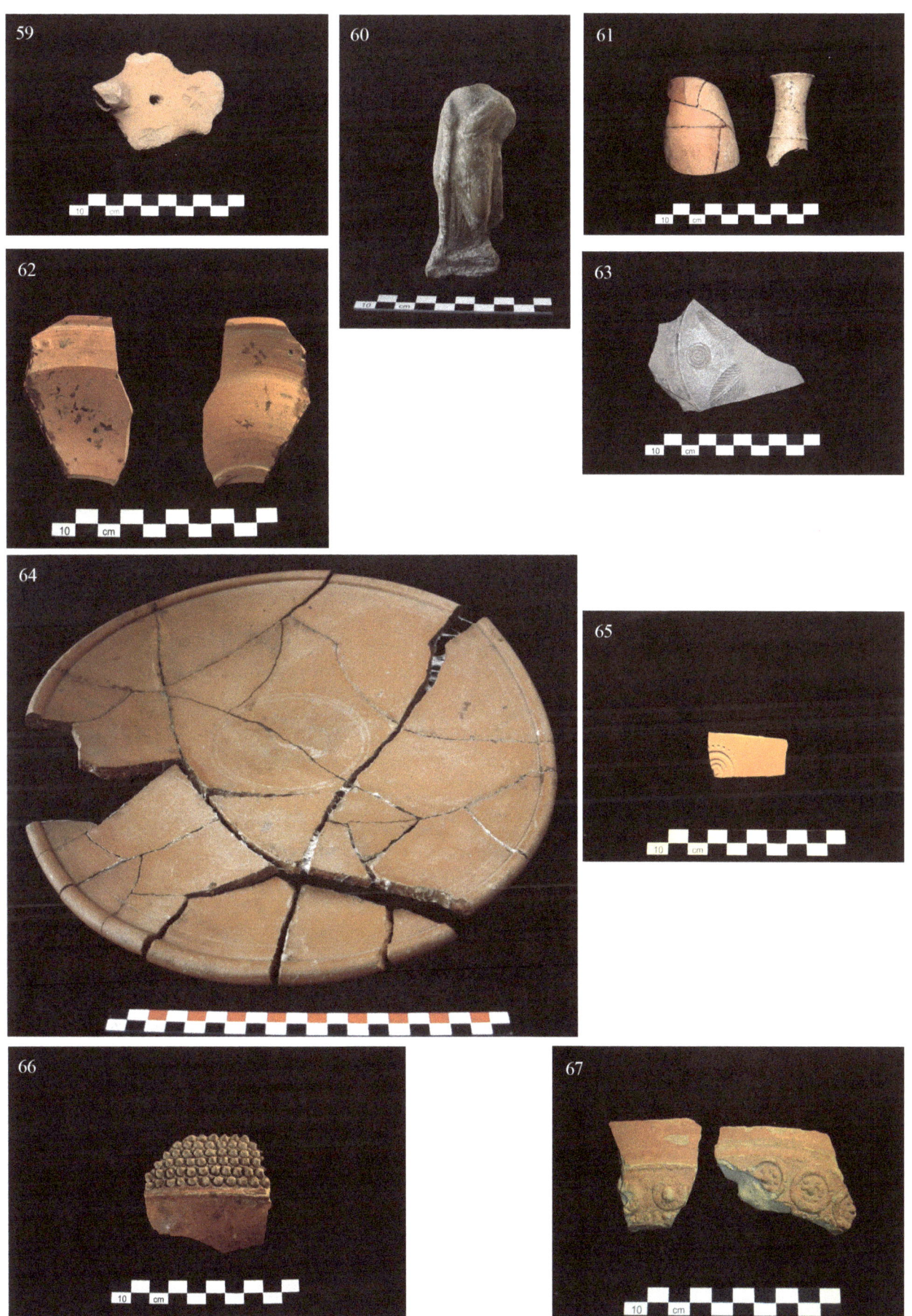

FIG. 11.59-67 IMPORTED CERAMIC ARTEFACTS IN THE NATIONAL MUSEUM OF ERITREA.

Three body fragments of the same ware and glaze characteristic of Sassanian tradition, one showing the attachment of a handle, could belong to an amphora (Figure 11.74).

Three base fragments of the same ware and glaze characteristic of Sassanian tradition could belong either to amphoras or bowls (Figure 11.75).

Sassanian open bowls and jars have also been found at Aksum in contexts dating prior to the mid-6th century AD (Phillips 2000: 326-327, figs. 284 e, g, h and 395-396, fig. 343 d).

Ampullae

Two fragmentary pink ware *ampullae* or flasks with preserved rim and handles, creamy-white slip on the external surface; one of the fragments has three decorative notches between the neck and shoulder, the diameter is about 1.5 cm (Figure 11.76). Two fragments of the same buff ware decorated with moulded strips and dots (Figure 11.79) probably correspond to the fragments described by Paribeni as widespread in Roman contexts and found in the upper layers of pit No. 138 associated with fragments of ribbed jars (Paribeni 1907: 447). These vessels can be identified with pilgrim flasks (cf. Kasser 1983, pl. CLIX n. 154-164).

Paribeni also reports the finding of Saint Menas flasks (Paribeni 1907: 538, fig. 54) used by pilgrims to carry water or oil home from the great pilgrimage site for Saint Menas, probably made in Egypt, at Abu Menas (Kazhdan 1991: 1340), widespread in the 6th-8th century AD (Kiss 1973: 137-154).

Lamps

Lamp fragments of African *sigillata* ware can be compared with lamps dating to the second half of the 4th and the second half of the 5th century, and can be compared with Italian and North African types.

Four fragments of *sigillata* ware (Figure 11.77) lamps are comparable to the African *sigillata* forms VIII C1 e or C1F (EAA 1988: 194-198, tab. CLVIII n. 1 and 5, cf. also Paribeni 1907: 522) and form VIII A2b (EAA 1988: 194 4 and CLVII n. 4) dating respectively to the second half of the 5th century AD and the second half of 4th - beginning of 5th century AD. This type of lamp characterized by the particular shape of the grip was widespread in Italy and in the Roman North African provinces.

Other lamps might date back to the early stages of the Muslim presence on the African coast of the Red Sea; in particular we refer to a ribbed fragment of the red ware lamp with a flat bottom and tapered body (Figures 11.78, cf. Paribani 1907: 535-536, fig. 52) comparable to a type found in Ayla/Aqaba (Khouri and Whitcomb 1992: 49).

Ribbed lamp with two spouts, usually found in Christian contexts (Figure 11.80, cf. Paribeni 1907: 523-526, figs. 42 and 45).

A red ware Late Roman lamp with close body, short spout, with Greek inscription around the body and four moulded crosses in the center. The inscription includes names of ecclesiastic people and, according to Paribeni, is a rare type of lamp, perhaps originally from Egyptian Christian contexts like the Saint Menas flasks (Figure 11.81, cf. Paribeni 1907: 499-500, fig. 28).

The local ceramic artefacts in the National Museum of Addis Ababa

The Anfray collection of ceramic artefacts from Adulis kept in the National Museum of Addis Ababa includes ca. 350 fragments of local pottery, as well as four complete vessels exposed in the display cabinet of the museum. The pottery collection includes local fragments of the Adulitan and Aksumite type grouped and described below by dating.

Local production contemporary to the Aksumite 1 (ca. 150 BC-150 AD)

Only four fragments can be tentatively attributed to an earlier phase, perhaps contemporary to the Aksumite 1 early Aksumite 2 on the basis of comparisons with finds from recent excavation conducted at the site (Adulis Fieldwork Report 2012), from comparisons with Paribeni's (1907) finds and pottery assemblages from the lower layers of Maṭarā dated by Anfray (1967 and 1968) to the 5th century BC to the 2nd century AD and of Haoulti dating from the 3rd-1st century BC (de Contenson 1963a: 50-51).

The collection includes:

Rim fragment of a black-gray ware unrestricted bowl with polished surfaces and incised decoration of small triangles under the rim, perhaps originally filled with a white paste. This fragment can be compared with the early Adulitan tradition of black-gray ware (ADU6083, south side, 0-0.60 m, Figure 12.1) (cf. Anfray 1967 Pl. XXXIX JE 3283 and JE 3282).

Body fragment of black-brown ware with decoration of incised triangles filled with oblique lines. This fragment can be compared with the early Adulitan tradition of black-brown ware (ADU6052-10f loc.8, Figure 12.2). Rim fragment of a reddish brown unrestricted bowl, similar in shape to the rim fragment ADU6083, south side, 0-0.60 m (ADU6113, Figure 12.3). It is characterized by external red slip, incised decoration of intersecting lines under the rim and a triangle filled with impressed dots and creamy slip. This fragment can be compared with the early Adulitan tradition of black-brown ware and a similar fragment found by Anfray at Maṭarā (Anfray 1967: 14-15, pl. L).

Fig. 11.68-75 Imported Ceramic artefacts in the National Museum of Eritrea.

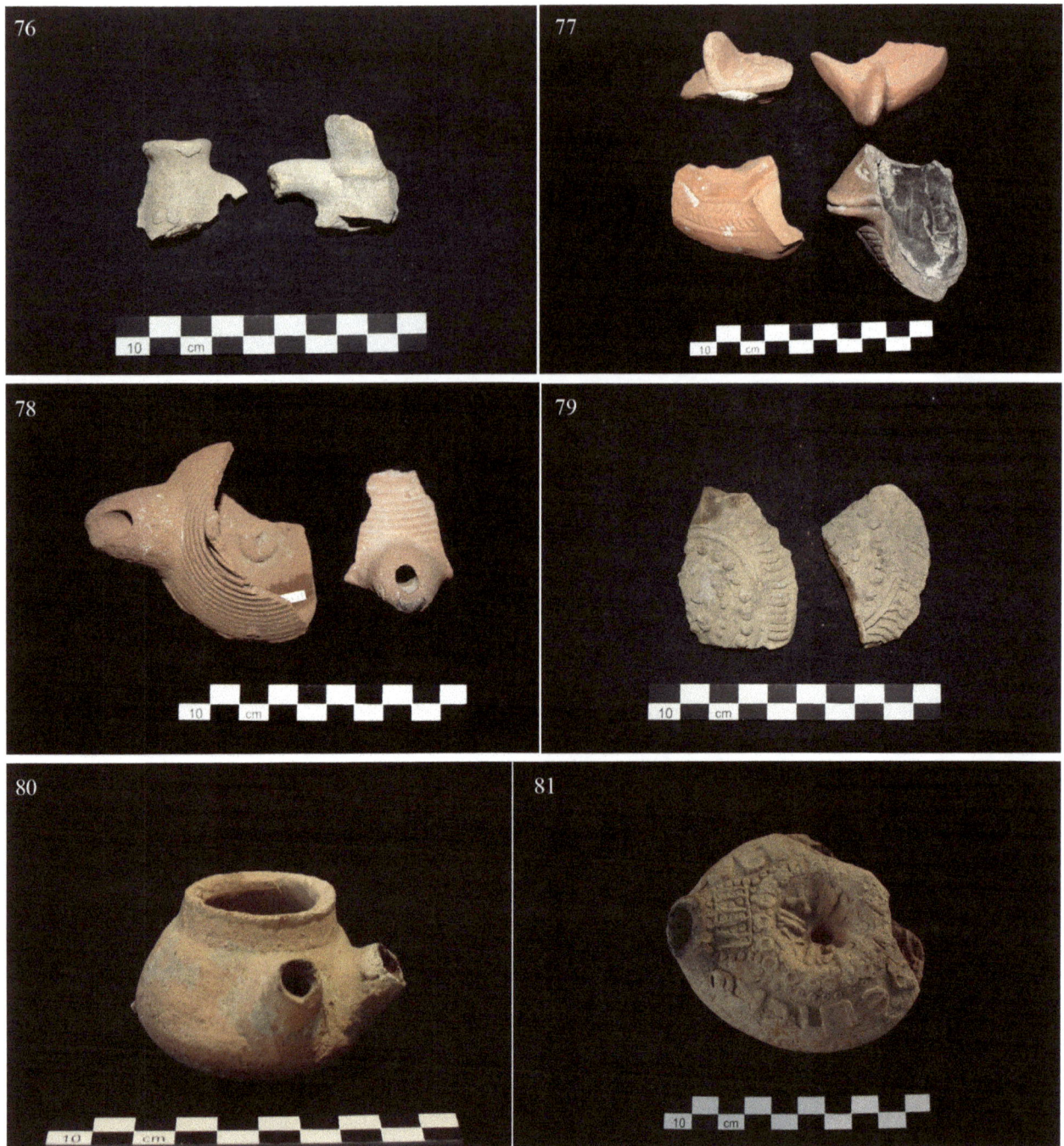

Fig. 11.76-81 Imported Ceramic artefacts in the National Museum of Eritrea.

Local and Aksumite 1-2 types (ca. 150-400/450 AD)

About six fragments are typologically similar to the ceramic material ascribed to Aksumite 1 and 2 (150 BC. -400/450 AD. AD), although the fabric seems to be slightly different (Perlingieri, personal communication).

Body fragment of orange-red ware, the outer surface shows vertical grooves and oval impressions. This decorative motif is typical of the classic Aksumite tradition and it is usually found on fine ware bowl, basins and jars (see Wilding 1989 and Phillips 2000). This fragment was found in the lower layers of of room 17, where Anfray observed the remains of earlier walls (Anfray 1974) (ADU6063_loc.17_2.5m, Figure 12.4).

Fragment of a possible pedestal characterized by orange-red ware polished surface and decoration of vertical grooves and oval impressions on a moulded ledge at the base. This object can be ascribed to the classical Aksumite tradition for the decoration pattern (see Wilding 1989 and Phillips 2000) but the shape cannot be compared firmly to any known type of pedestal so far (perhaps cf. Wilding 1989: 254, fig. 16.149) (ADU-6130-28f-loc.14 3.70 m, Figure 12.5).

Ledge rim fragment of orange-red ware characterized by impressions of vertical lines and oval dots (ADU-6062-236 loc. 8, Figure 12.6). This fragment is comparable to large basins with pot-stands (cf. Wilding 1989: 258 16. 164).

Fig. 12.1-10 Local Ceramic artefacts in the National Museum of Addis Ababa.

Ledge rim fragment of orange-red ware characterized by radial grooves (6136 ADU-5a-tr. level 2, Figure 12.7). This fragment is comparable to large basins with pot-stands (cf. Wilding 1989: 258, fig. 16.169). Fragment of unrestricted orange-red ware bowl with foot ring (ADU6060, Figure 12.8). This fragment can be compared with similar bowls found at Aksum and typical of the classical Aksumite phase (cf. Wilding 1989: 250, fig. 16. 122).

A body fragment of orange-red ware with decoration which can be compared to the typical globular jar with cylindrical neck of the Aksumite tradition (ADU 6066, Figure 12.9) (cf. Phillips 2000: 65, fig. 47 e).

Local and Aksumite 3-4 types (ca. 400 AD – 450/550 AD / 550 AD-700 AD)

Most of the pottery fragments present in the collection can be ascribed to the middle Aksumite tradition and to the contemporary Adulitan tradition. The fragments are grouped and described according to the different shapes. The fragments ascribed to the Aksumite tradition are fine ware bowls, cups and beakers and are usually decorated and show impressed or incised crosses, letters and flowers (Paribeni 1907 Fig. 60; de Contenson 1963b: 10).

The fragments attributable to the Adulitan tradition are strictly consistent with the housing quarter context in which they have been found. These are mainly large bowl, handled cauldrons, handled, necked and bag shaped jars and bottles often decorated with crossed incisions or chevrons.

Cauldrons

At least twenty fragments can be identified as a very characteristic type of red-orange ware cauldron with flat flaring rim and two or more horizontal handles with incised notches, widely diffused at Adulis (Adulis Fieldwork Report 2012) and in other Aksumite contexts. In particular a similar type of cauldrons is found in Aksum (Wilding 1989: 267-269, fig. 16.222). A complete cauldron from Adulis is on display in a showcase of the museum (Figure 12.10).

Jars

The collection includes around thirty fragments of red-orange ware jars. Jars typical of the Adulitan tradition are characterized by a flaring rim, cylindrical neck and vertical handles attached to the neck and to the shoulder, the body is globular (Figure 12.11) or bag shaped (Figure 12.12), the handle fragments that might belong to this type of jar are flat, rectangular in section, plain (ADU6113 and ADU6047, Figures 12.13 and 12.14) or they show decoration patterns of diagonal or crossed incised lines (ADU6048_15f_loc11_3-4m and ADU6106, Figures 12.15 and 12.16). Some twelve fragments present a moulded ledge with incised crossed lines on the junction of the neck and the shoulder (ADU 6041, Figure 12.17) which recalls the decoration of Late Aksumite (Aksumite 3-4) globular jars from Aksum (Phillips 2000: 318, fig. 275 e and f and 323, fig. 279 d and e; cf. also Wilding 1989 Fig. 16.408) or a filter (ADU6136_5a_tr.couche2, Figure 12.18) (cf. also Zazzaro and Manzo 2012, Adulis Fieldwork Report 2012). Some handles, circular in section sometimes showing vertical incised lines, probably belong to storage jars or amphoras (ADU6062__236_loc8 and ADU6063_2mars_loc17_2.5m, Figures 12.19 and 12.20).

Restricted Bowls

The collection includes several red-orange mineral tempered ware restricted bowls with rim diameter between 12-16 cm, the surface is usually burnished or covered with a dark red slip. Twenty nine show a narrowing and pointed rim and globular body, twenty three a vertical pointed rim and rounded base, nine show a flaring flat rim and three are body sherds. The usual decoration for these types of bowl is one or more incised line below the rim, vertical ribbing along the body, incisions of various types of crosses and letters. This type of restricted bowls was also found in the first level at Maṭarā (Anfray 1963 and 1967), in a large quantity, and at Aksum (cf. Wilding 1989: 296-298).

The globular bowls are usually characterized by a decoration on three registers: on the upper part, immediately below the rim, vertical or diagonal ribbings, in the middle part patterns of domed incisions or leaf motives, and the base is usually plain (ADU6054_6mars_loc8_2m, ADU6143_5mars_loc8, ADU6140, Figures 12.21, 12.22, 12.23). In some cases right below the rim are incisions of crosses and letters (ADU6078_19avril_loc7, ADU6114_12f_loc11.._1.5-2.5m, ADU6118_3.._loc8_1m, ADU6140, ADU6114_12f_loc11.._1.5-2.5m, Figures 12.24, 12.25, 12.26, 12.27, 12.28). This latter bears an incised Ge'ez letter *ma* without vocalization.

One of these bowls (ADU6128_10f_loc11_2m Figure 12.29) is almost identical to a bowl found at Maṭarā (JE2805 cf. Anfray 1967 Pl. XXVII, fig. 7), a type of bowl also common to other Aksumite contexts. Three bowls of this type are in black-gray ware, one showing a type of stylized cross characterized by six circles (ADU6062__236_loc8, Figure 12.30, cf. Anfray 1963 Pl. XCIII). Perhaps these black-grey ware bowls should be ascribed to a later tradition. Bowls with vertical profile and pointed rim are usually characterized by a simple decoration of crosses or letters and/or parallel lines incised below the rim (ADU6052_10f_loc8, ADU6078_19avril_loc7, ADU6106, ADU6126_17avril_mur_1-1.8m, ADU6146_2mars_loc8, ADU6143_5mars_loc8, Figures 12.31, 12.32, 12.33, 12.34, 12.35, 12.36). These bowls with a vertical rim are usually characterized by a flattened round base (ADU6063_2mars_loc17_2.5m, Figure 12.37).

Nine fragments show a vertical profile and flat flaring rim, ca. 5-10 cm in diameter, usually associated with incised decoration of crosses on the lip (ADU6041, ADU6052_10f_

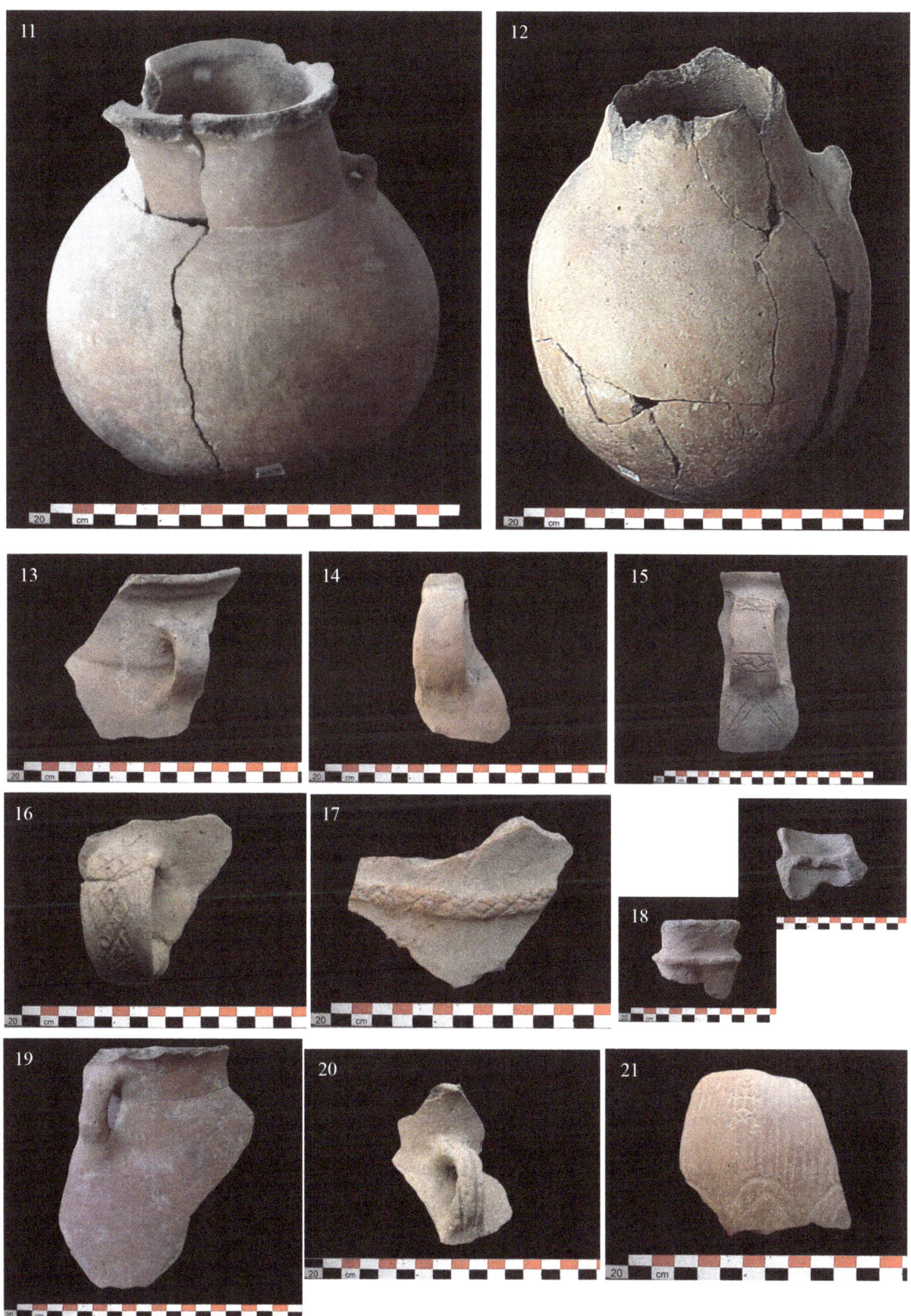

Fig. 12.11-21 Local Ceramics in the National Museum of Addis Ababa.

Fig. 12.22-39 Local Ceramics in the National Museum of Addis Ababa.

THE MUSEUM COLLECTIONS OF ADULITAN MATERIALS

FIG. 12.40-54 LOCAL CERAMICS IN THE NATIONAL MUSEUM OF ADDIS ABABA.

Fig. 12.55-67 Local Ceramics in the National Museum of Addis Ababa.

loc8, adu6097_4avril_tr_couche2, ADU6128_10f_loc11_2m, Figures 12.38, 12.39, 12.40, 12.41).

Unrestricted Bowls and Basins

Few fragments of unrestricted bowls are typical of the Aksumite tradition, while the majority of unrestricted bowls and basins included in this category show local characterizations.

Some ten fragments of orange-red fine ware bowls with external burnishing or red slip, characterized by a flaring rim, sometimes with a groove on the lip, can be ascribed to the Aksumite tradition imitating wheel-made bowls of African Red Slip ware occasionally found also on Aksumite sites (ADU6151_13f_loc8_1.60m, ADU6060, ADU6099, Figures 12.42, 12.43, 12.44 cf. Phillips 2000: 312-313, fig. 272). One of them can be readily compared to Hayes type 107/1 (Hayes 1972) dated to the early 6th century AD (Figure 12.42). One of these vessels bears an incision of the Ge'ez letter *ha*, without vocalization, on the lip (ADU6151_13f_loc8_1.60mt Figure 12.45). Another bowl fragment shows a moulded stud (ADU6063_2mars_loc17_2.5m, Figure 12.46, cf. Phillips 2000: 313, fig. 272c) and can be compared to Hayes type 72B (Hayes 1972: 122, fig. 21), another bowl fragment with flat flaring rim shows a series of three small studs that can also be compared to Hayes type 72 (Hayes 1972, ADU6063_2mars_loc17_2.5m, Figure 12.47). These bowls usually have a rounded base or foot-ring (ADU6048_15f_loc11_3-4m and ADU6060, Figures 12.48 and 12.49).

About twenty bowls can be ascribed to a local Adulitan tradition, characterized by red-orange ware, pointed vertical rim, round base and external and internal burnishing; a complete vessel of this type is on view in the museum (Figure 12.50). Other fragments are characterized by a very rough manufacture: vertical pointed rim vessels which might be decorated with incised lines parallel to the rim (ADU6102_7avril_loc3_bas, ADU6122_15avril_tr_0-1.3m, ADU6135_6avril_tr., Figures 12.51, 12.52, 12.53), other fragments show a slightly or completely flaring rim (ADU6042_11avril_tr_0-1.30m, ADU6147_13f_loc12_1.10mt, ADU6135_6avril_tr., ADU6051_27f_loc14_3.5m, ADU6063_2mars_loc17_2.5m, Figures 12.54, 12.55, 12.56, 12.57, 12.58), one showing a V shaped sign on the lip (ADU6066, Figure 12.59) and others showing a decoration of incised crossed lines on the lip (ADU6121_1avril_loc4_fond, ADU6069_17avril_1-1.80m, ADU6113, ADU6113, Figures 12.60, 12.61, 12.62, 12.63).

Similar to these latter bowls but with a thicker rim and a larger diameter are some forty coarse ware basin fragments all characterized by flat flaring thickened rim with incised cross lines decoration on the lip (ADU6044_28f_loc15_3m, ADU6058, ADU6078_19avril_loc7, ADU6048_15f_loc11_3-4m, ADU6048_15f_loc11_3-4m, ADU6110_27f_loc7_4.5m, ADU6048_15f_loc11_3-4m, ADU6067_17avril_loc3_fond, Figures 12.64, 12.65, 12.66).

Painted vessels

Some sherds are characterized by an extremely fine ware, very compact, yellow-orange in color and painted decoration of thick brown-purple parallel stripes sometimes alternating with cross motifs on a wet burnished surface (Phillips 2000: 330). A well preserved example is a vessel exposed in a showcase of the Addis Ababa Museum (Figure 12.67). This type of jars is typical of the Late Aksumite production; it is quite rare and was probably used by the elites.

Late and Post-Aksumite Black-Ware Types (ca. 700 AD)

Some fragments are attributable to the late Aksumite period on the basis of comparisons with the Late and Post Aksumite black ware pottery. These fragments belong to bowls, jars and basins and are characterized by smoothed and burnished surfaces and, in some cases, patterns of geometric incisions or crosses.

Some bowl fragments with vertical rim and flattened round base with parallel incised lines can be compared to Matara samples (cf. Anfray 1963, Pl. XCVI, ADU6062_236_loc8, ADU6063_2mars_loc17_2.5m, ADU6111_22f_t2_a7, Figures 12.68, 12.69, 12.70); a body sherd fragment can be compared to carinated bowls also found at Maṭarā (cf. Anfray 1963, Fig. 7, ADU6111_22f_t2_a7, Figure 12.71); about ten fragments belong to unrestricted bowls with thickened narrowing rim (ADU6147_13f_loc12_1.10m, Figure 12.72), with lateral grips (ADU6111_22f_t2.1_a.7, Figures 12.73) or with a sign incised on the lip (ADU6147_13f_loc12_1.10m, Figure 12.74) comparable to types found in the upper layers of Matara (Anfray 1963a, Pl. LXXXIVa); a small horizontal handle fragment might belong to a jar (ADU6058, Figure 12.75).

Unidentified, undetermined vessels

This category includes potsherds that currently cannot be identified with a specific ceramic tradition in terms of time and place.

Body sherd fragment of red ware with decoration of triangles incised and filled with crossing lines filled with white paste. Similar decorative patterns are also associated to potsherds found in the earliest levels of Maṭarā, associated with obsidian, dating from the 5th century BC to the 2nd century AD (Anfray 1967: 14-15, tav. L) (ADU6062_236_loc.8, Figure 12.77).

Unrestricted bowl fragment of red micaceous ware showing parallel lines incised on the body, the first two filled with diagonal incisions (ADU6062_236_loc.8, Figure 12.76).

Fragment of globular restricted bowl of red-brown ware with horizontal handle double pierced and diagonal and vertical incision along the body (ADU6085, Figure 12.78).

Fig. 12.68-85 Local Ceramics in the National Museum of Addis Ababa.

Restricted bowl fragment of red-orange ware with band incised below the rim and filled with vertical incised lines (ADU6146_2mars_loc8, Figure 12.79).

Unrestricted bowl fragment of red micaceous ware with rounded rim and oval grip decorated with incised dots on the top of the grip (ADU6150_26f_loc.8, Figure 12.80).

Unrestricted bowl fragment of light brown ware, rounded flaring rim and band of incised parallel lines below the rim filled with impressed dots (ADU6099, Figure 12.81).

Body fragment possibly of a globular jar, orange-red ware, horizontal moulded ledge along the body interrupted by pierced oval grips, the decoration consists in incised triangles filled with impressed dots (ADU6148, Figure 12.82).

Body fragment of black ware with irregular ribbing (ADU6052_10f_loc8, Figure 12.83).

Two similar unrestricted bowl or dish fragments of orange-red ware characterized by impressed dots along the internal rim (ADU6122_15avril_tr_0-1.3m, Figures 12.84 and 12.85).

Fragment of light brown ware globular jar with partially preserved cylindrical neck, characterized by moulded and incised crossed lines decoration between the neck and the shoulder and on the body (ADU6106, Figure 12.86).

Fragment of light brown ware globular jar with partially preserved cylindrical neck, characterized by an incised crossed line between the neck and the shoulder and vertical handle decorated with oval impressions (ADU6106, Figure 12.87).

Necked jar fragment of light brown ware darker on the rim, which is characterized by vertical lines incised all along the rim (ADU6063_2mars_loc17_2.5m, Figure 12.88).

Necked jar fragment of light brown ware characterized by incised band between the shoulder and the neck filled with impressed dots (ADU6102_7avril_loc3_bas, Figure 12.89).

Necked jar fragment of black ware characterized by a band of incised crossed lines below the rim (ADU6097_4avril_tr_couche2, Figure12.90).

Miscellaneous objects

The pottery from the Beth-Khalifa excavation also includes lamps, spout vessels, strainers, lids, incense burner and figurine fragments.

Lamp fragments are characterized by an oval body shape with pointed end usually showing traces of burning, they are all characterized by an orange mineral tempered ware (ADU6062__236_loc8, ADU6072_17avril_loc3_2o2.50m, ADU6085, ADU6098_26f_loc15_2.5m, ADU6129_20.._loc7_3m, ADU6146_2mars_loc8, Figures 12.91, 12.92, 12.93, 12.94, 12.95, 12.96, 12.97, 12.98).

Similar lamps were found in Late Aksumite contexts in Aksum (Wilding 1989: 288, figs. 329).

Five vessel fragments are characterized by the presence of a conical spout, they were perhaps originally part of globular jars, the ware is orange-red with visible micaceous inclusions; one fragment shows decoration of bands with incised crossed lines (ADU6042_11avril_tr_0-1.30m, ADU6067_17avril_loc3_fond, ADU6085, ADU6151_13f_loc8_1.60m, Figures 12.99, 12.100, 12.101, 12.102). Similar vessels were found also at Aksum (Wilding 1989 Figs. 16.449).

Three vessel fragments are characterized by large regular holes, thick body and rounded shape which suggest a function possibly as strainers, the ware is orange and mineral tempered (ADU6062__236_loc8, Figures 12.103, 12.104, 12.105). These fragments have all been found in the same context which suggests they were originally part of the same vessel, perhaps a pierced *dolium* or amphora.

The collection includes several possible fragments of footed incense burners, usually characterized by a cylindrical foot and vertical rim (ADU6138_21f_loc8, Figure 12.106) or foot-ring and flaring rim (ADU6136_5a_tr.couche2, ADU6140, Figures 12.107 and 12.108) sometimes decorated with impressed or incised crosses or stylized cross consisting of six dots around a circle comparable to a type found at Aksum and interpreted as a vessel foot (de Contenson 1963, Pl. XXd).

Two possible lid fragments are characterized by a foot-ring, one has a flat surface (ADU6113, Figure 12.109) while the other is slightly concave (ADU6103_23.., Figure 12.110); the incision of a letter inside and below the rim is comparable to similar objects with inscribed letters from Maṭarā (Anfray 1963b Pl. CXc). Similar objects have also been found at Aksum and interpreted as lids (Wilding 1989: 288, fig. 16.323).

A ceramic fragment resembles an animal head showing wavy signs, incised on a curved surface which might represent the mane of a lion. The fragment is pierced by holes which suggests the object was originally part of a filtered jar (ADU6067_17avril_loc3_fond, Figure 12.111).

The imported ceramic artefacts in the National Museum of Addis Ababa

The collection of imported pottery includes about 85 fragments of amphoras and vessels from Roman-Byzantine Egypt, the Mediterranean and the Middle East, as well as African Red Slip ware and *sigillata* ware, Eastern Desert pottery from Sudan, blue glazed pottery perhaps from the Sassanid regions and some vessel fragments that could come from other more distant destinations (India?).

Fig. 12.86-103 Local Ceramics in the National Museum of Addis Ababa.

Table and Cooking ware

This category includes north African red slip ware, African *sigillata* D, cooking ware from North-Africa and from the Eastern Mediterranean.

Five dish fragments of Italian sigillata ware characterized by two large concentric circles incised in the center of the dish (ADU6068 1f-loc.14 3.50m, ADU6078_19avril_loc7, Figure 12.112 and 12.113).

A series of bowl fragments characterized by red-orange ware and thick red slip can be ascribed to North African table ware tradition (ADU6044_28f_loc.15_3m, ADU6063_2mars_loc17_2.5m, ADU6112_16f_loc11_4m, ADU6060, ADU6122_15avril_tr_0-1.3m, ADU6140, (Figures 12.114, 12.115, 12.116, 12.117, 12.118, 12.119, 12.120, 12.121). A red ware fragment characterized by horizontal handle and horizontal ribs along the body may come from a cauldron perhaps from Eastern Mediterranean (ADU6150_26f_loc8, Figure 12.122).

Amphoras and Jars

Among the fragments identified as having belonged to amphorae are bases, handles and body. Most of the pottery sherds are characterized by a ribbing and orange-pink ware with a creamy-colored slip outside, characteristics typical of the Ayla-Aksum productions dating from the late 4th to the 7th century AD, a type perhaps produced in Aqaba (Whitcomb 1994: 23-25) and found in other Red Sea (Hayes 1996: 159-161) and Aksumite contexts (Phillipson 2000: 395, fig. 343a) and also in Eastern Mediterranean contexts dated to the 5th-7th century AD (Ballet 1996: 827 and Kuzmanov 1973).

Other amphora fragments are characterized by a lighter color ware and creamy-colored slip outside, vertical and slightly thick walls, some also showing black coat remains These fragments could be identified as wine amphoras from North Africa and dated to the Late Roman period.

Over fifteen fragments can be identified as ribbed Ayla/Aqaba amphoras including one rim (ADU6042_11avril_tr_0-1.30m, Figure 12.123), one base (ADU6072_17avril_loc3_2o2.50m and ADU6139, ADU6060, Figures 12.124) and several body sherds (ADU6060 and ADU6144 Figures 12.125, 12.126, 12.127, 12.128, 12.129), one characterized by red paint and others characterized by concentric ribs (ADU6097_4avril_tr_couche2, ADU6042_11avril_tr_0-1.30m, Figures 12.126 and 12.129) perhaps of a globular type of amphora found in the Island of Black Assarca shipwreck (cf. Pedersen 2000: 4, fig. 2) and observed in the storeroom of the Asmara Museum.

Five body fragments can be identified as Late Roman Amphora 2 or 4 type, for their characteristic pale brown or yellow surface and thin ribs on the body. This amphora was produced from the middle of 5th to the first half of the 7th century AD in the Eastern Mediterranean and used in the trade of Greek wine (ADU6041, ADU6042_11avril_tr_0-1.30m, ADU6136_5a_tr.couche2, Figures 12.130, 12.131 and 12.132). Other fragments show a more widely spaced ribbing and could be identified as Late Roman 5 or 7 amphora types also produced from the middle of 5th to the first half of the 7th century AD in the Eastern Mediterranean (ADU6079 and ADU6139, Figures 12.133 and 12.134). Several other body fragments have been readily identified as parts of amphoras although the type is difficult to identify: some types seem to be similar to Dressel 2-4 or 7-11 type of amphoras (cf. Peacock and Williams 1986, class 16). Among these is a fragment showing *tituli picta* in red on the outside surface and pitch traces on the inner surface (ADU6099, Figure 12.135).

Two potsherds of pink ware handles show a characteristic bifid shape typical of Dressel 2-4 type of amphoras (ADU6122-tr-0-1, 30m, Figure 12.136) produced in the 3rd century AD in Egypt (cf. Peacock and Williams 1986 and Empereur and Garlan 1986: 606).

A pink ware base and an amphora fragment bearing incision of two letters, probably A and D in a part which corresponds to the neck are perhaps a Dressel 2-4 or 7-11 amphora type (ADU6122_15avril_tr_0-1.3m, Figure 12.137 and 12.138).

Fragment of amphora base characterized by a pink paste, the shape can be compared to Dressel 2-4 or 7-11 amphora type bases (ADU6122_15avril_tr_0-1.3m).

Fragment of amphora pointed base characterized by a pink paste similar to Torpedo jars (Roberta Tomber, *pers. comm.* cf. Tomber 2007: 973-976, ADU6122_15avril_tr_0-1.3m, Figure 12.139).

Among jar fragments there are three filtered jars characterized by a pink paste and white slip. The fragments show double handles between the neck and the shoulder and three or four filter holes at the attachment between the neck and the shoulder (ADU6041, ADU-6147-13f-loc.12 1.10m, Figures 12.140, 12.141, 12.142). One of the fragments shows possible traces of waterproof coat on the outside. A copy of this type was also found in the cargo of the wreck of the Black Assarca island, associated with the Ayla-Aksum type of amphora (Pedersen 2000: 11, fig. 10). Similar jars are common to the Eastern Mediterranean region and Kellia in Egypt where they are dated to the Coptic period (Egloff 1977: 67-89). The collection includes three large storage jar fragments of unidentified origin (ADU6102_7avril_loc3_bas, ADU6130_28f_loc14_3.70m, Figures 12.143, 12.144); only one might be identified as a typical "center-Italic" *dolium*, a storage vessel used for the conservation of oil and rarely used for sea transportation (6129-20_loc.7-3m, Figure 12.145).

Fig. 12.104-121 Local and Imported Ceramics in the National Museum of Addis Ababa.

THE MUSEUM COLLECTIONS OF ADULITAN MATERIALS

FIG. 12.122-139 IMPORTED CERAMICS IN THE NATIONAL MUSEUM OF ADDIS ABABA.

Fig. 12.140-154 Imported Ceramics in the National Museum of Addis Ababa.

Pottery from Sudan and the Eastern Desert

Four fragments of the same vessel are characterized by a pink fine ware and decoration of alternating vertical lines of dark, red and yellow paint spots/drops; the surface also shows horizontal and parallel grooves. These fragments are comparable to the types 83-84, represented in plate 114 on the pottery from the tombs of Ballana and Qustul (Emery and Kirwan 1938 I, Pl. 114 n. 83-84; Adams 2000 Pl. 17, fig. 13-17, ADU6130_28f_loc.14 3.70m, Figure 12.146) also found in other Red Sea ports (Hayes 1996: 171, n. 40).

Two fragments of pink ware covered with a whitish-yellow slip and painted with concentric brown curls can be readily compared to a type of pottery found near the Wadi Shenshef, in Egypt (Hayes 1996: 174-175, n. 47, ADU_6143_5mars_loc.8, Figures 12.147 and 12.148).

Glazed pottery

Only four potsherds show clear traces of a thin white glaze with darker shades of yellow or golden which are most likely of Sassanian origin.

Two body fragments of glazed vessel similar to Sassanid vessels also found in late Aksumite contexts (Phillips 2000: 326-327, fig. 284 e, g, h, ADU6113 and ADU6121_1avril_loc4_fond, Figures 12.149 and 12.150).

Flat base fragment of open bowl covered with a thin white glaze comparable to small bowls and tableware of the Abbasid period, dating to the 9th century AD. This pottery was found at Athar also on the coast of Yemen and Siraf (Zarins & Zahrani 1985: 77, table 75, no. 10, ADU6139, Figure 12.151).

Unidentified imported pottery

Three fragments are certainly not of local production for the ware characteristics, shape and decoration. Some of them may be of Indian origin but a more precise identification has not been found so far (ADU6042_11avril_tr_0-1.30m, ADU6110_27f_loc7_4.5m, ADU6121_1avril_loc4_fond, Figures 12.152, 12.153, 12.154). The collar-like rim featured in Figure 12.153 recalls sherds from Sanjan, a port site at Gujarat, dating from the 8th to the 13th century AD (Gupta, Dalal, Dandekar, Mitra, Nanji, Pandey 2002: 98, fig. 8.6). The overall shape of the fragments is typical for the globular pots with narrow opening, dating to the 6th/7th century AD, called Form C in Tissamaharama, while the decoration seems to be so far unknown (Heidrun Schenk *pers. comm.*). This would be the first firm direct material indication of contacts with India.

Vessel Stoppers

The vessel stoppers observed in the Paribeni and Anfray collections are various. Some consist in a clay disc, originally placed in the neck of the amphora, in some cases overlapped by a layer of leaves, sealed with gypsum dropped inside and sometimes around the amphora lip. The diameter of the lids varies from 4 to 9 cm. Most of the gypsum seals show impressions or depictions of monograms, very popular in the Byzantine times, associated with Christian symbols, such as crosses and their derivates, as well as liturgical formulas, without any explicit indication of content or provenance.

Adulis vessel stoppers identified so far, fall into two categories:

- Plaster stoppers inserted into the neck of the amphora, not overlapping the lip, sometimes showing a pierced hole for the passage of an opening rope or sometimes associated with a clay disc.
- Plaster lids covering the entire inner and outer lip of the rim and part of the outer neck.

Vessel stoppers is a little studied class of object. The origin of this type of lid is perhaps Egyptian and the distribution is between the 4th and 7th century AD. The use of Greek, the language of commerce, testifies to the long-distance trade. The letters and the symbols on the seal might refer to the place of production of the vessel contents. Similar vessel stoppers are common also in other Red Sea ports such as Clysma / al-Qulzum (Bruyère 1966: 113-115), Quseir al-Qadim (Whitcomb and Johnson 1979: 233; cf. Thomas and Tomber 2006: 239) and Berenike (Sundelin 1996: 297-308), and in the Egyptian monastery of Epiphanius (Winlock and Crom 1973, I).

Vessel stoppers kept in the National Museum of Eritrea

The collection includes 32 vessel stoppers showing different characteristics, some with depicted red signs or various types of sealing impressions, and two lids still inserted in the rim and neck of Late Roman 2 types of amphoras (Figure 2.6, 2.7, 2.8) (cf. amphora types depicted in Peacock and Blue 2007: 97, fig. 8.16 n. 8).

Six vessel stoppers are characterised by the same sealing impression featuring a cross ending with an anchor and forked at the top, on the side underneath the arms two letters impressed, a Greek alpha on the right and a Greek p on the left (cf. Paribeni 1907: 520, fig. 39). Vessel stoppers showing one or more of this type of sealing were all originally fragments covering the full mouth of the vessel and part of the neck except the one still sealing the vessel fragment shown in Figure 13.1-3 that does not overlap the outer lip. This latter, and the vessel stopper in Figure 13.8, are both characterised by a hole, 1 to 0.5 cm in diameter, for the passage of a string to open the stopper. On the underside the impressions of a further layer of leaves sealing the lid are visible.

Seven vessel stoppers have red Christian monograms depicted on the upper face and fabric marks covering this face as a whole (Figures 13.11-13.15 and 13.16-13.17). Four of these stoppers show the depiction of a cross

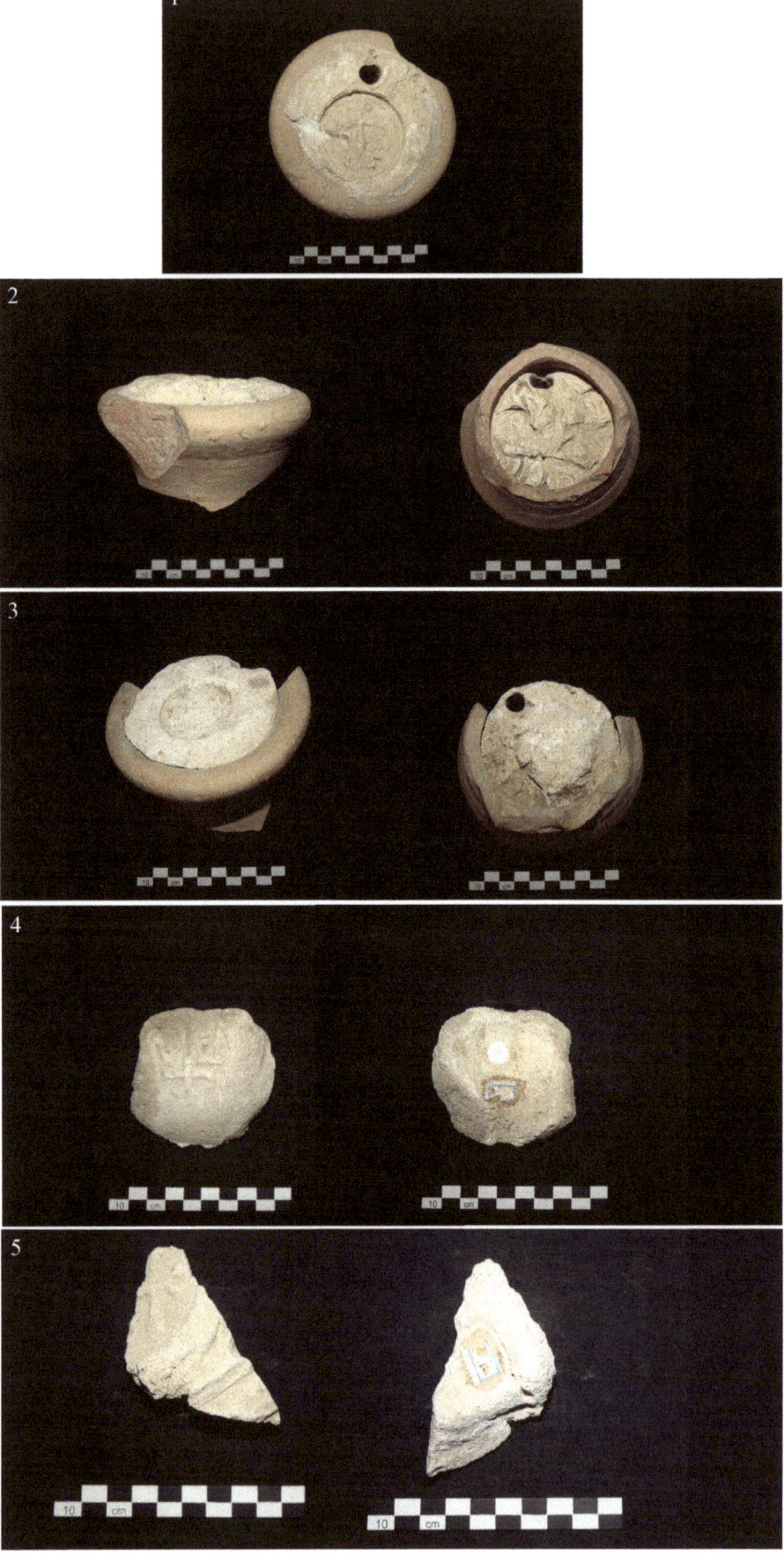

Fig. 13.1-5 Vessel Stoppers in the National Museum of Eritrea.

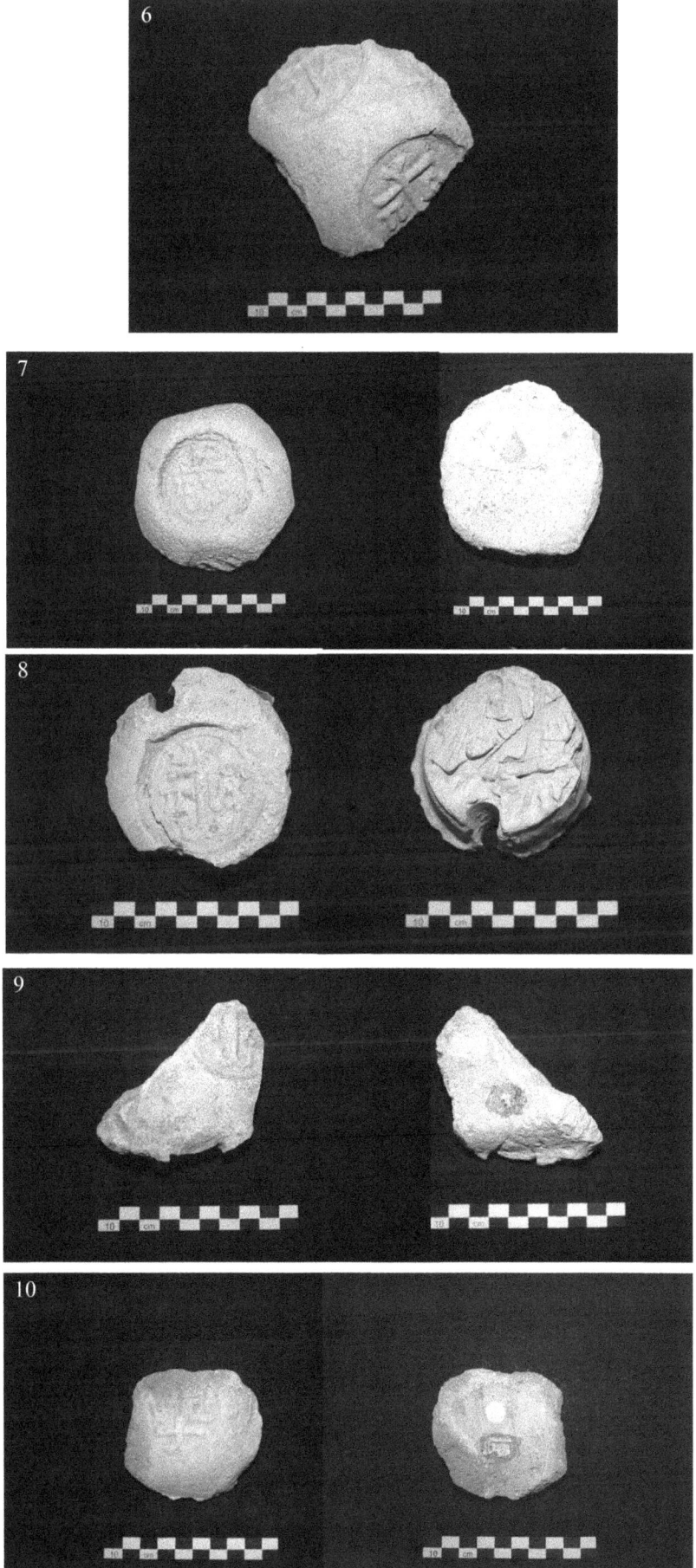

Fig. 13.6-10 Vessel Stoppers in the National Museum of Eritrea.

Fig. 13.11-15 Vessel Stoppers in the National Museum of Eritrea.

Fig. 13.16-20 Vessel Stoppers in the National Museum of Eritrea.

Fig. 13.21-25 Vessel Stoppers in the National Museum of Eritrea.

ending with short lines perpendicular to the arms (Figures 13.14-13.15 and 13.17) and only one is characterised by wide ending arms (Figure 13.13). The others show a fragmentary red sign, in form of a T encircled at the base (Figure 13.12). This is also a smaller lid compared to the others observed in the collection. Another shows the depiction of the Christian monogram P ending in the shape of a cross, the initials of Jesus Christ (Figure 13.11), which start to appear in the 5th century AD and it is often accompanied with the letters alpha and omega symbolising the beginning and the end. Most of these monograms show such an intricate combination of letters which is impossible to unravel. Further studies of this category of finds are crucial for understand the origin of the amphoras, in fact, some of those monograms might indicate the patron of the monastery. Evidence of the hole for the passage of the opening string, 0.15 cm is only visible in the vessel stopper in Figure 13.13, while the impression of a rope is visible on the upper surface of the vessel stopper featured in Figure 13.14. Two vessel stoppers in this group show impressions of leaves on the lower face (Figures 13.11 and 13.12), while two others have part of a clay lid still attached to the lower face (Figures 13.16 and 13.17). The two clay lids are different: one is beige-yellow in colour and has a ledge button in the centre, while the other looks like a pink ware disk. Both show the stamp bearing the old inventory number given by Paribeni.

Two fragmentary vessel stoppers are characterised by a type of sealing with an encircled Christian cross (Figures 13.18 and 13.19), outside of which there might have originally been impressed letters (cf. Paribeni 1907: 523-524, fig. 43); two others are characterised by a monogram which looks like a stylised letter M with a cross above it (Figures 13.21 and 13.22) (cf. Paribeni 1907: 456, fig. 4). The underside is characterised by the usual impression of leaves. Another fragmentary sealing shows three vertical lines, perhaps an E, as suggested by Paribeni (1907: 456) and a palm leaf below it (Figure 13.20). Two vessel stoppers show sealings possibly featuring a human figure, one also shows fabric marks and traces of red paint on the upper face (Figure 13.23), the other only shows a fabric impression and the human figure is clearer, showing part of the body and the arm perhaps holding a stick (Figure and 13.24). This latter sealing still has the Paribeni inventory number stamp.

Some vessel stoppers bear badly preserved sealings, the meanings of which are not clear (Figure 13.25-13.32). One shows the usual hole for the passage of the opening rope, two show possible stylized Christian crosses (Figures 13.29 and 13.30) and two clearly show the impressions of the clay disks and the rope all around them (Figures 13.26 and 13.27).

Vessel stoppers kept in the Addis Ababa National Museum

The Anfray collection include four plaster stoppers and seven clay discs. One plaster stopper is complete and shows three impressed letters.

Plaster fragment of an amphora vessel stopper perhaps originally associated with a clay disc. The marks of the amphora rim and the neck in which it was placed are still visible (ADU 24F-6057 loc. 13 to 3.30 m 1, Figure 13.31). The particularity of this stopper is the large amount of plaster which originally covered the entire outer part of the neck and the lip.

Plaster fragment of an amphora stopper with illegible inscription (ADU24f-6057-loc.13 3.30 m 2, Figure 13.32).

Plaster vessel stopper showing a convex side and the impression of fabric or other material used for sealing and traces of red painting (ADUtr.1 6135, Figure 13.33). The fabric impressions suggest that part of the fabric was left outside, presumably to facilitate the opening once the amphora arrived to destination. The other side shows the presence of clay fragments mixed with the plaster. Vessel stopper plaster fragment showing traces of a red paint band on one side (6106 ADU, Figure 13.33, bottom left).

Seven clay discs, three of which are from the same archaeological context. They have a characteristic light green-beige color, the edges are smoothed, suggesting that they have been shaped in a slightly concave shape before baking (ADU6148, ADU6126 mur 1 to 1.8 m, ADU6121 loc. 4 bottom, ADU6085 loc.7, ADU6078, Figure 13.34). The diameter of these objects varies from 6 to 10 cm. This kind of clay discs was inserted into the neck, under the plaster cast.

Metal artefacts

Various objects in gold, silver, bronze, copper and iron have been found at Adulis and are currently kept in the museums of Rome, Asmara, Addis Ababa and Stockholm. Although the stratigraphic and chronological context is unknown also for these objects, according to Phillipson (1998: 56) the number of metal objects found in the Aksumite contexts increases starting from the end of the 3rd century AD. Among the metal objects found at Adulis are elements of wood veneer, instruments for surgery and cosmetics, as well as scales and weights that can be compared to bronze objects widespread in the Romanized and Byzantine world. In particular, the range of metal objects from Adulis is typologically similar to the metal finds from the post-Meroitic Ballana and Qustul sites, perhaps made in Egypt and characterized by a strong Syrian and Byzantine artistic influence in the patterns and forms typical of the early 5th century AD (Emery and Kirwan 1938: 161-181). It is possible, however, that in the Christian kingdom of Aksum and Meroe as well as at Adulis there may have been a local production of metal objects that copied models distributed throughout the Christian world in Late Antiquity.

Most of the Adulitan metal objects seem to be made locally rather than imported. However, apart from the evidence of metalworking attested on the highlands (Todd and Charles 1978: 31-41), we still know little about the origin and working of metal in the coastal plains. The anonymous

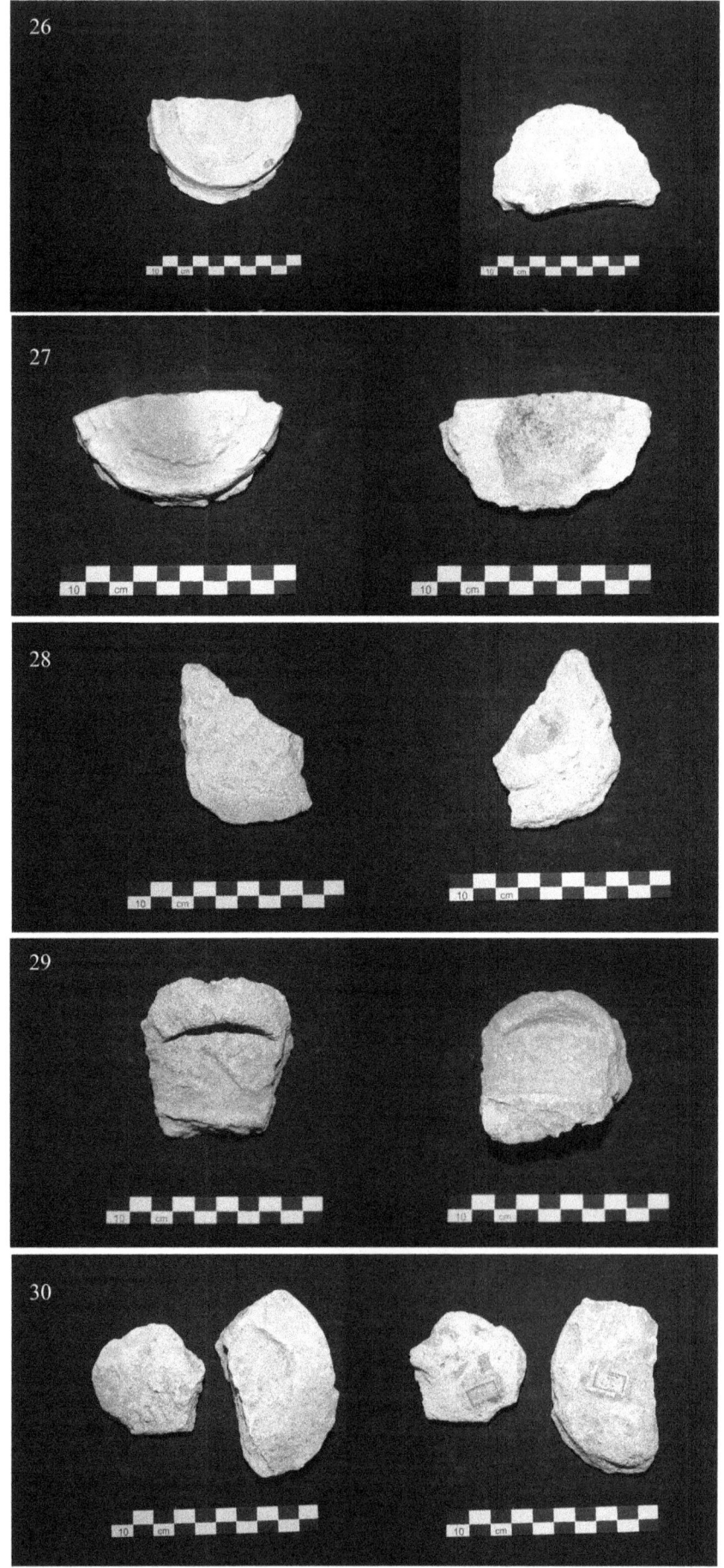

Fig. 13.26-30 Vessel Stoppers in the National Museum of Eritrea and in the National Museum of Addis Ababa.

Fig. 13.31-34 Vessel Stoppers in the National Museum of Eritrea and in the National Museum of Addis Ababa.

author of the Periplus of the Erythraean Sea stated that pig iron ingots were imported from India to Ethiopia/Eritrea (Casson 1989: 6.3.3-4). Cosmas Indicopleustes describes the existence on the Eritrean coastal plains of trade in cattle, salt and iron bars under the direct control of the kingdom of Aksum in exchange for gold from the Agaw, a region likely located between Meroe and Ethiopia (Mapunda 1997: 107-124 and 114-118). The discovery by Paribeni of goldsmith slate matrix in the upper strata of the survey No. 19 (Figure 4), shows that there might have been local metal working (Paribeni 1907: 461-462). Among the objects that are most likely to have been produced locally are iron spears and bronze rings and bracelets (cf. also Phillipson 1998: 98).

So far, gold artefacts have not been found in any of the collections examined evn though Paribeni found gold chains with cross pendants (Paribeni 1907: 487-491, figs. 20-21) and Anfray mentions the finding of "trésors d'objets en or" including cross and chains (Anfray 1974: 753). These objects were likely produced locally. Paribeni mentions evidence of local gold manufacture including the finding of unworked gold fragments and possible slags (Paribeni 1907: 483) and fragments of scales for weighing valuable goods (Paribeni 1907: 539-540, fig. 55) which would indicate the sale of gold at the site itself. The tiny gold fragment, perhaps slag, recently found at Adulis, also supports this hypothesis (Adulis Fieldwork Report 2012, unpublished).

Precious metal objects and coins were imported to the Aksumite kingdom as diplomatic gifts or as valuable goods for the local élite as attested by the finding of the golden coins of Kushana in the monastery of Debra Damo (Mordini 1960: 249-250). The gold earring featured in the Paribeni report could also have been brought from the Indian Ocean region as a gift, according to the type of manufacture (Paribeni 1907: 484, fig. 19).

So far we have reports of only a few metal objects from the Sundström collection of materials from Adulis kept in the Museum of Ethnography in Stockholm; the list mentions bronze fragments and a possible sounder (inventory numbers respectively 1907.59.0002 and 1907.59.0003). The sounder can be correctly identified as an object used to measure depth at sea because it is drafted next to the inventory number. It appears as a truncated cone shaped object with a hole on the top through which a rope passed to lower the weight into the water and measure how far down the seafloor was. Similar sounders are usually made in metal and are found in contemporary Mediterranean underwater contexts.

Metal objects from the other collections examined are inventoried and described below.

Metal artefacts kept in the National Museum of Eritrea

In the storeroom of the National Museum of Eritrea over 50 metal objects found by Paribeni at Adulis are preserved. The collection includes iron and bronze objects, most of which are ornaments, tools, weapons and nails. The presence of a dozen slag fragments and remelted lead and bronze indicate the existence of local metalwork processing. Such fragments were in fact found in the room H of the group of buildings to the north of the city, a room interpreted by Paribeni as a possible workshop of a goldsmith (Paribeni 1907: 486).

Bronze artefacts

Ornamental bronze artefacts include ten plain rings, most of which are circular in section, only one is characterized by a flattened ovoid part (Figure 14.1) and another is rectangular in section; two bracelets of about 5 cm in diameter, one with notches engraved decoration (Figure 14.2).

Among elements of wood veneer or decorative elements for leather or stone are a piece of perforated disk, six decorative nails and hemispherical studs (Figure 14.3), five thin plates of bronze, one still with nails and the other with possible letters in relief (Figure 14.1) (cf. also Paribeni 1907: 495-496, fig. 25), a small stylized leaf (Figure 14.1), perhaps used to decorate stone architectural elements, as in the case of a shale slab with carved decoration of leaves (Figure 16.2-4 cf. also Paribeni 1907: 507-508, fig. 32).

Among tools are five bent pins, about 6 cm long (Figure 14.4), six nails with diamond-shaped head and short pin, nine nails with rhomboid or domed head and medium pin similar to types dating to the late Aksumite phase (cf. Phillipson 2000: 343, fig. 299g) and four nails with flattened circular head (Figure 14.3). Elements of scales are also present in this collection, in particular, three arm fragments (Figure 14.5), seven possible fragments of the chain (Figure 14.6).

Among the surgical or cosmetic instruments are a decorative trowel probe with notches on the stem and a fragment of a small spatula or spoon and two sharp pins (Figure 14.5).

Two objects come from bronze vessels: one is a vertical flat rectangular handle and the other is a lid, semicircular in shape with a grip for the opening, a closing pin and a hook that originally attached the lid to the vessel (Figure 14.7).

The collection also includes about 20 unidentified fragmentary objects including possible vessel fragments ca. 0.3 cm in thickness, one of which seems to be a rim of an unrestricted bowl but with milled side, four tubular metal sheets, a possible fragment of support for a mirror and two fragments of dishes ca. 5 cm in diameter.

Iron artefacts

Iron objects include fragments of round or flattened rings, broken nails and very worn chain rings, some perforated plates used perhaps as joints or to fix elements of wooden frames, seven fragments of rods with circular flattened section, large folded rods, a plate with four holes and a broken rod ending with a spatula (Figures 14.8 and 9).

Among the weapons there are five spears that can be compared with similar types found at Aksum, characterized by a rib along the major axis, with a circular stalk and elongated shape (cf. Munro-Hay 1989a, fig. 15.133-134) or spears with elongated shape, square sectioned stalk and with no rib (cf. Munro-Hay 1989a, fig. 15.132) (Figure 14.10).

Metal artefacts kept in the National Museum of Addis Ababa

Metal objects from Adulis collected by Anfray are now kept in the National Museum of Addis Ababa. The collection includes only a few fragments of badly preserved iron and bronze nails (ADU 6079) and a bronze balance which is on exhibit (Figure 14.11). This type of portable steelyard balance is a type commonly used in trade for weighing bulky commodities. A similar balance has also been found in the Byzantine wreck of Yassi Ada (Kingsley 2004: 41). The balance found in the Eritrean wreck of the Assarca island includes a lead counterweight with a similar bronze hook (Pedersen 2000: 12, fig. 11).

Metal artefacts kept in the African Museum in Rome

Metal objects from the Paribeni collection kept in the African Museum in Rome include iron, lead and bronze objects, including parts of ornaments, vessels, surgical instruments, tools, scales and weights, weapons and bars (cf. Zazzaro 2004).

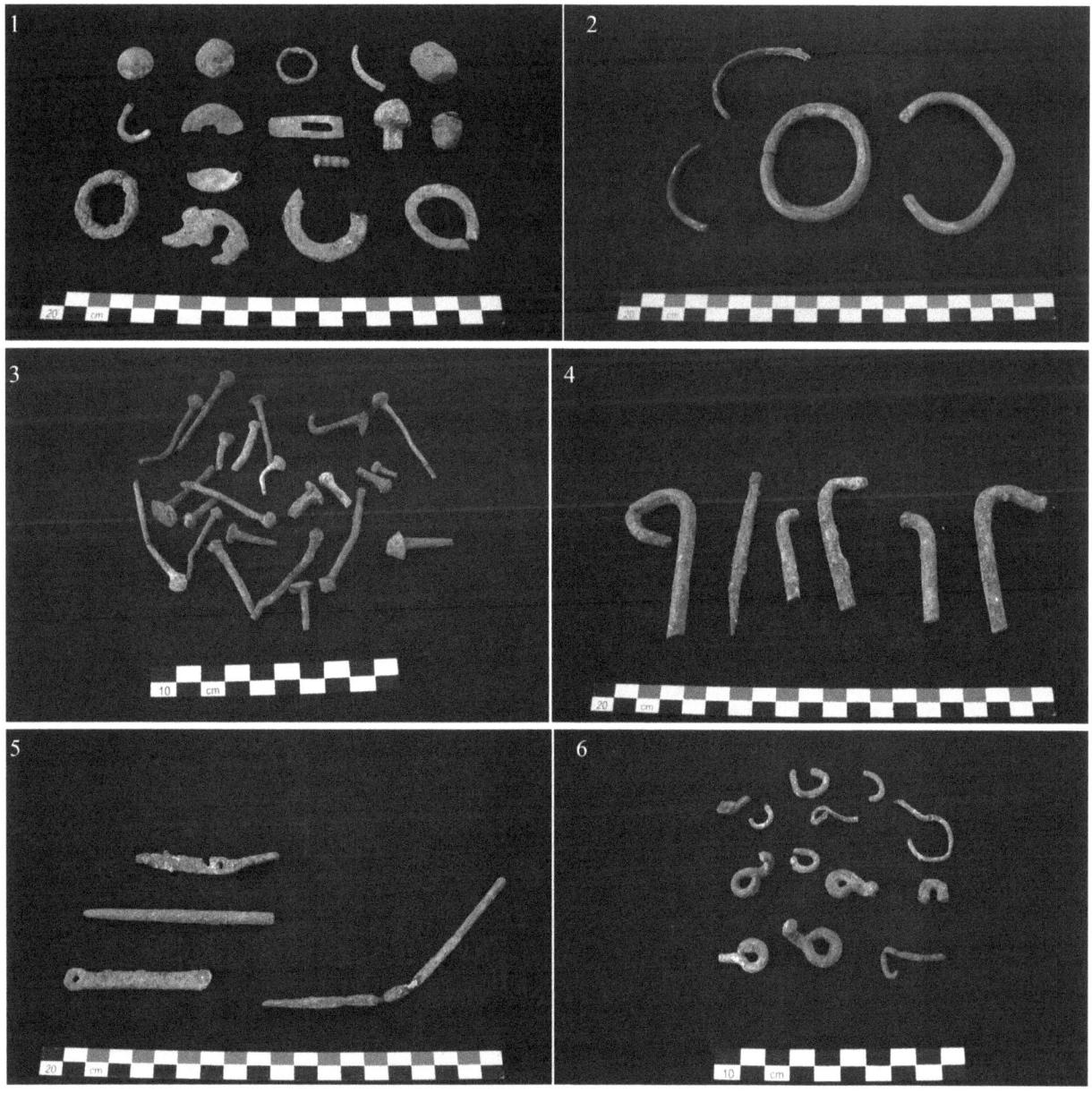

Fig. 14.1-6 Metal artefacts in the National Museum of Eritrea.

Bronze artefacts

The vessels collection includes a lamp with spoon-shaped unrestricted body bearing a tripod base, a vertical ring handle surmounted by the decoration of an ivy leaf (Figure 14.12.1) (cf. Paribeni 1907: 502, fig. 29). This lamp was found in the room S of a group of buildings adjacent to a church in the north sector of Adulis "[...] below fragments of sandstone slabs irregularly accumulated". The lamp seems to be of Mediterranean manufacture but it has a completely atypical shape except for the presence of the tripod base and for the unrestricted shape like other lamps throughout the Mediterranean area starting from the 8th century AD with the disappearance of the restricted lamps types (De Spagnoli and De Carolis 1983: 70).

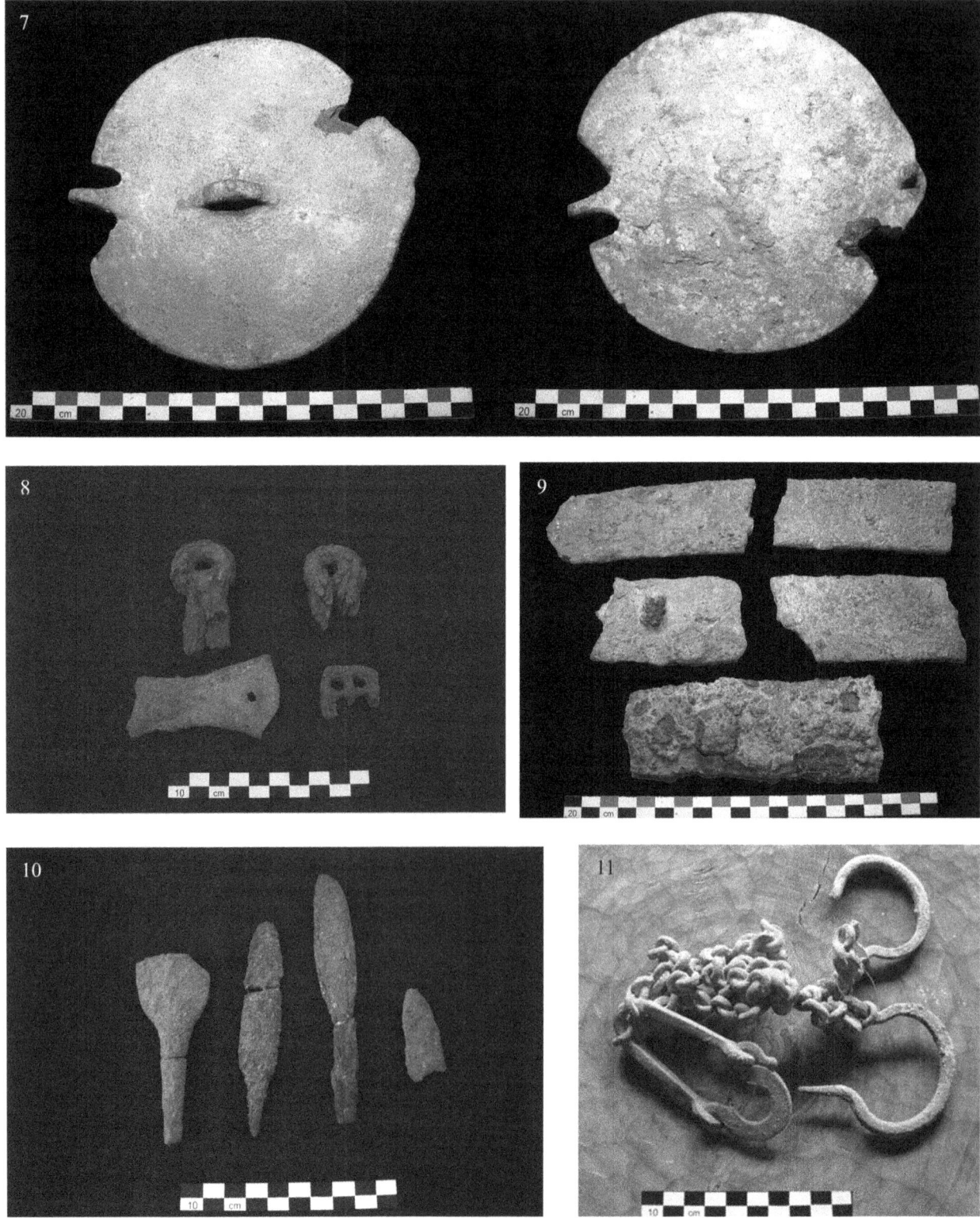

FIG. 14.7-11 METAL ARTEFACTS IN THE NATIONAL MUSEUM OF ERITREA, IN THE NATIONAL MUSEUM OF ADDIS ABABA.

The two *olpai* or *oinochoai* lateral handles of a bronze vessel decorated with leonine or canine head (Figure 14.12.2) (cf. Paribeni 1907: 558) seem also to be of Late Roman manufacture. Imported metal vessels from the Mediterranean area might have been widely diffused if we consider the number of imitations attested in several local pottery types (cf. Manzo 2003b).

Weighing instruments found by Paribeni are all combined on a single panel which includes three arms of scales, one of which is reconstructed combining the arm with some chain fragments, while at the bottom of the board there are nine weights (Figure 14.12.3). The scales worked by opposing weights at the same distance from the point of suspension; at the ends and at the center of the arms there are holes for the passage of chains for supporting suspended dishes. It is likely that the scale has been reconstructed by Paribeni using different copper object fragments found in the excavation. Similar scales are also found in the Tomb of Brick Arches at Aksum dating to the 3rd century AD (Munro-Hay 1989a, fig. 15.212-213) and in Meroitic contexts (Emery and Kirwan 1938, vol. 2, tab. 105). This type of scales called *trutina,* in the Roman world, was usually employed for weighing precious gems, pearls and gold. Paribeni reports that an almost complete scales was found in the church to the east of the city in a room to the right of the apse near the baptistery (Paribeni 1907: 539-540, fig. 55); two other fragments were found along the south and the east side of the altar (Paribeni 1907: 475-476 and 492). A pair of scales was also found during the British excavation (Markham 1869: 155, note 1). The presence of so many scales seems to testify the involvement of the town in the trade of precious commodities. Trade in gold at Adulis is in fact mentioned by Cosmas Indicopleustes (II.51.1-6).

The weights on the board correspond to the accurate description of the findings in the Paribeni report (Paribeni 1907: 562). A parallelepiped weight with "I B" engraved weighing one-twelfth of an ounce (Figure 14.12.3, the first weight from the left) seems to correspond to the description of a weight found by Paribeni in corridor L of the group of buildings in the south-west sector of the site (Paribeni 1907: 524); the two weights with three signs engraved, two upside down L (ΓΓ) and a cross in between them, weighing three ounces (Figure 14.12.3, third weight from left) are also mentioned in Paribeni's report (1907: 479 and 482). Three ounce weights with similar incisions were also found at Aksum by de Contenson together with another one-twelfth of an ounce weight with the incised sign "IIB" (de Contenson 1963: 12, tab. XX g and tab. XIV c). This type of weight is generally dated to the 6th-7th century AD. They were common in Roman and Late Roman contexts (Arena *et al.* 2001: 342-344) as well as in post-Meroitic sites (Emery and Kirwan 1938, vol. II, tab. 107, figs. E (B118-22) and G (80-108)) for weighing coins and precious commodities (Bendall 1996: 340).

The collection also includes several decorative or functional elements such as nails, hinges, pins and plates which were originally fixed to wooden frames.

Two studs are shaped in a zoomorphic leonine head, one still bearing the ring in the mouth (Figure 14.13.1). The two studs were found near the church in the east sector of the city, in the lobby after the central threshold between the remains of a burnt door, charcoal and ashes (Paribeni 1907: 535, fig. 53). These objects may therefore be dated to the last phase of occupation of the city that is around the 6th century AD. C. Similar objects were very common in the Eastern Roman art since the 2nd-3rd century AD (Comstock and Vermeule 1971: 460-462, figs. 673-674).

The bronze triangular stud with rounded corners and long spike, perhaps originally fixed to a wooden support (Figure 14.13.2), was found in one of the buildings to the east of the "altar of the sun" (Paribeni 1907: 492-493).

Hinges and decorative bronze plates are also part of the collection, originally attached perhaps to wooden boxes. Among those are a bronze hinge and hinge fragment belonging to the same type characterized by a rectangular tab terminating with a circular plate with knurled contour and a small nail in the center to fix it to the wooden support (Figure 14.12.3). This type of hinge is comparable to types found in the Tomb of Brick Arches of Aksum dating from the late 3rd century AD (Munro-Hay 1989a, fig. 15.208).

Two plates with carved decorations (Figure 14.13.4) originally adhering to a wooden support are similar to plates found in the Tomb of Brick Arches of Aksum (Phillipson 2000: 101-103, figs. 81b and 84). Two identical plates were found in a funeral chapel or small church at Maṭarā dating to the 6th-7th century AD (Anfray and Annequin 1965: 67-68, pl. LXVIII.4, J.E. 2847-2848).

Among other decorative elements are some discs measuring 2 to 4 cm in diameter with incision of concentric circles and holes for fixing them to wood or leather supports (Figure 14.14.3).

Seven small bronze nails are of the ornamental type and might have been employed to decorate wooden furniture or metal and fabric supports. The nail typology varies from types with hemispherical head similar to the nails used to fix the two studs with lion head to a wooden door (Figure 14.13.2), or flat rounded head with square or circular pin section (Figure 14.14.2). Bronze nails described by Paribeni in his report were found in various contexts, some associated with a knife handle made of bone (Paribeni 1907: 480).

Iron and bronze bracelets and rings are attested in various Eritrean-Ethiopian contexts, sometimes associated with burials (Anfray 1963b: 100, tab. LXXXI a and tab. LXXXII a, tab. CXI d, 184; Anfray 1967: pl. XVII, fig. 4; de Contenson 1963a: pl. XLII b2 and Leclant and Miquel 1959: tab. LVII a, c and tab. LVIII). The bracelets found at Adulis are generally open, triangular in section with curved sides or circular or oval in section (Figure 14.14.1).

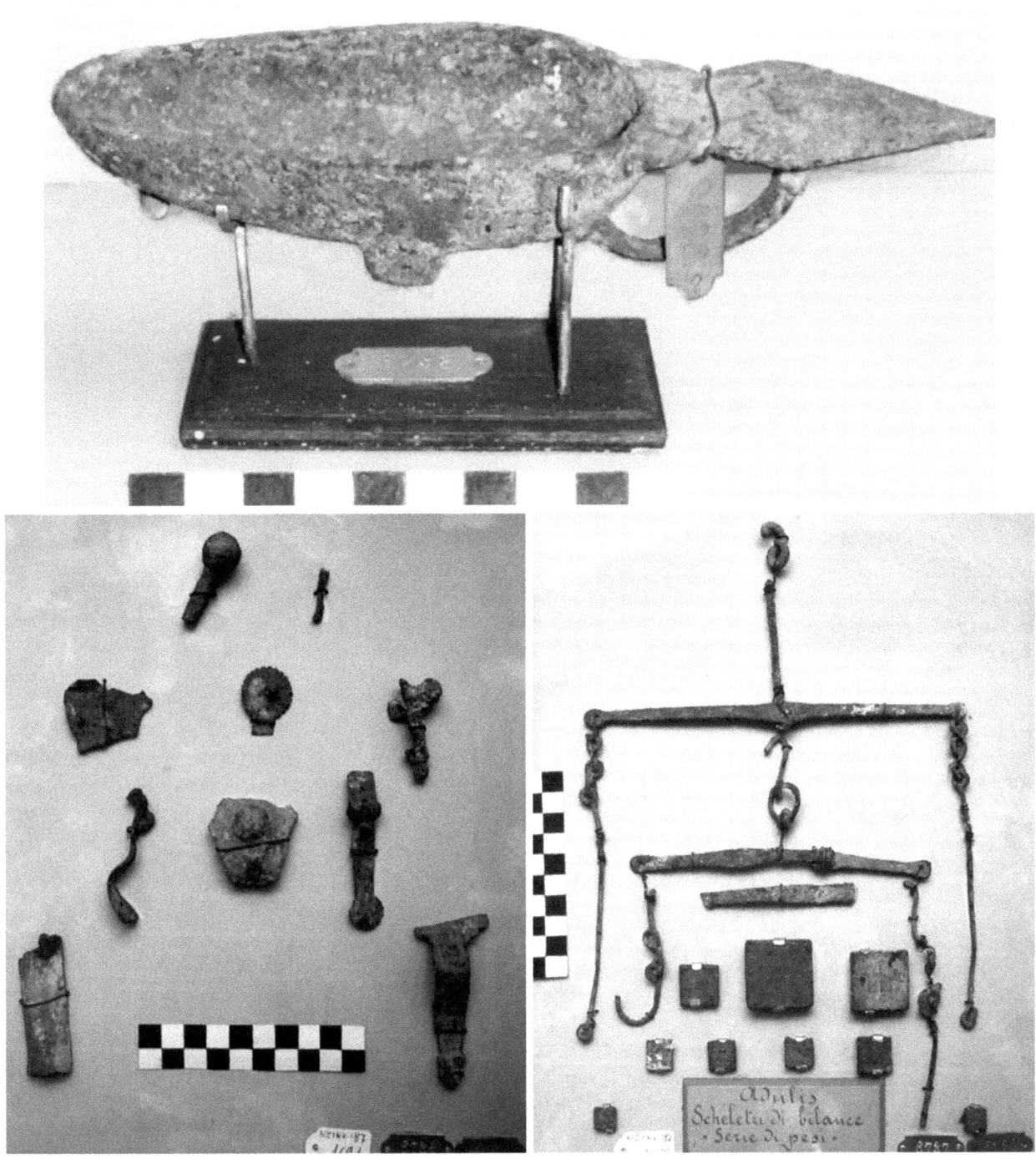

FIG. 14.12 METAL ARTEFACTS IN THE AFRICAN MUSEUM IN ROME.

A bronze object, the shape of which could not be determined, shows a ring on the top that could have been as a pendant (Figure 14.12.2).

Among surgical instruments are a probe, two fragments of probe and three or possibly four spatula probes (Figure 14.14.1-2). The thin cylindrical rod with grooves and a small knob, was found in the upper layers of room X in the group of buildings to the south-west. This object was perhaps employed to mix medicines or perfumes (Paribeni 1907: 520). A wide variety of similar instruments was found in Pompeii (Bliquez 2003: 322-330, fig. 1; Jackson 1990; Zampieri and Lavarone 2000), in later periods they are also found in Meroitic sites (Säve-Söderbergh 1981; Seele 1991 and Adams 2000) and worldwide.

The collection also includes numerous badly preserved fragments which are difficult to identify, including an object in the form of a bronze disc, ca. 5 cm in diameter and 1 cm in thickness (Figure 14.14.4). Bronze discs are described by Paribeni found in different contexts.

The Museum Collections of Adulitan Materials

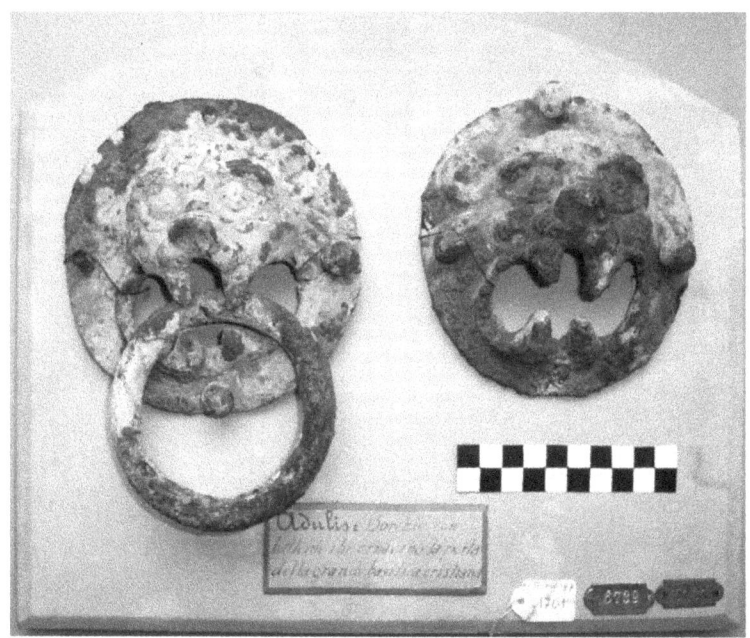

Fig. 14.13 Metal artefacts in the African Museum in Rome.

Iron artefacts

Among the iron artefacts there is a shovel, in poor condition, that could have been employed either as to clear out a grate or as an incense-shovel (*batillum*) (Figure 14.15.1). Similar shovels, but much more elaborate and refined, are generally dated to the 1st-2nd century AD and come from sacred contexts (Hayes 1984: 100-107, figs. 159, 163-168).

The six iron nails, five iron bars and an iron loop are poorly preserved (Figure 14.15.2). The nails were used for construction and they have been found in the buildings area in the south west sector of the city (Paribeni 1907: 522).

Four pieces of iron double dovetail shaped, with holes at both ends, in poor condition, could have originally belonged to a wooden box (Figure 14.15.3-4). They were found in the compartment U belonging to the group of buildings to the south-west and in the narthex of church located to the east of the site (Paribeni 1907: 524, 527 and 536).

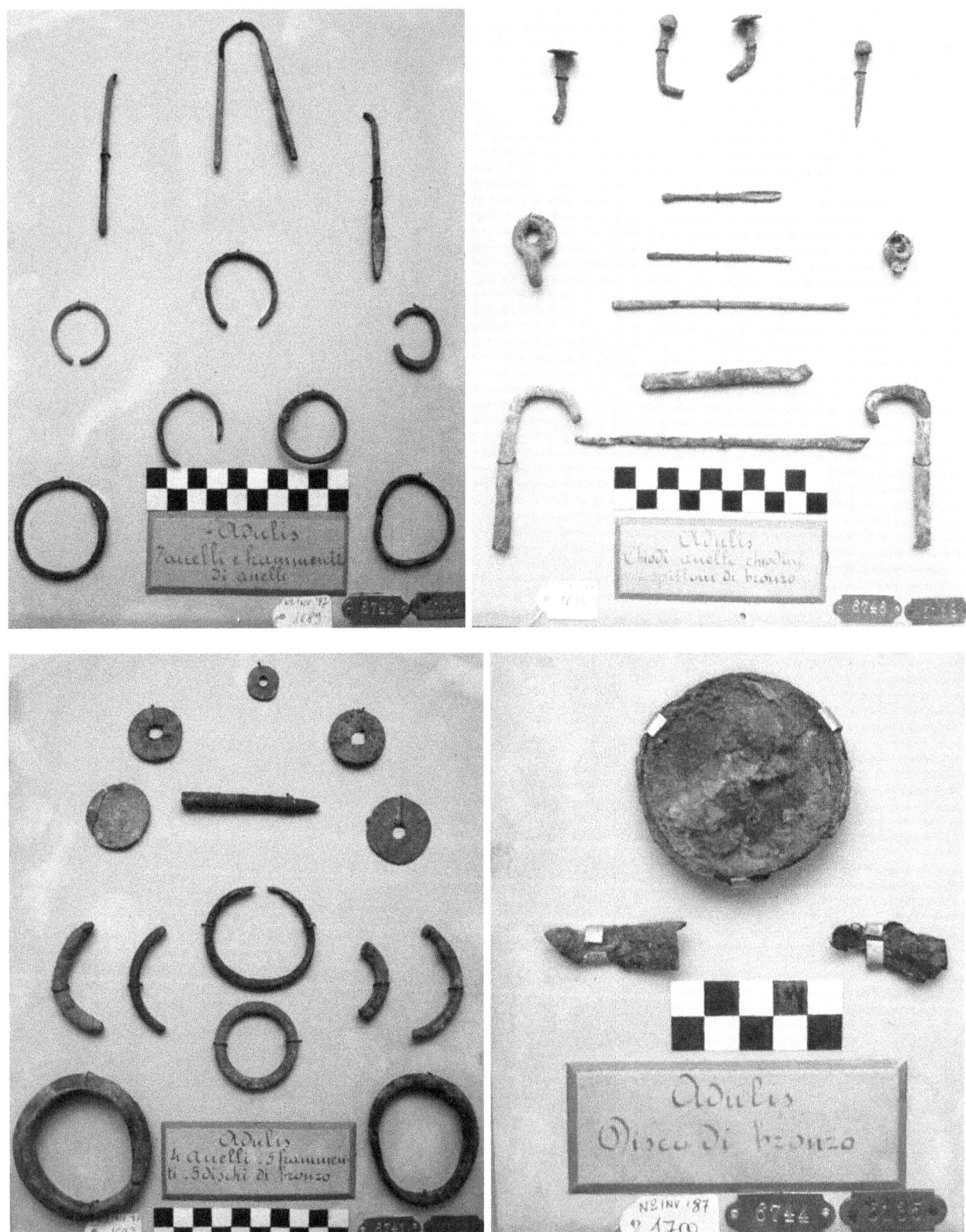

Fig. 14.14 Metal artefacts in the African Museum in Rome.

THE MUSEUM COLLECTIONS OF ADULITAN MATERIALS

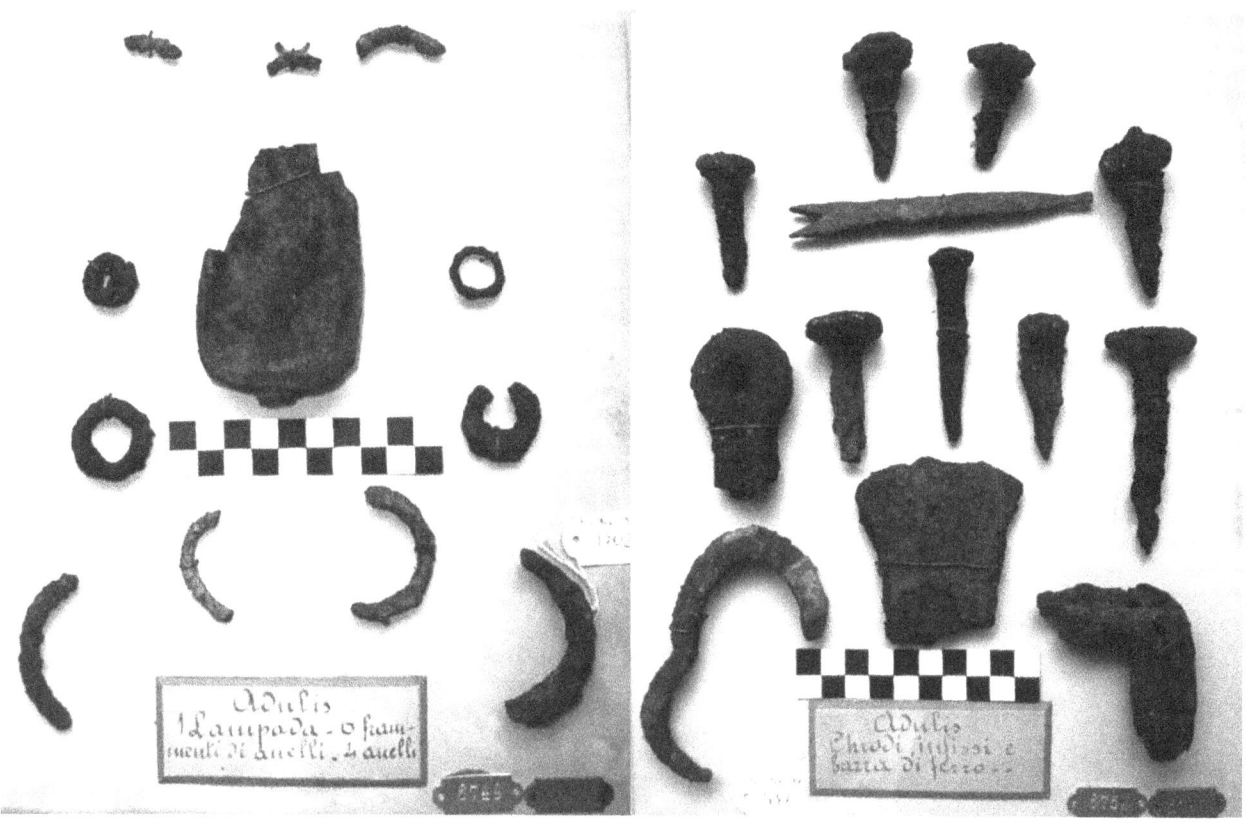

FIG. 14.15 METAL ARTEFACTS IN THE AFRICAN MUSEUM IN ROME.

Arrowheads found in various contexts at Adulis belong to the well known Aksumite type of "bay leaf" with central pivot (Figure 14.16.1) (Manzo 1998: 46; Munro-Hay 1989, fig. 15.133-134). The spearheads are comparable with similar types found at Aksum, characterized by a rib along the major axis, with a circular stalk and elongated shape (Munro-Hay 1989, fig. 15.133-134), or elongated and without ribs (Munro-Hay 1989, fig. 15.132). The board also bears three barely preserved atypical small arrowheads with rounded top (Figure 14.16.1). In addition to the arrowheads and spearheads there are also two cylindrical objects identified as tangs(?) as stated in Italian on the board (Figure 14.15.2).

Glass artefacts

Glass fragments have been found in large quantities on the site in the Paribeni and Anfray excavations. In particular, according to Paribeni, glass was second to the pottery in quantity for class of material recovered on the site. Glass fragments were found in different sectors of the site by Paribeni (1907: 451, 458, 517); he describes cylindrical or square jars, truncated conical vessels, rounded tips, calyx ring bases, bowls with handle, elongated and thin vessels with everted rim and rounded or flat base. He also describes thicker glass fragments found in the housing quarter near the Haddas. The colour varies from white to turquoise, yellow, marbled and decorated with lines, reticulate relief, elliptic cavities, spiral handles (Paribeni 1907: 558-560). In the deeper levels, associated with the local black ware pottery, Paribeni found a fragment of opaque glass with a blue nucleus encircled with a white and yellow stripe which could be dated to an earlier period, perhaps to the Pharaonic period as suggested by Fattovich (1996: 18). Such a large amount of glass evidence in Adulis is not surprising considering that glass vessels were in general common in other Aksumite contexts. Glass vessels were supposedly imported from the Mediterranean, Mesopotamia and Persia but they might also have been locally produced (Manzo 2005: 56). In fact, according to the anonymous author of the Periplus, glass was exported from Diospolis and Alexandria, in Egypt, to India, perhaps through Adulis (Casson 1989: 53).

Considering the very fragmentary condition of the glass assemblage and the luck of an exhaustive publication on late antiquity glass some inaccuracy in dating and in the identification of the form might occur, also considering that some are types that persisted over a long period. It is difficult to establish, for example, whether a glass vessel fragment was originally used as lamp, as drinking glass or as phials as these vessels may all have similar shapes. Sometimes the difference in thickness and the decoration might help in identifying the original use. Most of the glass fragments belong to common tableware vessels, of local production or imported from the eastern Mediterranean;

Fig. 14.16 Metal artefacts in the African Museum in Rome.

only one fragment could be originally from Persia. Several fragments might have been from oil lamps: glass vessels used as lighting devices were widely diffused in the liturgical context of early Christian churches and cemeteries dating to the 4th-7th century AD (Antonaras 2008: 23). Only the minority of the vessels was decorated, mainly bottles of the Byzantine period, with the most common type of horizontal wheel abraded lines.

Glass artefacts kept in the National Museum of Eritrea

The Paribeni collection in the National Museum of Eritrea includes about 40 glass fragments including fragments of flasks, bottles, phials, *unguentarium*, dishes and lamps.

Bottles

Three fragments have been identified possibly as bottles for their square section bases of which only one corner is preserved. Two of them show dark surfaces but they might have originally been translucent (Figures 15.1 and 15.2), one fragment has abraded decoration of horizontal and vertical lines (Figure 15.2) typical of the Late Roman production; another fragment in white translucent glass shows a spiral decoration converging in a bulb with convex centre (Figure 15.3): this can be identified as a bottle mark, common to bottles dating to the 2nd century AD (Isings 1971: 81 n. 156 and fig. 20).

Lamps or beakers

A series of rim fragments with prominent lips, globular or slightly vertical profile, can be identified as lamps or beakers. The body is very thin (ca. 0.1-0.2 mm), suggesting that these types are more likely to be identified as lamps rather than beakers. Also the distinctive lip-ledge shape suggests that these were hanging lamps suspended by handles or hooks (cf. Morrison 1989: 200). The diameters are ca. 3-4 cm, and the fabric is almost always colourless although some fragments show dark weathering (Figures 15.4 and 15.5). Similar fragments were also found at Maṭarā (Morrison 1989: 202-203 figs. 14.113-136), identified as possible lamps perhaps of Syrian-Palestinian provenance (Hayes 1975: 45 and 76 tav. 8 figs. 271-272) and dating from the 3rd-4th century AD. One yellow-green translucent glass base fragment shows a flattened large knob (Figure 15.8, above right); it can be compared to cylindrical vessels with tapering body of Uboldi type III.1 (Uboldi 1995) used as a lighting device and dating to the 5th-7th century AD.

Flasks or unguentarium

Round concave base thin-walled fragments, they can be identified as flasks or *unguentarium*, for their small dimensions and thickness. The base diameter varies from 4 to 5 cm, the thickness from 0.15 to 0.2 mm, they are colourless or in translucent brown (Figure 15.6) (cf. Morrison 1989: 189-191, fig. 14.15).

Phials

Base fragments of phials can be distinguished in a flat round base, 0.3 mm in thickness (Figure 15.7, left) or round drop shaped bases, 0.5 mm in thickness and 1.2 cm in diameter (Figure 15.7, right); the colour varies from translucent green, yellow to white. These types are also found in the highland contexts dating from the 3rd century AD (Morrison 1989: 195 and 200, figs. 101-112).

Drinking glasses

Rim fragments, similar in shape to lamp type vessels can be identified as a beaker for their thicker walls (Figure 15.4-5). Conical drinking glass were usually exported together with Sigillata ware dishes and bowls during the 4th-6th centuries AD (Isings 1957: 129-130 n. 106c). Among drinking glass fragments Paribeni found a faceted purple translucent base (Paribeni 1907: 458), perhaps the same thick-walled fragment with deeply cut facets, 3.5 cm in diameter, observed in the collection (Figure 15.13). Similar type vessels were usually produced on the eastern frontiers of the Roman Empire although it can also be compared to types dating from the 3rd-4th century AD (Isings 1957: 46-49 n. 32 and n. 35).

Miscellaneous fragments

A dark weathered green glass fragment of a possible bracelet (Figure 15.8.1).

A green translucent foot ring with part of the stem, 5.5 cm in diameter (Figure 15.8.3), could belong to a goblet, a flask or a bowl.

A dark weathered brown true ring base, 9 cm in diameter, 0.2 mm in thickness (Figure 15.8.4).

A series of weathered green, brown or colourless thin-walled vessel fragments some with evidence of abraded decoration (Figure 15.10).

A body fragment of white translucent glass showing a dark blue blob decoration, perhaps from a conical beaker (Fleming 1997: 32). This type of decoration was popular throughout the eastern provinces starting from the 4th century AD (Figure 15.11) (Weinberg 1988).

Several body fragments of small vessels are also attested, including a fragment in green translucent glass with horizontal wheel abraded lines typical of the Byzantine period (Figure 15.12) and a fragment in white translucent glass with grooved decoration (Figure 15.12) (Sternini 1999: 99, fig. 113).

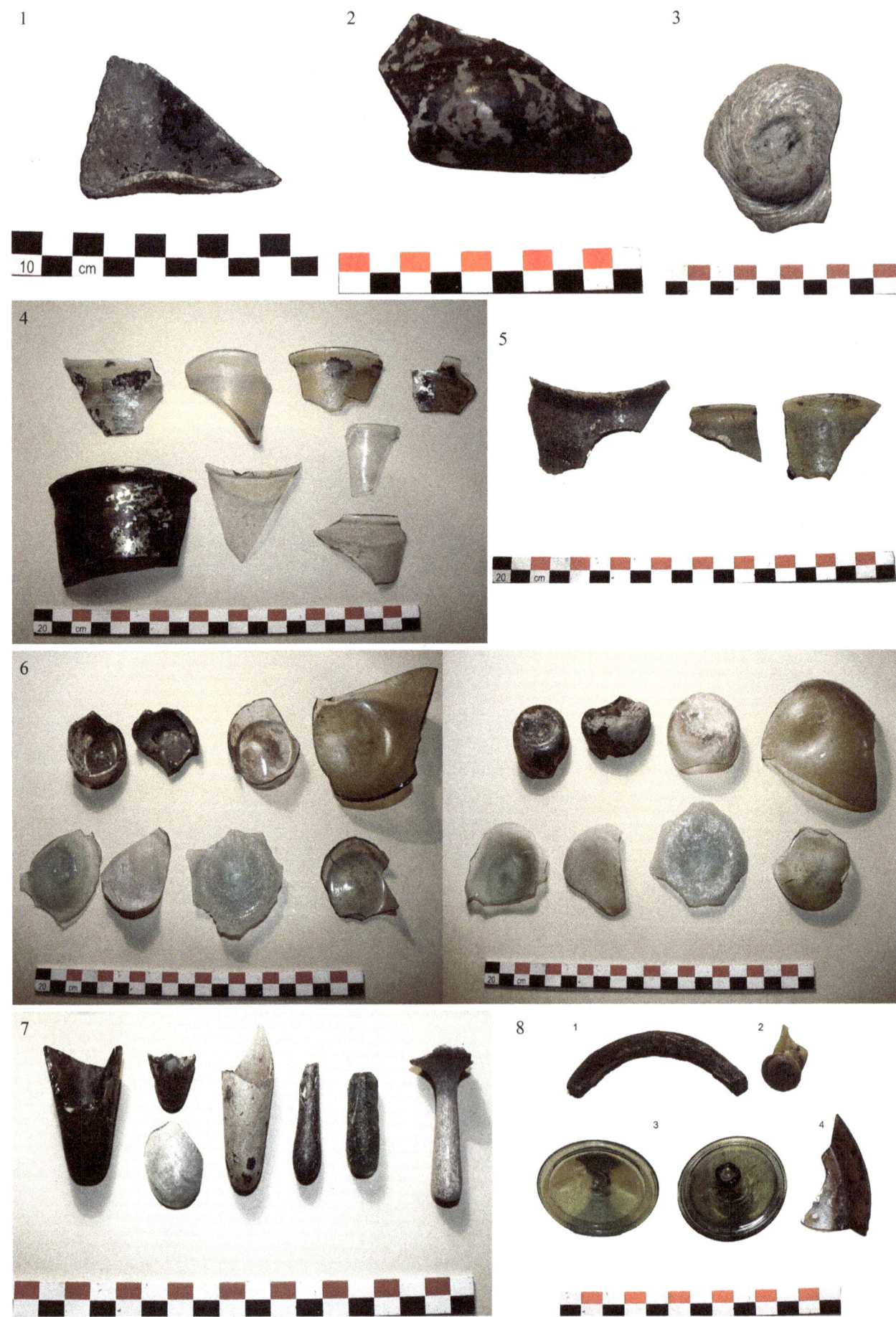

Fig. 15.4-8 Glass artefacts in the National Museum of Eritrea.

Fig. 15.9-14 Glass artefacts in the National Museum of Eritrea.

FIG. 15.15 GLASS ARTEFACTS FROM THE NATIONAL MUSEUM OF ADDIS ABABA

Four fragments of translucent glass vessel show moulded decoration also typical of the Byzantine period (Figures 15.12.1, 15.12.4, 15.12.7).

A weathered flat vertical handle, rectangular in section perhaps of a bottle or a flask (Figure 15.14).

Glass artefacts kept in the Addis Ababa Museum

Some 15 glass vessel fragments are kept in the storeroom of the Addis Ababa museum, including flasks, calix, ampoules, lamps and dishes.

Flasks

Four concave-conical bases of flasks or phials in green translucent glass, one with white patina, with conical lump in the centre, perhaps flask fragments, a type diffused starting from the 4th century AD (ADU6060, ADU6066, ADU6136 5a_tr.couche2_1, ADU6136 5atr.couche2_2, Figures 15.15.1, 15.15.2, 15.15.3) (cf. Sternini 1999: 99, n. 113).

Calix or cup

Fragment of a ring base in transparent glass with white patina, perhaps the base of a calix or a cup (ADU6147 13f_loc12_1.10mt, Figure 15.15.4).

Dish

One fragment of small dish and other three fragments perhaps from the same vessel, green glass with white patina (ADU6139 tranchée_couche2, ADU6099, Figures 15.15.5 and 15.15.6).

Unidentified fragments

Button-shaped tip fragment perhaps from a lamp with open walls, dark green glass, possibly a Late Antiquity type of lamp (ADU6085, Figure 15.15.7).

Fragments of green translucent glass base of an ampulla or lamp (Figure 15.15.8).

Flaring rim fragment from a flask or ampulla in green translucent glass (ADU6059 24f_loc7_mt3, Figure 15.15.9).

Stone artefacts kept in the National Museum of Eritrea

Stone artefacts found at Adulis include about 50 objects including grind stones, mortars, weights, vessels and other unidentified objects. The material varies from porous local volcanic stone to schist, serpentine, alabaster and marble (cf. Paribeni 1907: 452).

Lithic

The Paribeni collection includes obsidian flakes, found in the lower excavation layers (Paribeni 1907: 450-451). Among the approximately 20 flakes found in the storeroom of the museum it was possible to recognise:

Three convex very patinated handscrapers with long unidirectional retouch, trapezoidal shaped supports obtained from a multidirectional platform, the butts are plain and the bulbs are very protruding, they were produced by flaking using a strong hammer (Pelegrin 2000) (Figures 16.1.1, 16.1.2, 16.1.3).

Possible natural very patinated flake debitage, proximal reflected fracture, bulb and butt are absent, in the distal part there is an axial fracture (Figure 16.1.4).

Very patinated perforator on blade with reversed convergent retouch in the proximal part (Figure 16.1.5).

Very patinated possible natural debitage (Figures 16.1.6, 16.1.7, 16.1.8, 16.1.9).

This type of lithic industry is similar to that found in other Aksumite contexts.

Similar handscrapers but made in different material are also found on various sites of the Ethiopian-Eritrean highlands dating to the pre-Aksumite and Aksumite period (Phillipson 2009).

Miscellaneous objects

Among miscellaneous objects the collection includes:

Three fragments of basalt slabs with inlay decoration of metal leaves, now missing (Figures 16.2, 16.3 and 16.4) (cf. Paribeni 1907: 506-507, fig. 32).

A goldsmith slate matrix with incisions of crosses (Figure 16.5). This slate was found in the upper strata of the Paribeni's survey numbered 19 (cf. Paribeni 1907: 461-462, fig. 7) and may prove that metal working featured in local activities. This object can be compared to similar goldsmith slate matrix widespread in Mediterranean contexts dating to the 7th-10th century AD (cf. Arena *et al.* 2001: 54, fig. VI.10.31).

Eight local volcanic stone vessels found by Paribeni in the upper layers of the excavation (Paribeni 1907: 558) are circular or oval in shape 7-13 cm in length and 3.5-8 cm high, four of them are rounded at the base (Figure 16.6) while the other four are flat (Figures 16.7, 16.8, 16.9), two are characterised by a handle (Figures 16.7 and 16.9); they could have been used as incense burners or mortars, certainly not for liquids due to the porosity of the material. The finding of large circular turning volcano grind stones is well attested at the site (Paribeni 1907: 497-498, fig. 26). According to Anfray this type of grind stones are only seen at Adulis and in the area near Raheita, to the south on the Eritrean coast (see Puglisi 1969: 40, note 10 and Anfray 1970: 41-42, Pl. XX-XI), while they are elongated on the highland settlements (Anfray 1974: 752), although the author has seen a very similar grind stone in Farasan Island.

Seven ovoidal in shape grind stones, 6-15 cm in diameter, interpreted as bowls by Paribeni (1907: 558) but more likely to be mortars on account of the traces of use in the small central cavity (Figures 16.10 and 16.11).

Five small cylindrical pestles in pink granite 6-10 cm in dimensions (Figure 16.12).

The collection also includes stone weights among which one in grey-pink stone and parallelepiped shape weighing 84.7 gr which corresponds to Roman unit of measure *quadrans* (Figure 16.13, left); the other, cylindrical in shape, in marble, weighs 15.3 gr, corresponding to the Roman *quincunx* (Figure 16.13, centre) (Adams 2001: 12d2).

A possible porphyry mushroom shaped object ca. 4 by 3 cm in dimensions, perhaps a lid of a flask or bottle or a mace head (Figure 16.14).

One of the most interesting stone artefacts in the Paribeni collection is an alabaster lid (Figure 16.15), which can be compared with lids found in southern Arabia dating to the 3rd-2nd centuries BC (Hassell 1997: 248-9, fig. 2.C1). The find corroborates hypotheses on the early history of Adulis' trade connections with southern Arabia (Munro Hay 1996: 129; Fattovich 1995; 1996) and at least suggests the site was visited from this period on.

A granite (?) flat rounded sealing with a pierced grip and incised surface of concentric and radial lines (Figure 16.16). Similar objects, in clay or stone, have also been found in the most recent layer of occupation at Maṭarā and interpreted as possible sealings (Anfray 1967: 43, fig. 6).

A limestone or coral rock rounded object might have been employed as net weights for fishing (Figure 16.17).

Vessels

Stone vessels were found in large number by Paribeni (1907: 557). The collection includes five unrestricted bowls in serpentine stone with rounded bottom and rounded (Figure 16.18) or flat rim (Figure 16.22), with lateral grips (Figures 16.19 and 16.20). A small bowl characterised by a pointed bottom (Figure 16.21) was probably found in the Paribeni excavation sector No. 13 around the church, associated with material dating to the phase of abandonment of the site (Paribeni 1907: 459-460). In the same area around the church and particularly in the area near room H, a burial context, various fragments of alabaster and marble basins with flat bottom were found. These assemblage may have included the large unrestricted marble basin with flat flaring rim in the present collection (Figure 16.23).

Architectural elements

The most representative architectural elements of the collection were found in the early Christian church excavated by Paribeni in the north-west sector of the site and numbered as 13 on his plan (Paribeni 1907: 465-466). These are marble chancel posts, panels, screens and architraves all parts of a type of liturgical furnishing widely diffused in the Christianized regions during the 6th century AD and imported from the Byzantine empire. Most likely the raw material came from the Proconnesian islands in the Sea of Marmara (Heldman 1994: 239-252), worked somewhere in the regions of the Byzantine empire and exported by sea. In fact, similar divisor panels of Proconnesian marble were found in the Marzamemi shipwreck dating to the end of the 6th century AD. The ship was most likely carrying a complete set of church

FIG. 16.1-5 STONE ARTEFACTS IN THE NATIONAL MUSEUM OF ERITREA.

Fig. 16.6-11 Stone artefacts in the National Museum of Eritrea.

furnishing to be off-loaded in a Thessalian harbour or another north-African harbour (Kapitän 1980).

Three marble capitals, two carved with a tulip shaped flower (Figure 16.24 and 16.25), are similar to a marble capital from Nessana and from the St. Catherine monastery at Mount Sinai, perhaps dating to the 6th century AD (cf. Paribeni 1907: 495, fig. 24 and Heldman 1994: 242-243); a square capital of variegated marble shows a decoration of acanthus leaves (Figure 16.26), found by Paribeni in the area near the Christian church No. 13 (Paribeni 1907: 481, fig. 17) can be compared with a similar capital found in Aqaba and dated to the end of the Byzantine occupation and the beginning of the Islamic presence (Khouri-Whitcomb 1992: 61).

Architrave fragments with decoration of vine leafs and grapes (Figures 16.27) (cf. Paribeni 1907: 505, fig. 31 and fig. 35) and one with ivy leafs (Figure 16.28 and 16.29) (cf. Heldman 1994: 252, figs. 7 and 8) found in room M of the group of buildings near the church No. 13 (cf. Paribeni 1907: 509, fig. 34).

Three fragments of marble panels with a decoration of flowers (Figures 16.30, 16.31 and 16.32) were found inside the same church and interpreted as part of the pavement by Paribeni (1907: 503-504, fig. 30).

A marble panel fragment with the decoration of a six armed star (Figures 16.33) incorrectly interpreted as a solar disk by Paribani (cf. Paribeni 1907: 466, fig. 9), since the disk usually overlies a Christian cross in complete exemplars of the same type (cf. also for comparisons Heldman 1994: 247, fig. B).

A marble fragment with laurel wreath encircling a cross only partially visible (Figure 16.34). Most likely this was part of a chancel panel dating to the 6th century AD (cf. Heldman 1994: 250, fig. 4).

An alabaster fragment with incised sign in an unknown script (Figure 16.35). This object was found by Paribeni in the area of the church No. 13 (cf. sign on the right in Paribeni 1907: 543-544, fig. 57).

Two marble fragments of unidentified objects or decorative elements (Figure 16.36); angle fragment of a marble basin (Figure 16.37).

Apart from the above mentioned marble and alabaster fragments, all ascribable to the same Byzantine tradition and style, three other fragmentary decorative elements found in the same area were most likely discovered in the lower occupation layers in the western limit of the church. These include an alabaster fragment showing the stairs of a typical building facade decoration (Figure 16.39) similar to part of the decoration of a South Arabian altar found at Gobochela (Leclant 1959: Pl. XXXVIIIa); a small decorative alabaster fragment with triangular sectioned rabbets (Figure 16.40) and a fragment of a marble(?) basin with relief decoration (Figure 16.38) which differ from the others in style and material (Paribeni 1907: 491, fig. 22).

Stone artefacts kept in the Addis Ababa Museum

The Anfray collection of stone artefacts is very poor comparing to the others, not surprising considering that he did not excavated a monumental area but an housing quarter. The stone assemblage includes a pebble with a circular groove, perhaps a fishing weight (ADU6140, Figure 16.41), a marble fragment with red veins (ADU6148, Figure 16.42), a possible fragment of obsidian vessel (ADU6106, Figure 16.43), a basaltic stone basin with flat flaring rim and flat bottom (Figure 16.44) and a well preserved fragment of a typical marble or alabaster mortar with thick body, small cavity and four protruding elements, on display in the museum cabinet (ADU6095 Figure 16.45). This type of mortar was widely diffused in Nubia and in general in all Late Antiquity Christianized regions (see for example Kingsley 2004: 39).

Stone artefacts kept in the British Museum

In the collections of the Department of Prehistory and Europe in the British Museum are currently kept five marble fragments found during the excavation conducted by the British Army, under the auspices of the British Museum in 1868.

Two marble fragments with cross decorated in relief are most likely chancel panel typical of Early Byzantine furnishings, as seen in the church of Nessana (Heldman 1994: 239-259). The small fragment measures 27 x 23 cm and 3.6 cm in thickness (Inv. 1868.10.5.15) (Figure 16.48), the larger fragment measures 47 x 32 cm and it is 8 cm in thickness (Figure 16.49).

These marble fragments also appear among the sketch drawings of William West Goodfellow, Captain of the Royal Engineers expedition, who excavated the Byzantine church south-east of the site.

The collection also includes an octagonal alabaster column and a Byzantine capital (Munro-Hay 1989: 44, Pl. IV and V) similar to those that are illustrated in the volume of the French scientific mission led by Teophile Lefebvre in 1845 and they may be the same objects (Peacock and Blue 2007: 121, fig. 9.11).

The octagonal pillar (Inv. 1868 10.5.16), perhaps in alabaster, measures ca. 20 cm in diameter, one end is unfinished, the surface is rough with tool marks, the other end is broken. Each face of the octagon measures 7 x 5.5 x 3.5 cm, one face has a rectangular cavity (Figure 16.50). This pillar can be compared with similar types found in south Arabia and probably dating to the end of the 1st millennium BC – early 1st millennium AD (Bossert 1951; Rathjens and von Wissmann 1932).

Fig. 16.12-17 Stone artefacts in the National Museum of Eritrea.

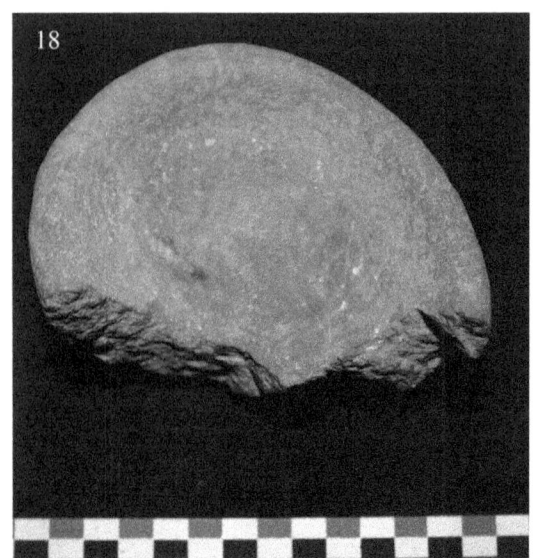

Fig. 16.18-23 Stone artefacts in the National Museum of Eritrea.

FIG. 16.24-34 STONE ARTEFACTS IN THE NATIONAL MUSEUM OF ERITREA.

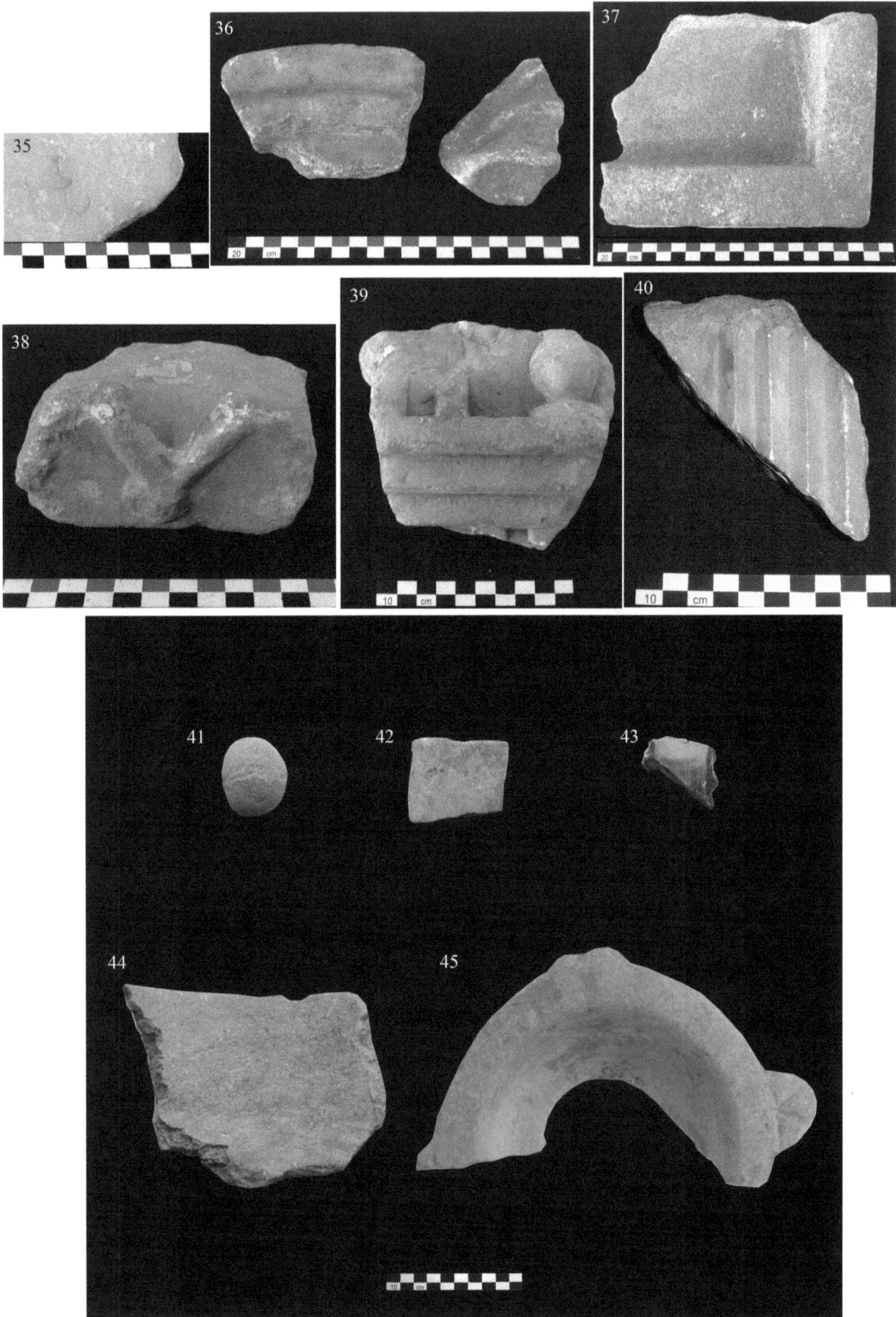

Fig. 16.35-45 Stone artefacts in the National Museum of Eritrea and in the National Museum of Addis Ababa.

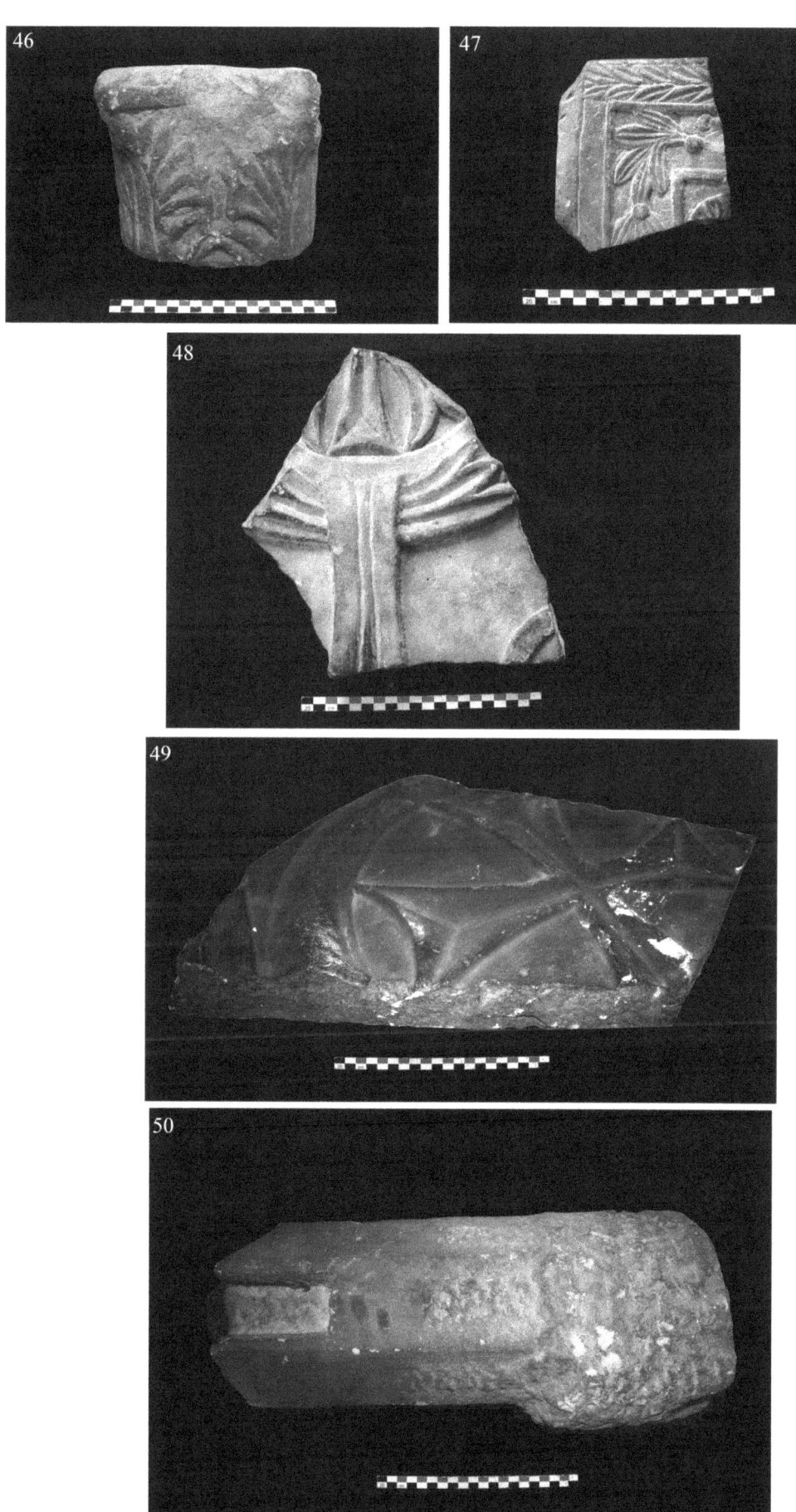

Fig. 16.46-50 Stone artefacts in the the British Museum.

The capital (Inv. 1868 10.5.12) is slightly flared and is banded by four prickly acanthus leaves, folded under the four corners of the abacus. The tips of the leaves come together to create opposing spaces geometrically shaped in lozenge, rectangle and triangle (Figure 16.46). The capital is fragmentary and it is 21 cm high, the square top measures 24 x 23 cm and the bottom 24 cm in diameter. It shows characteristics typical of the Byzantine style.

Another decorative panel fragment is in marble with yellow veins (Inv. 1868 10.5.16), it measures 14 x 13 cm and 3.4 cm in thickness and it features leaves along two concentric frames and chisel marks on the opposite side (Figure 16.47).

Shell artefacts and red coral kept in the National Museum of Eritrea

Paribeni collected a remarkable number of shell artefacts, most belonging to the species *Conus* and *Cypraea*, usually cut on the back and drilled or shaped in the form of rings. Other species mentioned by Paribeni but not all observed in the present collection are: *mactra, fusus, utriculus, murex, rostellaria, arca, bulla, pecten, spondylus, tapes, patella, neverita, pyrula, dosinia, cardium* and *nautilius* (Paribeni 1907: 561), all species that are widely diffused in the Red Sea and Indian Ocean (Peter Dance 1993).

A concentration of *Cypraea* sp. shells was found associated with gold fragments and ornaments including crosses, rods and earrings in the room H of a group of buildings excavated in the north sector of the site. This discovery suggested to Paribeni that this area might have been a workshop for shell manufacturing (Paribeni 1909: 485-486). Two fragments of polished shell rings were found by Paribeni in a living area near the shore of the river Haddas, one also showing inscribed letters (Paribeni 1909: 519 and 490). Unfortunately, no evidence of an inscribed ring, mentioned by Paribeni in his report, has been found in the present collection of the National Museum of Eritrea.

Shells are not mentioned among exports from Adulis in any literary source but the local consumption of sea products among people inhabiting the Red Sea costs, is well attested. Shells might have been collected and worked only for local and regional use.

At present the collection includes over 50 shells showing modification marks made by firing pins and smoothing tools, polishing, apical and lateral percussions in order to make necklace beads, rings, pendants and other ornaments (Figure 17.1). Sixteen *Cypraea* sp. shells, show a lateral carved opening on the back typical of *Cypraea* sp. shell worked still now by African population to decorate leather and cloths and to make ornaments (Figure 17.2, lower line); five worked shell disks are of the *Conus* sp. shells and they show an apical piercing (Figure 17.3, on the right), eleven *Oliva* sp. shells have longitudinal piercing (Figure 17.2, middle line) and five shells of the *Naticidae* family show a piercing on the back probably made by percussion (Figure 17.2, upper line).

Twenty fragments of polished oyster type shell, 0.15-0.2 cm in thickness, two with tiny holes, were possibly part of a decoration or an inlay, typical of the Byzantine decorative tradition (Figure 17.3, in the center). Two fragments were possibly part respectively of a fine small vessel and a small spoon (Figure 17.3, on the left and on the right) perhaps found in the living area on the river Haddas shore (Paribeni 1907: 519) A similar spoon artefact has also been found at Meinarti in Nubia (Adams 2002, tav. 37f). The variety and fine manufacture of these objects suggest the importance that this production might have had at Adulis.

The collection also includes two small fragmentary branches of red coral (Figure 17.4). Paribeni mentions the finding of several coral branches in rooms B and E of the housing quarter on the Haddas shore associated with sponges (Paribeni 1907: 561-562). The provenance of the coral, whether local or from the Mediterranean, is uncertain although the intense color and good quality and condition of the specimen might suggest that it was imported from the Mediterranean.

This is not surprising if we consider the fact that Mediterranean coral was exported from Alexandria to India, where it was widely employed in jewelry and as decoration on various supports, already in the 2nd-1st century BC. Later on, Pliny mentions the availability of coral, probably of inferior quality, also in the Red Sea (XXXII, 21 4) probably because demand in India had increased. Part of the exportation of Mediterranean coral might have passed through the Red Sea following the main trade routes of the Roman period (De Romanis 2001). The anonymous author of the *Periplus Maris Erythraei* (Casson 1989: paragraph 28) mentions the imports of coral at Qane, in South Arabia, the final destination of which might have been India, but nothing is said about possible exports or imports of coral in Adulis.

Bone and ivory artefacts kept in the National Museum of Eritrea

Ivory and bone artefacts are very common finds in Adulis. Paribeni mentioned in his report the finding of a portion of elephant tusk, ten ivory disks for playing and some other small objects that unfortunately were not observed in the present collection (Paribeni 1907: 560-561). A complete elephant tusk was also found by Anfray in 1962 (Anfray 1981: 379) and not identified in the present museum collection.

The exportation of ivory and rhinoceros horns is mentioned in the sources. Rhinoceros horn was as a particularity of Adulis, as well as hippopotamus skin (Pliny the Elder *Naturalis Historia* 1982: VI.173) although to date skins, horns or horn artefacts have not yet been identified in archaeological contexts or in the museum collections.

Fig. 17.1-7 Shell, red coral, ivory and bone artefacts in the National Museum of Eritrea.

Ivory is mentioned among exports from Adulis by Pliny (*Naturalis Historia* VI.173). The anonymous author of the *Periplus Maris Erytraei* only states that at Ptolemais Theron a type of ivory similar to the Adulitan ivory was available (Casson 1989: 50-51). Ivory was certainly systematically exported from this region by sea to India, Persia, Himyar and Rome at the time of Cosmas Indicopleustes (*Christian Topography* XIm 33). In fact literary sources attest the disappearance of elephants from north-Africa in the 1st century AD (Scullard 1974), since then, the Roman Empire might have started to look for new sources of ivory further south, most likely in the Sudanese and Ethiopian-Eritrean lowlands, particularly in the 5th-6th century AD (Phillipson 2000: 483). Considering that ivory for exportation was available in large pieces, the finding of whole tusks and large portions at Adulis suggests that this was exported. The examination of the ivory objects from the Paribeni collection also suggests the existence of a local manufacture.

The collection includes fragments of a *pyxides* (Figure 17.5) and other unidentified small vessels and box fragments (Figures 17.5, 17.6 and 17.7) similar to those found at Aksum and locally manufactured. The lid of the *pyxides* shows the typical scrape marks due to the use of a scraper, also attested in other Aksumite contexts and called "Guidit scraper". This evidence suggests that ivory artefacts were worked locally and not imported (Phillipson 2000: 460-467).

An undetermined bone fragment is characterised by a decorative pattern of hearts similar to some 5th century AD decoration on Roman vessels (Hayes 1978: 246-248 figs. 44 p-q) (Figure 17.8).

Conclusion

Adulis was the gateway for the most crucial cultural innovations to occur in the northern Horn of Africa during antiquity if we consider the contribution of cultural exchanges with South Arabia and the introduction of Christianity to the development of a sense of political unity in the region. The complexity of the Adulitan involvement in the Red Sea and Indian Ocean trade and the impact that trade contacts had on the rest of the inland territory is far from being completely tracked; the potential for archaeological investigation in this area is still enormous, with plenty of implications for the African and Red Sea maritime archaeology and history.

The regional autonomy of Adulis and the Eritrean coast from the Aksumite kingdom in the earlier phases, is a reality, as transpires from both literary and more recent archaeological evidence. The maritime component of the ancient Eritrean coastal people is an aspect that should no longer be neglected, and needs to be investigated also in its ethnographic and linguistic manifestations and in relation to the agro-pastoral component of the highland settlement culture.

The type of interaction between Adulis and the rest of the coastal regions and Aksum has been so far only hypothesized: future archaeological investigations need to be conducted in key areas identified in this book on the Eritrean coast and on the eastern lowlands.

So far it has not been possible to precisely locate all place-names mentioned in the ancient sources, presumably to be identified with locations situated on the Eritrean coast south of Massawa. The contribution that travellers' accounts and colonial exploration gave to the European environmental and cultural knowledge of the ancient and present coast of Eritrea are still the only source of reference for starting new archaeological investigations in the area. Archaeological and environmental evidence attests the presence of several harbours and coastal areas that are probably to be identified with the settlements mentioned in the sources as elephant-hunting stations, watchtowers, fortifications and harbours. The comparative analysis of archaeological evidence, historical sources and environmental characteristics has shown a certain connection among inland sources of ivory, obsidian, volcanos, salt and the bays, as well as a connection between marine resources available on the islands and coastal sites. This analysis has suggested the existence of an intense regional interconnectivity in the past on the Eritrean coast. Small harbours may have been trading posts for products coming from volcanic areas and salt plains that were otherwise not easy to reach, while navigational routes were probably more convenient than overland routes. The desert and maritime routes, as well as caravan routes to the interior, have to be tracked though archaeological surveys. Archaeological evidence in key coastal settlements such as those identified in the region around Raheita, in souther Eritrea, has to be systematically investigated.

Among the most interesting aspects of southern Red Sea archaeology are the various systems of water storage installations adopted over a long period of time and, in some cases, still in use today. These are among the most important ancient technological advances recorded so far in the region and are still essential elements for local subsistence. An understanding of their functioning can help to improve the present management of modern and ancient water storage systems, all too often rendered useless by the inability to maintain them. A future systematic investigation of the Dahlak islands water storage systems and of the other structures located in the region, allied to a programme of consolidation and conservation, might help to improve the present management of water resources in the region and the quality of life for people inhabiting these arid lands.

The analysis of the Adulis collections of materials has suggested new interpretations of the origin, different phases and end of the Red Sea international trade and related flourishing of the town. These materials have also provided information on the region's ancient occupation, the local economy and strategies of subsistence.

According to Paribeni, who conducted the more extensive excavation in Adulis, the site underwent to four occupation phases: the so-called pre-Ptolemaic period, the Greco-Roman Pagan period, the early Christian period followed by an interruption and a reprise (Paribeni 1907: 565). This analysis has been revised on the basis of the author's re-examination of the finds.

Very little is still known about the site of Adulis before the 1st century AD. The black-grey ware pottery seems to be representative of the most ancient phase of occupation at Adulis, although the suggested dating to the 2nd-1st millennium BC for this pottery is still under discussion. Pottery recently found at Adulis seems to provide firmer stratigraphic evidence that the site was occupied much earlier than previously suggested, perhaps in the 2nd-1st millennium BC, and that it was involved in the circuit of exchange linking Egypt, Sudan and South Arabia. If confirmed by further excavation and ceramic analysis, this would be not only relevant for a first outline of the absolute chronology of the Adulitan ceramic tradition, but it will also show that since the very beginning of its history Adulis played a crucial part both in the Red Sea dynamics and as a gateway to the highlands (Zazzaro and Manzo 2012: 238).

The presence of a South Arabian alabaster lid that the author was able to recognize in the Paribeni collection of the National Museum of Eritrea seems to demonstrate that the site had contact with the opposite coast at least from the 3rd century BC according to comparison with similar objects found in South Arabia (Zazzaro 2009, 50 fig. 6.1). Other findings like an unguentarium, an opaque glass fragment and a glass scarab respectively described and depicted in Paribeni's report could be imported from Egypt and date from the Hellenistic period or before (Paribeni 1907: 450). Unfortunately, no trace of the Egyptian-type scarab described by Paribeni has been found in the present museum collection in Asmara. Vessels ascribed to the proto-Aksumite tradition (ca. 400 – 50/40 BC) also provide material evidence that the site was inhabited in the early centuries BC. All these data call into question the hypothesis that the Ptolemy the 3rd inscription copied by Cosmas Indicopleustes at Adulis was originally brought from somewhere else in the region (Krebs 1969: 168-169; Desanges 1978: 85) and support the hypothesis that a settlement existed at Adulis also during the Hellenistic period.

According to recent excavation work conducted at the site, an early building phase might be dated to the 2nd-4th century AD, while the latest and the most evident on the site surface can be ascribed to a second flourishing period dating to the 5th-7th century AD (Adulis Fieldwork Report 2012, unpublished). Imported pottery and glass identified in the museum collections also attest the level of intense trade activity of Adulis with the Mediterranean, especially in the 5th-7th century AD. Although statistical analysis cannot be applied to such a collection of materials. Analysis of the imported artefacts and their find context on the basis of written excavation reports suggests that the town might have experienced two main peaks of trade contacts with two different Mediterranean areas.

Imported materials dating to the 4th-5th century AD are mainly from north Africa. In fact the African Red Slip and sigillata ware, present in the collection, date from between the second half of the 4th and early 5th century AD, while imported materials dating to the 5th – 7th century AD are prevalently from the Eastern Mediterranean and only in part from north Africa. The amphora lids and the Saint Menas ampoules may suggest a close connection with the centres of monasticism of the Egyptian Eastern Desert and north Egypt. This seems to be consistent with the trend of imports prevalently from the Eastern Mediterranean attested at Aksum in the same period (Manzo 1996). The presence of the examined early Byzantine style marble chancel posts, panels, screens, capital and architrave fragments, also present in the collection, suggests that Adulitan churches were provided with marble liturgical furnishing imported from the Eastern Mediterranean (Heldman 1994: 243-244). Further, the building technique of Adulitan churches is typical of the region but the internal repartition consisting in a presbytery divided by a screen and a tripartite plan is typical of the Eastern Church tradition.

Among imported finds of the collections are also sherds comparable to pottery from the Sudanese sites of Ballana and Qustul and from the Egyptian Eastern Desert which suggests the existence of contacts also with inland people from nearby regions outside the northern Horn of Africa.

Interestingly, nothing comparable to the highland ceramics dating to the late 1st-early 2nd millennium AD was present in the collection, confirming that at that time the town was abandoned (Anfray 1974). The presence of almost complete vessels of an unidentified pottery tradition, at the surface levels, though, might suggest that the site was visited after its sudden abandonment, possibly by local people or by the Arab people that took over the Red Sea trade in the 8th century AD. After being abandoned, the site was reused as an Islamic cemetery only in recent times.

The presence of Aksumite-style pottery in the collection and in the assemblages from recent excavations needs to be clarified through further studies on ware composition in order to determine whether a local production of Aksumite-style pottery might have existed at Adulis or whether this type of pottery was imported from the highlands. These studies will better clarify the nature of the relationship among these two regions.

Fine artefacts such as ivory pyxides, shell bracelets and rings, bronze decorative elements and vessels, attest the presence of an intense local manufacture. In this regard, Paribeni identified in some excavated layers possible evidence of a manufacturing area for gold and shells. Such an intense production was probably designed both for trade and for exportation by sea although it is not clearly mentioned by ancient literary sources. The metal and ivory manufacture and production can be compared to the one attested on the highlands while the shells manufacturing seems to be a locally developed skill. Shells might have had an important part in the economy of coastal people both for subsistence and as exported products. Mother of pearl it is not mentioned among exported products but it was possibly employed as part of boxes inlay and jewellery decoration which might have traveled as goods and gifts.

Archaeological sites and materials described in this book intended to provide sufficient basis and an effective contribution to further studies. A long term continuation of archaeological research at Adulis is more than desirable both for local scholars engaged in the enhancement of their archaeological heritage and historical identity and for international scholars interested in the study of ancient interconnectivity among Africa, the Mediterranean and the East.

Bibliography

Primary Sources

Acta Sanctorum 1869. *Martyrium Sancti Arethae et sociorum In Civitate Negran Caput VII*, Acta Sanctorum, Octobris, Tomus Decimus, Pariis et Romae.

Antinori, O., M. Bonati (ed.) 2000. *Viaggio nei Bogos*. Perugia.

Bausi, A. and A. Gori, (ed. and tr.) 2006. *Tradizioni Orientali del "Martirio di Areta". La prima recensione araba e la versione etiopica. Edizione critica e traduzione.* Quaderni di Semitistica 27. Firenze: Dipartimento di Linguistica, Università di Firenze.

Cosmas Indicopleustes, W. Wolska-Conus (ed. and tr.) 1968. *La Topographie Chrétienne*, Paris: Editions du CERF.

Photius, R. Henry (ed.) 1974. *Bibliothéque VII*. Paris.

Periplus Maris Erythraei, L. Casson (ed. and tr.) 1989. *The Periplus Maris Erythraei. Text with introduction, translation and commentary.* Princeton: Princeton University Press.

Periplus Maris Erythraei, G.W.B. Huntingford (ed. and transl.) 1980. *The Periplus of the Erythraean Sea*. Hakluyt Society.

Gaio Plinio Secondo, G. B. Conte (ed.) 1982. *Storia Naturale*. Torino: Giulio Enaudi Editore.

Procopius, H. B. Dewing (tr.) 1954. *History of the Wars* I. London: W. Heinemann.

Strabo, H. L. Jones (tr. and ed.) 1960. *Geography*. London: William Heinemann.

Secondary Sources

Acton, R. 1868. The Abyssinia Expedition and the Life and Reign of King Theodore, in *The Illustrated London News*. London.

Adams, W.Y. 2000. *Meinrati I. The Late Meroitic, Ballana and Transitional Occupation*. London.

Adams, W.Y. 2002. *Meinrati III. The Late and Terminal Christian Phases*. London.

Adulis Fieldwork Report 2011 (unpublished report). The National Museum of Eritrea (ed.).

Adulis Fieldwork Report 2011 (unpublished report). Ce.R.D.O (ed.).

Adulis Fieldwork Report 2012 (unpublished report). Ce.R.D.O (ed.).

Agius, A., Cooper, J. and Zazzaro, C. 2009. *Fieldwork in the Republic of Djibouti*. http://projects.exeter.ac.uk/mares/FieldworkDjibouti.htm.

Alpozen, T. O., Ozdas, A. H., Berkaya, B. 1995. *Commercial Amphoras of the Bodrum Museum of Undewater Archaeology*. Bodrum.

Anfray, F. 1963a. La première campagne de fouille à Maṭarā près de Sénafé, in *Annales d'Ethiopie* 5: 87-166.

Anfray, F. 1963b. Une campagne de fouille à Yēhā, in *Annales d'Ethiopie* 5: 171-234.

Anfray, F. 1965. Le musée archéologique d'Asmara, in *Rassegna di Studi Etiopici* 21: 5-15.

Anfray, F. 1966. La poterie de Maṭarā, in *Rassegna di Studi Etiopici* 23: 5-74.

Anfray, F. 1967. Maṭarā, *Annales d'Ethiopie* 7: 33-88.

Anfray, F. 1970. Notes Archéologiques, in *Annales d'Ethiopie* 8: 31-53.

Anfray, F. 1974. Deux villes axoumites: Adoulis et Maṭarā, in *IV Congresso Internazionale di Studi Etiopici*, 1: 745-765. Roma.

Anfray, F. 1981. The Civilization of Aksum from the First to Seventh Century, in G. Mokhtar (ed.) *General History of Africa I: Ancient Civilizations of Africa*, pp. 362-380.

Anfray, F. and Annequin, G. 1965. Maṭarā. Deuxième, troisième et quatrième campagne de fouille, in *Annales d'Ethiopie* 6: 49-86.

Anfray, F. 2003. Navigation en Mer Rouge dans les temps anciens, in *Massawa et la Mer Rouge*, Paris 2003.

Antonaras, A. 2008. *Glass Lamps of the Roman and Early Christian Periods. Evidence from the Thessaloniki Area*, in *Zalau, Clui-Napoca (ed.) Lychological Acts 2. Acts of the 2nd International Study Congress on Antique Lighting*. Editura Mega.

Anzani, A. 1928-1929. Numismatica e Storia d'Etiopia, estratto da *Rivista Italiana di Numismatica*, 5-6, S 3.

Arena, M. S. *et al.* (ed.) 2001. *Roma: Dall'Antichità al Medioevo: Archeologia e storia nel Museo Nazionale Romano Cripta Balbi*. Milano.

Arslan, E. A. 1996. Monete axumite di imitazione nel deposito del cortile della sinagoga di Cafarnao, in *Liber Annus* 46: 307-316.

Ballet, R. 2001. Céramique hellénistiques et romaines d'Égypte, in P. Lévêque e J.P. Morel (eds) *Céramique Hellénistiques et Romaines* III: 105-144. Paris.

Baldry, J. 1978. Foreign Interventions and Occupation of Kamaran Island, in *Arabian Studies* 4: 89-111.

Bard, K. A. 1997. *The Environmental History and Human Ecology of Northern Ethiopia in the Late Holocene*. Napoli.

Barkay, R. 1981. An Axumite Coin from Jerusalem, in *Israel Numismatic Journal* 5: 57-59.

Barthoux, J. 2007. Recherches en mer Rouge méridionale (1961-1962): ports ptolémaïques et terrains de chasse, in *Pount* 1: 47-87.

Bass, G. A. 1972. *History of Seafaring and underwater archaeology: based on underwater archaeology*. London.

Beeston, A. F. L. 1985. Two Bi'r Ḥimā Inscriptions Re-Examined, in *Bulletin of the School of Oriental and African Studies, University of London* 48.1: 42-52.

Beeston, A. F. L. 1989. The Chain of al-Mandab, in *On both sides of al-Mandab. Ethiopian, South-Arabic and Islamic Studies presented to Oscar Lofgren on his nineteenth birthday, 13 May 1988, by colleagues and friends* 1-6. Istanbul: Swedish Research Institute in Istanbul.

Bendall, S. 1996. *Byzantine weights. An introduction*. London.

Bendall, S. 1987. A note on an Axumite coin from Jerusalem, in *International Numismatic Journal* 9: 17-20.

Bigliardi, G., Cappelli, S., Cocca, E. 2013. Tecnologie digitali integrate per lo studio del sito archeologico di Adulis (Eritrea), in *Archeologia e Calcolatori* 24.

Blanc, A. B. 1952. L'industrie sur obsidienne des îles Dahlac (Mer Rouge), in *Actes du II Congrès Panafricain de Préhistoire* pp. 355-347. Algiers.

Bliquez, L. J. 2003. Roman Surgical spoon probes and their ancient names, in *Journal of Roman Archaeology* 16: 322-330.

Blue, L. 2007. Locating the Harbour: Myos Hormos/Quseir al-Qadim: a Roman and Islamic Port on the Red Sea Coast of Egypt, in *The International Journal of Nautical Archaeology* 36.2: 265-281.

Bloss, J. F. E. 1936. The History of Suakin, in *Sudan Notes and Records* 19: 271-280.

Bossert, H. Th. 1951. *Altsyrien*, Tubinga.

Bresson, A. 1991. Les cite grecques et leur emporia, in A. Bresson and P. Rouillard (eds) *L'Emporion*. Centre Pierre: Paris.

Bruce, J. 1790. *Travels to Discover the Source of the Nile, in the Years 1768, 1769, 1770, 1771, 1772, and 1773*. 5 vols. Edinburgh: G.G.J. and J. Robinson.

Bruyère, B. 1930-1932. *Fouille de Clysma-Qolozoum (Suez)*. Le Caire.

Buffa, V. 2007. *Malayba et l'Âge du Bronze du Yémen, Archäologische Berichte aus dem Yemen*, 12. Wiesbaden: Reichert Verlag.

Bury, J. B. 1958. *History of the Later Roman Empire*, New York: Dover Publications Inc.

Butzer, K. W. 1981. Rise and fall of Aksum, Ethiopia: a geo-archaeological interpretation, in *American Antiquity* 46 – 3: 472-495.

Cerulli, E. 1933. Vestigia di Antiche Civiltà. *La Rassegna Italiana* 184-185: 152-156.

Chittick, N. 1976. An Archeological Reconnaissance in the Horn: the British–Somali Expedition, 1975, in *Azania* 11: 117-139.

Chittick, H. N. 1981. A cistern in Suakin and some remark on burnt bricks, in *Azania* 16: 181-183.

Comstock, M. and Vermeule, C. 1971. *Greek, Etruscan and Roman Bronzes in the Museum of Fine Arts*. Boston.

de Contenson, H. 1961. Les fouilles à Haoulti-Melazo en 1958, in *Annales d'Ethiopie* 4: 39-60.

de Contenson, H. 1963a. Les fouilles de Haoulti en 1959, in *Annales d'Ethiopie* 5: 41-86.

de Contenson, H. 1963b. Les fouilles à Axoum en 1958, in *Annales d'Ethiopie* 5: 1-40.

Conti Rossini, C. 1900. Ricerche e Studi sull'Etiopia, in *Bollettino della Società Geografica Italiana* 37.2: 104-120.

Conti Rossini, C. 1922. Antiche rovine sulle Rore eritree, in *Rendiconti della Reale Accademia Nazionale dei Lincei* 31: 291-298.

Conti Rossini, C. 1944-1945. Pubblicazioni Etiopistiche dal 1936 al 1945, in *Rassegna di Studi Etiopici* 4: 1-132.

Cremaschi, M., D'Alessandro A., Fattovich, R. & Piperno M. 1985. Gash Delta Archaeological Project: 1985 Field Season, in *Nyame akuma* 27: 45-48.

Cressey, G. B. 1958. Qanats, Karez, and Foggaras, in *The Geographical Review*, 48: 27-44.

Crowfoot, J. W. 1911. Some Red Sea ports in the Anglo-egyptian Sudan, in *Geographical Journal* 37.5: 523-550.

D'Abbadie, A. 1868. *Douze ans de séjour dans la Haute Ethiopie (Abyssinie)*. Paris 1868.

Dainelli, G. and Marinelli, O. 1912. *Risultati di un viaggio nella Colonia Eritrea*. Roma.

Davidde B. and Petriaggi, R. 1996. Prospezioni subacquee nella regione del Dhofar, in *Egitto e Vicino Oriente Antico* 19: 212-216.

De Amezaga, C. 1880. Assab, in *Bollettino della Società Geografica Italiana* 8: 1-57.

Department of Statistics and Documentation of Northern Red Sea, 06/09/2008.

De Romanis, F. 1996. *Cassia, cinnamomo, ossidiana. Uomini e merci tra Mediterraneo e oceano Indiano*. Roma 1996.

De Romanis, F. 2001. Esportazioni di corallo mediterraneo in India nell'età ellenistico romana. Redazione Archaeogate, 23-09-2001. http://www.archaeogate.org/subacquea/article/84/2/esportazioni-di-corallo-mediterraneo-in-india-nelleta-e.html

Desanges, H. 1978. Enquêtes and Découvertes d'Obok à Doumeira, in *Annales d'Ethiopie* 11: 75-82.

Desanges, J. and Reddé, M. 1994. La côte africaine du Bab el-Mandeb dans l'antiquité, in *Hommage à Jean Leclant, Etudes Isiaques* 3, *Bibliothèque d'étude* 106/3: 161-195.

De Spagnoli, M. and De Carolis, E. 1983. *Museo Nazionale Romano. I Bronzi. Le Lucerne* 4.1. Roma.

Dunn, R. E. 1986. *The Adventures of Ibn Battuta. A Muslim Traveler of the 14th century*. Berkeley.

E.A.A. 1985. *Enciclopedia dell'arte antica classica e orientale: Atlante delle forme ceramiche, diretta da Giovanni Pugliese Carratelli*. Roma.

Egloff, M. 1977. *Kellia. La Poterie Copte*. Geneve.

Emery, W. B. and Kirwan, L. P. 1938. *The Royal Tombs of Ballana and Qustul*. Cairo.

Fattovich, R. 1992. Lineamenti di storia dell'archeologia dell'Etiopia e della Somalia, 72, in *Annali dell'Istituto Universitario Orientale* 52.2. Napoli: I.U.O.

Fattovich, R. 1995. L'archeologia del Mar Rosso: problemi e prospettive, in *Annali dell'Istituto Universitario Orientale* 55.2: 158-176. Napoli: I.U.O.

Fattovich, R. 1996. The Afro-Arabian circuit: contacts between the Horn of Africa and southern Arabia in the 3rd-2nd millennia BC, in *Interregional contacts in the later prehistory of Northeastern Africa*, pp. 395-402. Poznan.

Fattovich, R. 1997. The Contacts between southern Arabia and the Horn of Africa in the Late Prehistoric and Early Historical Times: a view from Africa, in A. Avanzini (ed.) *Profumi d'Arabia: atti del convegno*, Roma: L'Erma di Bretschineider, pp. 273-286.

Fattovich, R. 2007. Aqiq: a coastal site in the Red sea, Sudan, in B. Gratien (ed.) *Mélanges offerts à Francis Geus. Égypte-Soudan*, pp. 87-97.

Fattovich, R., Bard, K. et al. 2000. *The Aksum archaeological area: A preliminary assessment.* Napoli: Centro Interdipartimentale di Servizi per l'Archeologia.

Fattovich, R., 2013. The Northern Horn of Africa in the First Millennium BCE: Local Traditions and External Connections, in *Rassegna di Studi Etiopici* 4: 1-60.

Fleming, S. J. 1997. Later Roman Glass at the University of Pennsylvania Museum: A Photo Essay, in *Expedition* 39.2: 25-41.

Franchini, V. 1953. Stazioni litiche di superficie in Eritrea, in *Il Bollettino* 1: 25-30. Asmara.

Franchini, V. 1957. Notizie Varie, in *Il Bollettino* 2: 47-51. Asmara.

Franchini, V. 1963. Riordinamento del Museo della Biblioteca Italiana di Asmara, in *Il Bollettino* 3: 67. Asmara.

Gabriel, G. 1953. Il Museo Archeologico di Asmara, in *Il Bollettino* 1: 13-16. Asmara.

Gallina, F. and Paribeni, R. 1907. La missione archeologica in Eritrea, in *Bollettino Ufficiale della Colonia Eritrea* 16.19: 90-92 (reprint in *Bollettino della Società Africana d'Italia)*.

Gascoigne, A. L. 2007 Amphorae from Old Cairo: a preliminary note, in *Cahiers de la Céramique Égyptienne* 8.1: 161-174.

Gautier, J. 1976. Etude de poterie provenant d'Ethiopie (periodes pre-axoumite et axoumite) effectué par le laboratoire de recherche des Musées de France, in *Annales d'Ethiopie* 10: 57-69.

Glover, J. C.1996. Contacts between India and Southeast Asia, in H. P. Ray and J-F. Salles (eds) *Tradition and Archaeology. Early Maritime Contanct in the Indian Ocean, Proceedings of the International Seminar Techno-Archaeological Perspectives of Seafaring in the Indian Ocean 4th cent. BC 15th cent. AD. New Delhi, Feb. 28-March 4, 1994*, pp. 129-158. Lyon/New Delhi.

Guida AOI 1938. Consociazione Turistica Italiana, *Guida dell'Africa Orientale Italiana.* Milano.

Gupta, S.P., Dalal, K.F., Dandekar, A., Mitra, R., Nanji, P., Pandey, R. 2002. A Preliminary Report on the Excavations at Sanjan, in *Puratattva* 32: 182-198.

Gutherz, X., Joussaume, R., Amblard, S. and Mohammed, G. (in collaboration with Bonnefille, R., Duday, H., Gouraud, G., Thiebault, S., Thiam, I., El Hadji, and Van Neer, W.) 1996. Le site d'Asa Koma (République de Djibouti) et les premiers producteurs dans la corne de l'Afrique, in *Journal des africanistes* 66: 255-297.

Hassell, J. 1997. Alabaster Beehive-Shaped Vessels from the Arabian Penisula: Interpretations from a Comparative Study of Characteristics, Contexts and Associated Finds, in *Arabian Archaeology and Epigraphy* 8: 245-281.

Hayes, J. W. 1972. *Late Roman Pottery.* London: British School at Rome.

Hayes, J. W. 1996. The Pottery, in S. E. Sidebotham-W. Z. Wendrich *Berenike '95 Preliminary Report of the Excavations at Berenike (Egyptian Red Sea Coast) and the Survey of the Eastern Desert*, pp. 147-178. Leiden.

Hebbert, H. E. 1936. El-Rih – a Red Sea Island, in *Sudan Notes and Records* 19: 306-313.

Hein, C.J., FitzGerald, D., Bard, K.A., Fattovich, R., and Zazzaro, C. 2008. *Geological Investigations of a Middle Kingdom Harbor: Wadi Gawasis, Egypt*, in Geological Society of America Abstracts with programs 40.6: 384.

Heldman, M. E. 1994. Early Byzantine Sculptural Fragments from Adulis, in *Etudes Ethiopiennes* 1: 239-259.

Heuglin, Th. Von 1877. *Reise in Nordost-Afrika.* Brunswick.

Holland, T. J. and Hozier, H. M. 1870. *Record of the Expedition to Abyssinia.* London.

Hourani, G. F. 1995. *Arab Seafaring in the Indian Ocean in Ancient and Early Medieval Times.* Beirut.

Hunter, J. R. 1994. Maritime Culture: notes from the land, in *The International Journal of Nautical Archaeology* 23.4: 261-264.

Huningford, G.B.W. 1989. *The Historical Geography of the Ethiopia. From the First Century AD to 1704.* New York.

Illustrazione Italiana 1923. L'inaugurazione del Museo Coloniale a Roma, in *Illustrazione Italiana* 46, 18 November 1923.

Insoll, T. 1997. An Archaeological Reconnaissance Made to Dahlak Kebir, the Dahlak Island, Eritrea: Preliminary Observations, in *Papers of the XIIIth International Conference of Ethiopian Studies, Kyoto 12-17 December 1997*, pp. 382-388. Kyoto.

Insoll, T. 2001. Dahlak Kebir, Eritrea: From Aksumite to Ottoman, in *Adumatu* 3: 39-50.

Isings, C. 1957. *Roman Glass.* Groningen/Djakarta.

Isings, C. 1971. *Roman Glass in Limburg.* Groningen.

Issel, A. 1885. *Viaggio nel Mar Rosso e tra i Bogos.* Milano.

Jackson, R. 1990. Roman doctors and their instruments: recent research into ancient practice, in *Journal of Roman Archaeology* 3: 5-27.

Kapitän, G. 1980. Elementi architettonici per una basilica dal relitto navale del VI secolo di Marzamemi (Siracusa), *Università degli Studi di Bologna Istituto di Antichità Ravennati e Bizantine* 27: 71-136.

Kapitän, G. 1969. The Church Wreck off Marzamemi, in *Archaeology* 22.2: 122-123.

Karein Osman, R. A. and Sidebotham, S. E. 2000. Geomorphology and archaeology of the central Eastern Desert of Egypt, in *Sahara* 12: 7-30.

Kasser, R. 1983. *Survey Archéologique des Kellia (Basse-Egypte). Rapport de la campagne 1981*, fascicule II.

Kawatoko, M. 1993. *Preliminary Survey of 'Aidhab and Badi' Sites, in Kush 16*.

Kazhdan, A. P. (ed.) 1991. *The Oxford Dictionary of Byzantium*. New York: Oxford University Press.

Khouri, G. and Whitcomb, D. 1992. *Petra, Wadi Ramm, Aqaba*. Amman.

Kingsley, S. 2004. *Encyclopedia of Underwater Archaeology. Barbarian Sea. Late Roman to Islam.* Periplus: London.

Kirwan, L. P. 1972. The Christian Topography and the Kingdom of Aksum, in *Geographical Journal* 138: 167.

Kiss, Z. 1973 Les amphores de St. Ménas découvertes à Kôm-el-Dikka (Alexandrie) en 1969 in *Études et Travaux* VII, tomo 14, 1973, pp. 137-154

Kobischanov, Yu. M. 1965. On the problem of sea voyages of ancient Africans in the India Ocean, in *Journal of African History* 6.

Kobischanov, Yu. M. 1966. The sea voyages of ancient Ethiopians in the Indian Ocean, in *Proceedings of The Third International Conference of the Ethiopian Studies, Addis Ababa 1966*, pp. 19-23.

Krebs, Von W. 1969. Adulis – ein antiker Hafen am Roten Meer, in *Altertum* 15: 162-169.

Kuzmanov, G. 1973. Tipologiya i Kronologiya na Rannovizantiyskite Amfori (IV, VI, V), in *Arkheologiya* 1: 14-21.

Labrousse, H. 1978. Enquêtes et découvertes d'Obock à Doumeira, in *Annales d'Ethiopie* 11: 75-82.

Lanzoni, A. 1920. Escursione nel Marghebla, in *Bollettino della Società Geografica Italiana* 9: 249-258

Lapage, C. 1973. Recherches sur l'art chrétien d'Ethiopie du X au XV s. Résultats et perspectives, in *Abbay* 4: 39-58.

Leclant, J. 1959. Les fouilles à Axoum en 1955-1956. Rapport préliminaire, in *Annales d'Ethiopie* 3: 3-23.

Leclant, J. and Miquel, A. 1959. Reconnaissances dans l'Agané: Goulo-Makeda et Sabéa, in *Annales d'Ethiopie*, 3: 107-130.

Lefebvre, T. 1845. 1839-1843. *Voyage en Abyssina*. Paris.

Lejean, G. 1865. Le Sennaheit, souvenir d'un voyage dans le désert nubien, in *Revue des Deux Mondes* 35: 744-752 and 77-83.

Mallinson, M. 2004. Suakin 2003/2004, in *Sudan and Nubia* 8: 90-94.

Mancini, E. 1908. Gli avanzi antichi dell'antica Adulis. Scavi e scoperte archeologiche nella colonia Eritrea, in *Illustrazione Italiana,* 30 agosto 1908, pp. 206-20.

Manzo, A. 1995. Breve notizia su un viaggio di studio in Eritrea, in *Rassegna di Studi Etiopici* 37: 115-134.

Manzo, A. 1996a. Culture e ambiente: l'Africa nord-orientale nei dati archeologici e nella letteratura geografica ellenistica, in *Annali dell'Istituto Orientale di Napoli* 56: 87.2. Napoli: I.U.O.

Manzo, A. 1996b. Progress Report on the Imported Ceramics and Glass from Bieta Giyorgis (Aksum, Ethiopia), in *8th Biennial Conference of Africanist Archaeologists*. Poznan.

Manzo, A. 1998. *Ancora su Aksum e Meroe: Riconsiderazione di alcune evidenze dalla Necropoli di Mai Heggià e del loro significato*. Centro Studi Archeologia Africana, pp. 44-54.

Manzo, A. 2002. Note su alcuni oggetti sudarabici rinvenuti in Etiopia, in *Rassegna di Studi Etiopici* 42: 45-61.

Manzo, A. 2003a. Note sulla più antica fase archeologica aksumita, in *Rassegna di Studi Etiopici* 43: pp. 37-50.

Manzo, A. 2003b. Skeumorphism in Aksumite Pottery? Remark on the Origins and Meanings of some Ceramic Types, in *Aethiopica* 6: 7-46.

Manzo, A. 2005. Aksumite Trade and Red Sea Exchange Network: A View from Bieta Giyorgis (Aksum), in J. C. M. Starkey (ed.) *People of the Red Sea. Proceedings of Red Sea Project II. Held in the British Museum, October 2004*, pp. 51-66. Oxford: BAR Publishing.

Manzo, A. 2010. Exotic Ceramic Materials from Mersa Gawasis, Red Sea, Egypt. In W. Godlewski and A. Łatjar (eds), in *Between the Cataracts. Proceedings of the 11th Conference of Nubian Studies*, Part 2.2, *Polish Archaeology in the Mediterranean Supplement Series*. Warsaw: Polish Centre of Mediterranean Archaeology – University of Warsaw, 439-453.

Manzo, A. 2012. Nubians and the others on the Red Sea. An Update on the Exotic Ceramic Materials from the Middle Kingdom harbour of Mersa/Wadi Gawasis, Red Sea, Egypt. In D.A. Agius, J.P. Cooper, C. Zazzaro, *Red Sea Project V: Navigated spaces, connected places. Proceedings of the Red Sea Project V*, held in the University of Exeter, September 2010. Society for Arabian Studies Monographs, BAR International Series. Oxford: BAR Publishing.

Mapunda, B.B. 1997. Patching Up Evidence for Ironworking in the Horn, in *African Archaeological Review* 4.2: 107-124.

Marini, A. 1903. Colonia Eritrea. Escursione lungo le coste settentrionali della penisola di Buri e isole adiacenti, in *Bollettino della Società Geografica Italiana* 60: 374-400.

Markham, C. R. 1869. *A history of the Abyssinian Expedition*. London.

Margariti, R. 2002. *Like the Place of Congregation on Judgment Day: Maritime Trade and Urban Organization in Medieval Aden, ca. 1080-1229*. Ph.D. Dissertation Princeton University.

Martin de, S. M. V. 1863. Eclaircissement géographiques et historiques sur l'inscription d'Adoulis et sur quelques points des inscriptions d'Axoum, in *Journal Asiatique* 2: 337.

Meshorer, Y. 1966. An Axumite Coin from Cesarea, in *Israel Numismatic Journal* 3: 32-36.

Monneret de Villard, U. 1937-38. Note sulle influenze asiatiche nell'Africa Orientale, in *Rivista degli Studi Orientali 17.4:* 303-349.

Monneret de Villard, U. 1947. Mosè vescovo di Adulis, in *Orientalia Christiana Periodica* 13: 613-623.

Mordini, A. 1960. Gli aurei di Kushana del convento di Debra Damo, in *Atti del Convegno Internazionale di Studi Etiopici, Roma 1959*, pp. 253-267.

Morrison, H. M. 1989. The Beads, in Munro-Hay (ed.) *Excavation at Aksum*. London: British Institute in Eastern Africa, pp. 168-178.

Morrison, H. M. 1989. The Glass, in Munro-Hay (ed.) *Excavation at Aksum*. London: British Institute in Eastern Africa, pp. 188-209.

Munro-Hay, S. 1982. The foreign trade of the Aksumite port of Adulis, in *Azania* 17: 107-125.

Munro-Hay, S. 1989. *Excavation at Aksum*. London: British Institute in Eastern Africa.

Munro-Hay, S. 1991a. Aksumite overseas interests, in *Northeast African Studies* 13.2-3: 127-140.

Munro-Hay, S. 1991b. *Aksum: An African Civilisation of Late Antiquity*. [put online with permission by Alan Light, <alight@vnet.net>].

Munro-Hay, S. and Yuel-Jensen B. 1995. *Aksumite Coinage*. London.

Murray, G. W. 1926. 'Aidhab, in *Geographical Journal* 68: 235-240.

O'Mahoney, K. 1970. The Salt Trail, in *Journal of Ethiopian Studie* 8.2: 147-153.

Nappo, D. 2009. Roman Policy in the Red Sea between Anastasius and Justinian, in L. Blue, J. Cooper, R. Thomas and J. Whitewright (eds), *Connected Hinterlands: Proceedings of Red Sea IV, 25-26 September 2008*, pp. 71–77. Society for Arabian Studies Monographs 8; BAR International Series 2052. Oxford; BAR Publishing.

Odorizzi, D. 1911. *Colonia Eritrea: Il Commissariato Regionale di Massaua al 1° Gennaio 1910*. Asmara.

Oman, G. 1976. *La necropoli islamica di Dahlak Kebir.* Napoli.

Paribeni, R. 1907. Ricerche sul luogo dell'antica Adulis (Colonia Eritrea), in *Monumenti Antichi* 18: 437-572.

Peacock, D. and Blue, L. eds. 2007. *The Ancient Red Sea Port of Adulis, Eritrea Report of the Eritro-British Expedition, 2004-5.* Oxford: Oxbow Books.

Peacock D. and Peacock, A. 2007. The Enigma of 'Aydhab: a Medieval Islamic Port on the Red Sea Coast, in *The International Journal of Nautical Archaeology* 37.1: 32-48.

Pedersen, R. K. 2000. Under the Erythraean Sea: An Ancient Shipwreck in Eritrea, in *INA Quarterly* 27. 2/3: 3-12.

Pedersen, R. K. 2008. The Byzantine-Aksumite Period Shipwreck at Black Assarca Island, Eritrea, in *Azania* 63: 77-94.

Pedroni, L. 2000. Una collezione di monete aksumite. Catalogo. Analisi microchimiche di Guido Devoto, in *Bollettino di Numismatica* 28-29: 7-150.

Pelegrin, J. 2000. Les techniques de débitage laminaire au Tardiglaciaire: critères de diagnose et quelques réflexions, in B. Valentin, P. Bodu et M. Christensen (eds.), *L'Europe centrale et septentrionale au Tardiglaciaire. Confrontation des modèles régionaux de peuplement. Actes de la table-ronde de Nemours, mai 1997. Nemours, APRAIF, Mémoire du Musée de Préhistoire d'Ile-de-France* 7: 73-86.

Perlingieri, C. 1999 (unpublished). *La ceramica aksumita da Bieta Giyorgis, Aksum (Tigray, Etiopia). Tipologia ed implicazioni storico-culturali e socio-economiche*, PhD Thesis, Università degli Studi di Napoli "L'Orientale", Napoli 1999.

Peter Dance, S. 1993. *Conchiglie*. Milano: Fabbri.

Phillips, J. 2000a. Pottery and Other Clay Objects. In D.W. Phillipson, *Archaeology at Aksum, Ethiopia, 1993-7*. London: The Society of Antiquaries, 57-77.

Phillips, J. 2000b. The Pottery. In D.W. Phillipson, *Archaeology at Aksum, Ethiopia, 1993-7*. London: The Society of Antiquaries, 194-196.

Phillips, J. 2000c. The Pottery and Clay Objects. In D.W. Phillipson, *Archaeology at Aksum, Ethiopia, 1993-7*. London: The Society of Antiquaries, 303-337.

Phillipson, D. W. 1998. *Ancient Ethiopia*. London.

Phillipson, L. 2009. *Using stone tools: the Evidence from Aksum, Ethiopia*. British Archaeological Reports Series 1926 Oxford: BAR Publishing.

Phillipson, D. W. 2000. *Archaeology at Aksum*, London 2000.

Phillipson, D. W. 2011. *Foundations of an African Civilisation*: Aksum and the northern Horn, 1000 BC-AD 1300. Eastern Africa Series Woodbridge, Suffolk: James Currey.

Puglisi, G. 1953. Le cisterne di Dahlac Chebir e di Adal nell'arcipelago delle Dahlac, in *Il Bollettino* 1: 53-70. Asmara.

Puglisi, G. 1958. La necropoli di Dessèt el-Banaia ed una leggenda sul Cubbet es-Saladin, in *Il Bollettino* 2. Asmara.

Puglisi, G. 1969. Alcuni vestigi dell'isola Dahlac Chebir e la leggenda dei Furs, in *Proceedings of the Third International Congress of Ethiopian Studies, Addis Abeba*, pp. 35-47.

Rathjens, C., von Wissmann, H. 1932. Vorislamische Altertømer. Rathjens - v. Wissmannsche Sødarabien-Reise, Band 2. Hamburg: Hamburgische Universität - Abhandlungen aus dem Gebiet der Auslanskunde.

Ray, H.P. 1994. *The Wind of Change*. Kolkata.

Red Sea Pilot 1909. *The Red Sea and Gulf of Aden Pilot.* London: Printed for the Hydrographic Office Admiralty by Eyre & Spottiswoode, Ltd.

Red Sea and the Persian Gulf, published by the National Imagery and Mapping Agency, Bethesda, Maryland, 1997

Reinisch L. 1885. Zula (Adulis), una città scomparsa del Mar Rosso, in *Bollettino della Societa Geografica*

Italiana 10.1: 584-587.

Ricci, L. 1983. Museo Archeologico di Asmara, in *Istituto Italo Africano* 7. Roma.

De Rivoire, D. 1868. La baie d'Adulis et ses alentours. *Bulletin de la Société de Géographie* 15: 249-253.

Rodziewicz, M. 1976. Un quartier d'habitation gréco-romain à Kom el-Dikka, in *Études et Travaux* 9: 169-210.

Roubet, C. 1970. Prospection et découverte de documents préhistoriques en Dankalie (Ethiopie Septentrionale), in *Annales d'Ethiopie* 8: 13-20.

Rüppel, E. 1830-1840. *Reise in Abyssinien*. Frankfurt and Main.

Salles, J-F. and Sedov A. V. 2010. *Qāni'. Le port antique du Hadramawt entre la Meditrranee, l'Afrique et l'Inde. Fouilles rousses 1972, 1985-1989, 1991, 1993-1994*. Lyon: Brepols.

Salt, H. 1814. *A Voyage to Abyssinia and Travel into the interior of that country executed under the order of the British Government in the year 1809 and 1810*. London: W. Bulmer & Co.

Sapeto, G. 1857. *Viaggio e Missione Cattolica fra i Mensa, i Bogos gli Habab. Con un cenno geografico e storico dell'Abissinia*. Roma.

Sapeto, G. 1871. Ambasciata mandata nel 1869 dal Governo francese al Negussié Degiazmate del Tigré e del Samièn, in *Bollettino della Società Geografica Italiana* 6: 22-71.

Säve-Söderbergh, T. 1981. *Late Nubian Cemeteries*. Scandinavian University.

Sauter, R. 1957-1961 (unpublished manuscript). *Project d'article sur Adoulis (1957 déc.) remanié en 1961 (avril)*. Library of the Centre for African Studies in Asmara.

Schmidt, P.R., Curtis, M.C., Zelalem Teka 2008. *The Archaeology of Ancient Eritrea*. Trenton, NJ: Red Sea Press.

Schneider, M. 1983. *Stèles funéraires musulmanes des îles Dahlak (mer Rouge)*. Le Caire: Institut français d'archéologie orientale du Caire.

Sleeswyk, A.W. 1983. On the location of the land of Pwnt on two Renaissance maps, in *The International Journal of Nautical Archaeology* 12.4: 279-291.

Scullard, H.H. 1974. *The elephant in the Greek and Roman world*. London: Thames and Hudson.

Sedov, A. V. 1996. Qana (Yemen) and the Indian Ocean the archaeological evidence, in H. P. Rayand and J-F. Salles (eds) *Tradition and Archaeology. Early Maritime Contanct in the Indian Ocean, Proceedings of the International Seminar Techno-Archaeological Perspectives of Seafaring in the Indian Ocean 4th cent. B.C. – 15th cent. A.D. New Delhi, Feb. 28-March 4 1994*, pp. 11-35. Lyon/New Delhi.

Seeger, J.A., S.E. *Sidebotham*, J.A. *Harrell*, and *Pons*, M. 2006. A brief archaeological survey of the Aqiq Region (Red Sea Coast), Sudan, in *Sahara* 17: 7–18.

Seele, K. C. 1991. *Excavation between Abu Simbel and the Sudan Frontier*. Chicago.

Seguid, A. 2005 (unpublished report). *Adulis: An Ancient Port City, March 2005*. National Museum of Eritrea. Asmara.

Serjeant, R. B. 1969. South Arabia and Ethiopia – African elements in the South Arabian population, in *Proceedings of the Third International Congress of Ethiopian Studies, Addis Abeba*, pp. 35-47.

Shiferaou, A. 1955. Rapport sur la découverte d'antiquités trouvées dans les locaux du gouvernement général de Maqallé, in *Annales d'Ethiopie* 1: 13-15.

Sidebotham, S. E. 1987. Ports of the Red Sea and the Arabia-India Trade, in *L'Arabie prèislamique et son environnement historique et culturel*, pp. 195-223.

Sidebotham, S. E. 2002. Berenike 1999-2001, in *Sahara* 13.

Sidebotham, S. E. & Wendrich, W. Z. 1996. *Berenike '95 Preliminary Report of the Excavations at Berenike (Egyptian Red Sea Coast) and the Survey of the Eastern Desert*. Leiden: Research School CNWS.

Sidebotham, S. E. 2011. *Berenike and the Ancient Maritime Spice Route*. California World History Library, 18. Berkeley/Los Angeles/London: University of California Press.

Sternini, M. 1999. I vetri provenienti dagli scavi della missione italiana a Cartagine (1973-1977), in *Journal of Glass Studies* 41: 83-104.

Sundelin, L.K.R. *1996*. Plaster Jar Stoppers, in Sidebotham and Wendrich (eds) *Berenike ,95, Preliminary Report of the Excavations at Berenike (Egyptian Red Sea Coast) and the Survey of the and the Survey of the Eastern Desert*, pp. 297-308. Leiden: CNWS.

Sundström, R. 1907. Preliminary Report of the Princeton University Expedition to Abyssinia, in *Zeitschrift für Assyrologie* 20: 151-182.

Tedeschi, S. 1969. Note storiche sulle isole Dahlac, in *Proceedings of the Third International Congress of Ethiopian Studies*, pp. 49-57.

Thomas, R. I. and Tomber, R. S. 2006. Vessel stoppers. In *Survey and excavation, Mons Claudianus: Volume III ceramic vessels and related objects*, V. Maxfield & D. P. S. Peacock (eds.), pp. 239-60. Cairo: IFAO.

Todd, J.A. and Charles, J.A. 1978. Metallurgy as a contribution to archaeology in Ethiopia, in *Abbay* 9: 31-42.

Tomber, R. S. 2007. Aksumite Sherds from Berenike 1996-2000, in S. E. Sidebotham and W. Wendrich (eds) *Berenike 1999/2000. Report on the excavations at Berenike, including excavations in Wadi Kalalat and Siket, and the survey of the Mons Smaragdus region*, pp. 175-182. Cotsen Institute of Archaeology, University of California: Los Angeles.

Tringali, G. (1984) Orecchini in pietra ritrovati nella zona di Sembel Cuscet (Asmara), *Quaderni di Studi Etiopici* 5, 93-95.

Tringali, G. 1985-1986. Elenco commentato dei reperti archeologici custoditi nel museo del Collegio "La Salle" in Asmara, in *Quaderni di Studi Etiopici* 6-7: 143-157

Trucca, B. 1971 (unpublished manuscript). *Diario Archeologico*. Library of the Centre for African Studies in Asmara.

Uboldi, M. 1995. Diffusione delle lampade vitree in età tardo antica e alto medievale e spunti per una tipologia, in *Archeologia Medievale* 22: 93-145.

Ward, C. 2012. Ancient Egyptian Seafaring Ships Archaeological and Experimental Evidence, in *P. Tallet and el-Sayed Mahfuz (eds) The Red Sea in Pharaonic Times Recent discoveries along the Red Sea coast*, pp. 1-17. Institut français d'archéologie orientale.

Weinberg, G. D. (ed.) 1988. *Excavation at Jalame: Site of a Glass Factory in Later Roman Palestina*. Columbia: University of Missouri Press.

Westerdahl, C. 1994. Maritime cultures and ship types: brief comments on the significance of maritime archaeology, in *The International Journal of Nautical Archaeology* 23.4: 265-270.

Western Arabia and the Red Sea 1946. *Western Arabia and the Red Sea: June 1946*. Oxford : Naval Intelligence Division.

Whitcomb, D. and Johnson, J. H. 1979. *Quseir al-Qadim 1978: Preliminary Report*. Cairo.

Wilding, R.F. (with contributions by S.C. Munro-Hay) 1989. The pottery. In S.C. Munro-Hay (ed.), *Excavations at Aksum, BIEA Memoir* 10. London: The British Institute in Eastern Africa, 235-316.

Winlock, H. E. and Crum, W. E. 1973. *Monastery of Epiphanius at Thebes, The Archaeological Matrial, the Literary Material*. Part 1. New York.

Withcomb, D. 1994. *Ayla. Art and Industry in the Islamic Port of Aqaba*. Chicago.

Zampieri, G. and Lavarone, B. 2000. *Bronzi Antichi del Museo del Museo archeologico di Padova*. Roma.

Zarins, J. 1990. Obsidian and the Red Sea Trade. Prehistoric Aspects, in *South Asian Archaeology*, 507-541. Rome.

Zarins, J. & Zahrani, A. 1985. Recent Archaeological Investigation in the Southern Thiama Plain, in *Atlal* 9: 65-107.

Zazzaro, C. 2006. Oggetti in metallo da Adulis (Eritrea) nella collezione archeologica del Museo Africano di Roma, in *Africa* 61.3-4: 454-482.

Zazzaro, C. 2006 (unpublished). *Il Mar Rosso e il Corno d'Africa nell'antichità. Un approccio archeologico: navigazioni, siti e materiali*. Ph.D. Thesis discussed at the University of Napoli "L'Orientale" in 2006. Napoli.

Zazzaro, C. 2009. Adulis and the Eritrean coast in the museum collections and in the Italian and European travellers' records, in L. Blue, J. Cooper, R. Thomas and J. Whitewright (eds), *Connected Hinterlands: Proceedings of Red Sea IV, 25-26 September 2008*, 49–59. Society for Arabian Studies Monographs 8; BAR International Series 2052. Oxford.

Zazzaro, C. and Manzo, A. 2012. The pottery assemblage from the port town of Adulis (Eritrea) in the museums collections and recent findings, in *British Museum Studies in Ancient Egypt and Sudan* 18, 233-246.

Zazzaro, C. 2012. Historical and archaeological records to reflect on the maritime components of the Aksumite society in A. Bausi, A. Brita, A. Manzo (eds) *Aethiopica et Orientalia Studi in Onore di Yacob Beyene, Studi Africanistici. Serie Etiopica* 9 vol. 2, pp. 625-642. Napoli: Università degli Studi di Napoli "L'Orientale".

Cartographic Sources

Zula C. 4. in *Carta Topografica della Colonia Eritrea* 1:50000, incomplete. Istituto Geografico Militare 1890-1909.

Carta della Colonia Eritrea 1:100000 in 35 sheets. Istituto Geografico Militare 1909-1934.

Carta della Colonia Eritrea 1:400000 in 12 sheets. Istituto Geografico Militare 1934.